Practical Counselling Skills

An Integrative Approach

Kathryn Geldard

and

David Geldard

palgrave
macmillan

First published 2005 by
PALGRAVE MACMILLAN
Houndmills, Basingstoke, Hampshire RG21 6XS and
175 Fifth Avenue, New York, N. Y. 10010
Companies and representatives throughout the world

PALGRAVE MACMILLAN is the global academic imprint of the Palgrave
Macmillan division of St. Martin's Press, LLC and of Palgrave Macmillan Ltd.
Macmillan® is a registered trademark in the United States, United Kingdom
and other countries. Palgrave is a registered trademark in the European
Union and other countries.

ISBN-13: 978–1–4039–4513–6
ISBN-10: 1–4039–4513–6

This book is printed on paper suitable for recycling and made from
fully managed and sustained forest sources. Logging, pulping and
manufacturing processes are expected to conform to the environmenta
regulations of the country of origin.

A catalogue record for this book is available from the British Library.

9   8   7   6   5   4
13 12 11 10 09

Printed in China

Contents

Part I

Counselling – An Overview

Chapter 1

What is Counselling?

We, Kathryn and David Geldard, are a husband and wife team who work as counsellors, trainers, and authors. As we started to write this book we asked ourselves the question, 'What is counselling?' When we thought about this question we realised that counselling is just one way of helping people, but it is a special way which involves the use of particular skills for specific purposes.

There are many different ways of helping other people. Perhaps the most common of these involves giving others practical help. In our society there are many individuals who spontaneously help others in this way. Additionally, some people belong to organisations which have been set up to provide help to specific groups such as the elderly, the disabled, and those with mental health problems. Most importantly, there are many professions such as nursing, occupational therapy, and social work which involve professionals who are trained to provide and/or organise practical help for others.

While helping other people in a practical way many volunteer and professional helpers also make use of some counselling skills. Using these skills can be very useful in enabling people to feel better as described in our book *Counselling Skills in Everyday Life* (Geldard and Geldard, 2003). However, it needs to be recognised that just being able to make use of some counselling skills does not qualify a person as a counsellor.

Counsellor training

In order to qualify as a counsellor, a person needs to complete an accredited course of study and training, have ongoing supervision, and

3

meet the full requirements of the British Association for Counselling and Psychotherapy (BACP), or of the relevant counselling professional body in their country of residence if they do not live in the United Kingdom. They need to have knowledge in the areas of psychology, human development and the processes of change. They are trained to use advanced counselling skills in the context of the particular therapeutic approach of their choice.

A wide variety of therapeutic approaches are described by Feltham and Horton (2000). They have grouped the most commonly used approaches under the headings psychodynamic, cognitive-behavioural, humanistic-existential, and eclectic-integrative. We ourselves prefer to use an eclectic-integrative approach in which we integrate skills from a number of different approaches in order to create a counselling process which we believe maximises the benefit for the client.

> An integrative approach combines skills from various therapeutic approaches

We should make it clear that it is not sufficient for counsellors just to complete an academic training course. Additionally their training needs to include personal therapy, experiential groupwork, personal growth experiences, and attendance at counselling related workshops. Both during and subsequent to training all counsellors need ongoing supervision so that they can debrief, discuss their work, improve their skills, and address personal issues that might be triggered as a consequence of counselling others. Counsellors may often find themselves in the position of client in a supervision session as they seek to resolve their own personal issues which may have been triggered by their work with their own clients.

Counsellors are required to maintain their current accreditation by undergoing professional development activities to demonstrate a commitment to ongoing training and development. Most importantly they are required to practise in accordance with the Ethical Framework for Good Practice in Counselling and Psychotherapy (BACP, 2002), or in accordance with the relevant code of ethics for counsellors in their own state or country.

We believe that after completing an accredited course of study and training, the best way to start practising as a counsellor is to undertake closely supervised work with individual adults. After gaining experience in working with adults many counsellors learn additional skills to enable them to counsel couples, families, and children. Readers who are interested in the possibility of working with children or adolescents might like to read our books *Counselling Children* (2002), *Counselling Adolescents* (2004), or *Working with Children in Groups* (2001). Readers who are interested in counselling families might like to read Eddy Street's *Counselling for Family Problems* (1994).

Why do people seek counselling?

In seeking to answer this question we realised that, generally, people who live satisfying and fulfilling lives and are not confronted by any particular crisis do not seek counselling. However, even people who live satisfying and fulfilling lives will at certain times be troubled emotionally and may seek help. Many people, if not all, will at some time encounter physical and/or emotional crises. It is at times like these that people may seek counselling.

It needs to be recognised that people deal with troubling times in their lives in their own unique ways. Some people are very adaptive, and are able to resolve their emotional problems by thinking things through on their own. Other people may talk with a partner, family member, or friend. However, there are many people who either have no one to talk to about personal issues, or who prefer to deal with their issues by talking to a counsellor rather than someone who knows them well. Sometimes, it may be easier for a person to talk to a counsellor about extremely personal matters than to risk straining a relationship by disclosing intimate personal information to someone who knows them well.

Our personal experience suggests that the most common reasons why people come to see counsellors relate either to relationships or to developmental life changes. Many people experience emotional crisis when they are in a difficult relationship, when they have lost a relationship, or when they seek a relationship but are unable to find a satisfactory one. Similarly, developmental life changes frequently cause high levels of stress and/or emotional distress. Examples of such developmental changes include getting married, having a first child, being promoted at work, and reaching midlife. Of course, there are many other reasons why people might seek counselling. These include having experienced physical or emotional trauma, being troubled by illness, or as a consequence of many types of loss.

> People come to counselling for help in resolving their problems

Clearly, people usually come to see counsellors when they are emotionally troubled, and believe that they are unable to solve their problems and resolve their distress without outside help. In coming to counselling, they expect that they will be able to talk to someone else in confidence about their problems with the hope of finding solutions and feeling better. It follows that central to the counselling process is the client–counsellor relationship.

Counselling involves a relationship

Counselling involves a special type of relationship between the counsellor and the person seeking help. The characteristics of this relationship will be discussed in detail in Chapter 2. Sometimes the client–counsellor relationship is a face-to-face relationship and sometimes it is conducted by phone. Occasionally, a counselling relationship will be a relationship which is limited to writing letters between the client and counsellor. In our modern Internet world, this may occur electronically. Whatever the way in which the relationship is conducted, it is a relationship with a purpose.

> The client–counsellor relationship is central to the counselling process

In this book, we will try to parallel some of the qualities of the counselling relationship by remembering that you, the reader, and we, the authors, are engaging together in a relationship with a purpose. We also need to remember that we each have our own unique personalities, so inevitably we will sometimes think similarly and sometimes differently, and that is OK.

People receiving help from counsellors like to know something about the person who is helping them so that they can have confidence in the help being offered. Sometimes it is sufficient for them to know that the counsellor concerned works for a reputable agency and is a fully qualified. When this is not the case, they may want to know about the counsellor's training, experience, and/or qualifications.

As authors, our relationship with you, the reader, is not the same as a client–counsellor relationship. However, just as clients want to know something about their counsellors, you may want to know something about us, the authors. Much as we would in a counselling session, we will begin by introducing and sharing something about ourselves. First, Kathryn will tell you who she is and how she became a counsellor:

I started my professional life not as a counsellor, but as an occupational therapist. However, my professional interests led me to train to work with young people in a psychiatric setting. As a consequence I inevitably became interested in psychotherapy and as an occupational therapist focused on working with children and young people who had behavioural and/or emotional problems. As time progressed, I began to realise that my focus had shifted towards counselling. This shift led me to undertake counsellor training and as a result complete a Master's degree in counselling. It is interesting for me to recognise that perhaps the most important thing I learnt during my academic training was that theoretical knowledge on its own does not make a counsellor, and that being prepared to face my own issues in supervision was essential. Now that I have many years experience as a counsellor I am convinced that the most significant attribute needed in counselling is the ability to build a trusting relationship.

Now it is time for David to introduce himself:

I should start by explaining that right from the time I was a young person I had ambitions to be a counsellor. Unfortunately, I lacked confidence and self-esteem and didn't think I was capable of being a counsellor. Instead I trained as a mechanical engineer as my parents and teachers told me that I was better suited to working with machines than people. I believed them. This was a very bad mistake because I was not suited to engineering. I did however appear to succeed in my job by being able to join with other people who were more competent as engineers than I was! My relationship skills probably saved me from either being demoted or sacked for incompetence! Much later, at a very low point in my life I embarked on a long period of personal growth as a result of help from a skilled counsellor. My interest in helping people therapeutically was rekindled. After looking at course options I decided to go back to university to study and train as a counselling psychologist. In time I graduated as a psychologist, trained initially as a person-centred counsellor, and then as a gestalt therapist. With further training and supervision I then moved into using an integrative counselling approach. In my early work as a counsellor, I focused on counselling adults who had personal problems, and later trained to work with couples, families, then children. I find counselling very satisfying as it encourages me to be creative and to use myself as a person. Generally it is stimulating and satisfying, but I must admit that at times it can be stressful and demanding.

Why do you want to be a counsellor?

We hope you will enjoy reading this book and find it useful. Because you are reading it, we assume that you may be intending to train as a counsellor. Now that we have told you how we became counsellors, we will ask you to think about the question, 'Why do you want to be a counsellor?' As we write we remember how we felt when we first started our training. Our feelings and attitudes then were very different from those we have now. However, it was those feelings and attitudes which motivated us to go ahead. We wonder how you feel as you think about your decision to train as a counsellor. What are your motivations? Stop for a minute and think. As we have suggested, you might ask yourself the question, 'Why do I want to be a counsellor?' and, if you have the energy and inclination, write your answer on a sheet of paper so that you can refer to it later.

Your answer is, of course, individually yours, but it is quite probable that it fits into one of two moulds. It could be that you wrote a statement about your *own* needs. Possibly you have the idea that being a counsellor will give you status, power or satisfaction. Perhaps you think that counselling will add a new quality and richness to your life. It may be, though, that when you wrote your answer you were not thinking about your own needs at all. You may have decided to become a counsellor so that you can satisfy the needs of other people. You may have written down something like, 'I want to be a counsellor because I care about other people and want to help them.' Most counsellors are very caring people and helping others is an important part of their motivation. However, it's important for all of us to remember that even if we become counsellors with the primary goal of satisfying other people's needs, we will *also* be satisfying some of our *own* needs. We will, for example, get satisfaction for ourselves out of caring for others. This discussion may not seem important right now, but it is, because if we are not careful, our motivations for becoming counsellors may negatively influence the way in which we will function as counsellors. While it probably doesn't matter greatly what our personal motivations are, it is important that we are aware of these motivations and of the needs of our own that we hope to satisfy. With this awareness we will be better able to avoid letting the satisfaction of our own needs interfere with the counselling process, and with our ability to meet the needs of clients.

Purposes and goals of counselling

As counsellors, if we are to meet the needs of clients we must have a clear understanding of the purposes and goals of the counselling process. Additionally, to be effective counsellors we need to have an understanding of what it means to be effective.

For most people it is not easy to make an appointment and then go to see a counsellor. Although attitudes are starting to change many people still hold the view that it's a sign of weakness if people need outside help in order to be able to cope with their problems. This tends to make it difficult for those with significant work responsibilities to come for counselling. Such people often believe that, if they admitted to seeking help from a counsellor, their colleagues would think that they were inadequate and not capable of taking responsibility. Consequently, many people are reluctant to seek counselling help unless they are in such a disturbed emotional state that their ability to carry out their normal daily tasks is significantly impaired, and they are no longer able to hide their pain and emotional distress from others.

If we take note of the fact that generally clients come to see us in a state of raised anxiety and distress, then we must assume that the central purpose of counselling is to help clients feel better. However, just helping them to feel better in the short term is not sufficient. It is not going to be useful for clients if they feel better in the short term only to return to their previous uncomfortable emotional state later. A major goal of the counselling process therefore needs to be to help clients change. Clients need to be able to make changes in the way they think and/or the things they do, so that they are less likely to repeat patterns of thinking and behaving which lead to negative consequences for them.

> Effective counselling helps people change

Judging the effectiveness of counselling is usually subjective and there are clearly two different perspectives – the client's and the counsellor's. It may be that the client will perceive effectiveness in a different way from the counsellor, so we will ask you, the reader, to spend a few minutes considering first the client's expectations and then the counsellor's.

The client's perspective

Many clients who are not used to the counselling process go to counsellors expecting that the counsellor will give them direct advice and tell them exactly what they should do, so that at the end of the counselling session they can go away having been told how to solve their problems. This is generally not the case. Most experienced counsellors agree that it is usually, although not always, unhelpful to give advice. In fact, in many situations there may be real disadvantages for a client if a counsellor does try to give advice and provide solutions to problems.

There are several dangers inherent in giving advice. Firstly, human beings are remarkably resistant to advice. In fact, some counsellors have become so impressed by the way that clients resist advice, that in advanced counselling sessions they will use paradoxical methods to suggest that a client should do exactly the reverse of what the counsellor really believes is best! We need to say that we ourselves do not use paradoxical methods because we believe that they would compromise both our authenticity and our relationship with the client.

Unfortunately, giving advice may be counterproductive even if the client follows the advice. If the advice turns out to be inappropriate, then quite clearly the counsellor has done the client a disservice and that client will not be impressed. On the other hand, if the advice has positive consequences then there may still be negative consequences in the long term. Instead of having worked things out for themselves, the client has accepted the counsellor's advice and may now regard the counsellor as a superior expert who needs to be consulted whenever major decisions are to be made. This is likely to compromise the client's ability to be self-reliant and to personally make use of adaptive decision-making processes.

> Giving advice is often unhelpful

We do need to make it clear that there are counselling situations where direct advice by the counsellor is required. For example, in medical emergencies, crisis situations, or situations where a person's safety is compromised, quick decisions may be required, and it may be imperative for counsellors to be directive.

If we as counsellors are generally not willing to give clients advice, then we do need to try to understand what the client is seeking when expecting advice. If we were to ask the client, as we sometimes do, 'What would you like to achieve by coming to counselling?', what do you think the answer would reflect? Generally, it seems to us that clients want to feel better emotionally, and in order for this to happen they often believe that they need to find solutions to problems.

If we don't usually give clients advice, how can we help them feel better? Often, clients will feel better just because they have had an opportunity to share their problems with another person who is prepared to listen. Listening is the most important way in which a counsellor can meet the client's needs. Additionally, if clients are able to discover for themselves, during counselling sessions, better ways of thinking about, responding to, dealing with, and managing their problems, then they are likely to feel better. They are also likely to feel satisfied with the outcome, even though they may not have received any advice.

The counsellor's perspective

If we are to be effective counsellors, we need to have a clear idea of our goals. A useful short-term goal is to help clients to feel better, or at least to feel more comfortable. In the long term, it is sensible to help clients to discover for themselves how to become more self-sufficient, and how to deal with ongoing and future life situations in a constructive way without requiring continual help. It is very much in both the client's and the counsellor's interests to promote enduring long-term change, rather than to engage in short-term problem-solving. A counsellor is clearly going to feel very frustrated if clients keep returning for counselling each time new problems are encountered. It is important, if counsellors are to feel a sense of satisfaction in their work, that clients change and grow in such a way that they learn to cope, as much as is realistically possible, on their own. Additionally, a counsellor might be seen to be more effective if change occurs more quickly. However, we need to be aware of the danger of producing short-term transitory change which is not sustainable, and which fails to enable the client to cope more effectively with future crises.

Encouraging self-reliance

It is not helpful for clients to perceive counsellors as superior experts who have the answers to other people's problems. Such perceptions are undesirable because they disempower clients instead of helping them to learn self-reliant ways of behaving. Thus, an important goal for a counsellor may be to help clients to discover for themselves how to become more self-reliant and how to feel confident about their own ability to make decisions. In the long term it is certainly not helpful for a client to become dependent on a counsellor's advice. It is far better for the client to become self-reliant, and capable of making and trusting their own decisions.

> Counsellors empower clients so that they can make their own decisions

As we have discussed, in most situations counsellors usually don't give direct advice, don't 'problem-solve' for clients, and don't seek to produce quick short-term solutions without long-term gain. Instead they help clients sort out their own confusion, and by doing this enable them to discover for themselves solutions to their problems that fit for them. This is a process that is empowering for clients. Sometimes the counsellor may think that the client's solutions are not the most sensible or appropriate ones. However, it is important for clients to make decisions that are right for them. They can then test their decisions and learn from their own experiences, rather than learning to rely on the 'wisdom' of the counsellor.

Contracting with the client

From the previous discussion it is obvious that at times there may be a mismatch between the client's and the counsellor's expectations. One way of dealing with this mismatch when it occurs would be to ignore it and just allow the counselling process to proceed. However, a more respectful approach is to discuss expectations openly with the client and to agree on a counselling contract that is mutually acceptable.

> Contracting helps make the counselling process transparent

A counselling contract may include an agreement regarding issues such as those related to confidentiality, general and specific goals, the counselling process, the counselling methods to be used by the counsellor, and issues to be discussed. At the contracting stage we like to make it clear that the client's wishes will be respected with regard to what issues will and will not be discussed. This is very important for some clients who may fear that they will be pressured in subtle ways to discuss issues which they do not wish to explore.

Sometimes a contract will involve an agreement to attend counselling sessions at regular intervals; for example weekly or fortnightly for a particular number of sessions, with a review of the counselling process occurring at set times.

LEARNING SUMMARY

- Many helpers make use of some counselling skills; this is useful but that doesn't make them counsellors.
- Counsellors need to complete an accredited course of study and training, have ongoing supervision, and meet the requirements of the relevant counselling body in their state or country (the BACP in the UK).
- Counsellors may use a single therapeutic approach or an integrative approach.
- Counsellors are bound by a code of ethics determined by the relevant professional body.
- Most people seek counselling only when they encounter physical or emotional crisis.
- A central feature of counselling is the client–counsellor relationship.
- A counsellor's motivation inevitably influences their effectiveness.
- Client expectations may be at variance with counsellor goals.
- Clients often ask for direct advice and solutions to their problems.
- Counsellors generally try to empower clients so that they can become self-sufficient and discover their own solutions rather than be dependent on someone else's advice.
- Goals of the counselling process include working collaboratively with the client to help the client sort out their problems and discover solutions, helping the client to change their thinking and/or behaviours, empowering the client to become self-sufficient, and helping the client to feel better.

References and further reading

Bor, R. and Palmer, S. (2001) *A Beginner's Guide to Training in Counselling and Psychotherapy*, London: Sage.

British Association for Counselling and Psychotherapy (2002) *Ethical Framework for Good Practice in Counselling and Psychotherapy*, Rugby, Warwickshire: BACP.

Dryden, W. (ed.) (2002) *Handbook of Individual Therapy*, fourth edition, London: Sage.

Feltham, C. and Horton, I. (eds) (2000) *Handbook of Counselling and Psychotherapy*, London: Sage.

Geldard, K. and Geldard, D. (2001) *Working with Children in Groups: A Handbook for Counsellors, Educators, and Community Workers*, London: Palgrave.

Geldard, K. and Geldard, D. (2002) *Counselling Children: A Practical Introduction*, second edition. Basingstoke. London: Sage.

Geldard, K. and Geldard, D. (2003) *Counselling Skills in Everyday Life*, Basingstoke: Palgrave Macmillan.

Geldard, K. and Geldard, D. (2004) *Counselling Adolescents: The Pro-active Approach*, second edition. London: Sage.

Street, E. (1994) *Counselling for Family Problems*, London: Sage.

Chapter 2

The Counselling Relationship

You may not be surprised to learn that most counsellors believe that the effectiveness of counselling is highly dependent on the quality of the relationship between the client and the counsellor. This belief is supported by a number of research studies which have been discussed in some detail by Roxanne Agnew-Davies (1999), who made a comprehensive review of the relevant research literature. Additionally, a meta-analysis showed that the presence of identifiable components of good quality relationships is statistically correlated with successful counselling outcomes (Horvath and Symonds, 1991). We can therefore confidently say that the quality of the counselling relationship has a major influence on counselling outcomes.

> Effective counselling depends on the quality of the relationship

Perhaps you, the reader, would like to spend a few moments thinking about what sort of counselling relationship you would like if you were a client, before reading on.

Desirable qualities of the counselling relationship

It is obvious that the relationship between a client and counsellor is dependent on the counsellor's personality, beliefs, attitudes, and behaviours. These personal characteristics of the counsellor are certain to influence the relationship they have with their client.

What is good and what is not so good in this picture?

Many years ago Carl Rogers identified a number of counsellor characteristics which he believed were important in a counselling relationship. He described these in his book *Client-Centered Therapy*, published in 1955, and developed his ideas further in subsequent publications. Interestingly, some time after writing *Client-Centered Therapy* Rogers preferred to call his approach '*Person*-Centred Counselling', because he placed a very strong emphasis on the need for counsellors to think of their clients as people rather than impersonal entities. He saw the client–counsellor relationship as a person-to-person relationship where the person seeking help is respected and valued. Rogers' ideas are still relevant today and in particular his understanding of what is required in a counselling relationship is both powerful and useful. Rogers identified a number of important characteristics of the counselling relationship which he believed were required for effective outcomes (Rogers, 1957). Later, in his 1961 book *On Becoming a Person*, he emphasised three of these characteristics as necessary for effective outcomes. These were *congruence, empathic understanding* (now generally referred to as 'empathy'), and *unconditional positive regard*. He also believed that people have within themselves the ability to find their own solutions. This belief demands that the counsellor show respect for client competence.

David Howe (1999) describes the counselling relationship as working in conjunction with what he calls a therapeutic alliance. He describes the alliance as involving more than the presence of Rogers' three core conditions. In his view the alliance involves mutual *collaboration* by both counsellor and client. The alliance is an expression of the positive bond between the client and the counsellor, who is perceived as a supportive person (Luborsky, 1994). According to Howe therapist qualities and characteristics required for an effective alliance include being *warm, supportive, attentive, empathic, understanding, clarificatory, helpful, purposive, involved, collaborative, sensitive*, and *having good rapport*.

It has to be recognised that good human relations alone are not necessarily sufficient to produce effective counselling outcomes. As suggested by Gerard Egan (1994), skill and an active, methodical, pragmatic approach are also necessary.

It is clear that the counselling relationship is complex depending on the counsellor's personal qualities and the way the counsellor behaves as they interact with the client.

Desirable counsellor qualities when using an integrative approach

We believe that for an effective counselling relationship to be achieved counsellors using an integrative approach should strive to be:

1. congruent;
2. empathic, warm, and sensitive with good rapport;
3. non-judgemental with unconditional positive regard;
4. attentive, understanding and supportive;
5. collaborative while showing respect for the client's competence; and
6. proficient in using counselling skills purposefully.

We recognise that if you are a reader who already has a detailed understanding of the various counselling approaches you may be particularly interested in the way in which a counsellor can be collaborative while showing respect for the client's competence (5 in the above list). We will discuss this in some detail later in the chapter as it is of particular importance when using an integrative approach.

Being congruent

To be congruent the counsellor must be genuinely themselves: a complete, integrated and whole person. Everything about the counsellor as a person must ring true. For example, there is only one Kathryn Geldard, even though she has a variety of roles. She is a wife, mother, and sister, a counsellor, a friend, a patient, a customer, and a trainer, in addition to many other roles. It is clearly true that there are differences in the way that she behaves in each of these roles, and in different situations. While she is playing with a child she is happy to wear causual clothes and romp around on the floor, but when she is attending a professional meeting of counsellors she prefers to dress more conservatively and behave in a more formal way. However, in both situations she has a choice. If she chooses, she can be an actor playing a role or she can in the fullest sense really be herself. She can either stay fully in contact with herself as a person and be genuine, without the need to change, or, if she chooses, she can disown parts of herself, wear a mask, and pretend to be different from who she really is. Similarly, as a counsellor she could pretend to be an expert who has all the answers and no vulnerabilities, or she could throw away her 'counsellor mask' and be true to herself, a real person complete with strengths and weaknesses. When a client comes to see her, in her counsellor role, then two people meet. It is a person-to-person relationship. For the client to feel valued, she, the counsellor, needs to be congruently herself, genuine in all regards. If this happens, then the relationship will be enhanced and the counselling process is likely to be more effective.

Each time Kathryn enters a counselling relationship she brings with her that part of herself which is a parent, that part of her which is a professional counsellor; that part of her which is childlike and likes to have fun. She also brings the serious side of herself. She is, within her own limitations, genuinely herself and tries to avoid pretending to be different from her real self. Naturally, when working as a counsellor she makes use of those parts of her personality which are most relevant in the counselling relationship, and other parts of her may remain out of sight. These are not deliberately concealed from the client, but are available only if they can be appropriately used.

> **Be real!**

In the way that Kathryn tries to be congruently herself, David does the same. Some time ago he was invited to run a counsellor training group, and in that group were two people who had known him in another context. During the training he gave a demonstration of counselling. The two people concerned had never seen him act as a counsellor before. After the session, one of them said to him, 'I was really surprised because when you acted as a counsellor all I saw was the same person that I knew previously, and I expected to find someone different.'

A similar situation occurred when a lecturer friend of ours at our local university was teaching counselling skills. One of the students, early on in the course, said to the lecturer, 'How about you show us how you counsel by giving us a demonstration? You've been teaching us counselling micro-skills, but you've never actually sat down in front of us and demonstrated how to counsel.' The lecturer readily agreed, sat down and, as counsellor, helped a young student client to resolve a difficult and painful issue. After the session was over, the student who'd asked the lecturer to give the demonstration seemed to be amazed and delighted. She said to the lecturer, 'You know, I really can't believe it. It was just as though you were being yourself, and Irene [invented name] and you were talking together like friends.' Yes, that's how it was; the lecturer was being totally congruent and was relating to Irene as she related to other people in her daily life, as a real person. Of course, it wasn't quite the same, because in daily life we generally behave as though our own needs are equally as important as other people's needs, whereas in a counselling relationship the counsellor focuses on the client's needs rather than their own. After all, the counselling situation is not the appropriate place for a counsellor to work through their own problems; rather it's the place where the central focus is the client.

Self-disclosure

We believe that being congruent may sometimes require a counsellor to be willing to self-disclose a limited amount of personal information, as otherwise the client may experience an excessive lack of equality in the relationship. It must be acknowledged that in reality there is inevitably to some degree a lack of equality in a counselling relationship, because in the counselling situation the roles of client and counsellor are different. However, if the counsellor is able to respond openly and at times to disclose information which may be relevant to the counselling conversation, this can be helpful in enabling the client to feel at ease. As in every relationship, sensible boundaries need to be established. It would not be appropriate for a counsellor to disclose information of a highly personal nature. Additionally, self-disclosure needs to be used sparingly so that the focus is on the client's issues and the possibility that the client's issues might become contaminated by the counsellor's issues is avoided. It is essential for counsellors to ensure that they do not use counselling sessions with clients in order to work through their own issues. Excessive and inappropriate self-disclosure by a counsellor would be likely to move the focus onto the counsellor's issues rather than the client's.

Being empathic, warm, and sensitive with good rapport

A good metaphor for the counselling process is for the counsellor to imagine that the client is walking along a path. Sometimes the client may wander away from the path, go into the woods, trip over, climb over rocks, wander through valleys, cross streams and generally explore. Sometimes they may go around in a circle and come back to the same point again. As counsellors we are neither followers nor leaders most of the time, although at times we will follow and at times we will lead. Most of the time, what we try to do is to walk alongside the client – to go where they choose to go, to explore those things that the client chooses to explore, and to be warm, open, friendly, concerned, caring, real, and genuine. This way, trust develops between the client and ourselves and we experience the world in almost the same way that the client experiences it. We try to think and feel the way the client does, so that we can share with the client what they are discovering about themselves. We develop good rapport by going on a journey with them, listening to everything they say with sensitivity, matching their every move, and being right beside them. This is what is meant by empathy.

> Walk alongside your client

Being empathic means having a togetherness with the client, and as a consequence creating a trusting environment in which the client feels cared for and safe. In such an environment clients can talk about their darkest secrets, their innermost feelings, and the things that seem to them to be so terrible or so personal that they have not yet dared to talk to others about them.

Being non-judgemental with unconditional positive regard

Now that we have discussed congruence and empathy which Rogers believed were essential counsellor qualities for effective counselling, we should consider the third counsellor characteristic which he identified as necessary. This is what he called 'unconditional positive regard'. This involves accepting the client completely, in a non-judgemental way, as the person they are, with all their frailties and weaknesses, and with all their strengths and positive qualities. Having unconditional positive regard doesn't mean that I agree with or accept the values of the client for myself, but it does mean that I accept the client as he or she is now, that I value them as a person, am non-judgemental about their behaviour, and do not try to put my values onto them. I consequently enable them to feel free to be open in exploring their inner processes without censoring them for fear of criticism. This gives them the best opportunity for increased personal awareness and consequent personal growth.

Unconditional positive regard isn't always easy to achieve, and sometimes it is just not possible. However, attempting to achieve it is an excellent goal, as when it is achieved counselling outcomes are more likely to be effective. The first step in attempting to achieve unconditional positive regard is to try to see the world through the eyes of the client. By doing this, we are better able to understand the client's motivations and to be more accepting of their behaviour. The longer we have been counsellors, the more convinced we have become that even the most terrible behaviour is often understandable if we first understand the world that the client lives in and has lived in. We try to take the view that inside every person, behind the facade that the world sees, there is somebody who has the potential to be a good, creative, loving person. We are rarely disappointed by this expectation.

> Remember – most people are doing the best they can

By caring for each person who talks with us in a similar way to the way in which we would like to be cared for ourselves, we are better able to be accepting and non-judgemental. We are not going to pretend that this is easy, because sometimes it isn't. On occasions in counselling sessions clients will discuss their behaviours, beliefs or attitudes in ways which conflict with, or are offensive to, our own value systems. At these times, it is really hard for us to be non-judgemental and also to remain congruent, but it is a goal that we strive for. We have found that if we are able to see the world from the client's perspective without judging, then the client is more likely to feel safe in being open and honest with us while exploring troubling issues. Our belief is, that by being as non-judgemental as is possible, we maximise the possibility that our client will feel free to fully disclose important information, and we increase the likelihood that the client will change. Only by being non-judgemental can we expect to earn the total trust of the client and to really see the world in the way the client does. Unfortunately, when we can't do this, and sometimes we can't, we may fail to facilitate change effectively because the client will not perceive us as accepting and understanding.

Clearly, being non-judgemental and accepting clients with unconditional positive regard is not easily achieved. Moreover it will be very difficult for us to create the relationships we need to have with clients and to be non-judgemental unless first we are very clear about who we are and what our own values are. If we have not sorted out our own value conflicts, then there is a risk that our own confusion will interfere with our ability to focus on the client's confusion, and we may inadvertently end up using the counselling session to resolve our own conflicts rather than the client's. To get a better understanding of our own values we have had to explore them, to scrutinise them and to question them. We have needed to carefully consider different values from our own and to understand where our feelings about those different values come from. This is an ongoing process that will never be finished. We have found that when we have had extremely polarised views, this has sometimes been because we have been afraid to look at the opposite point of view and to seek to understand it. Through sorting out our own value system, understanding ourselves better, and consequently being less threatened by views diametrically opposed to ours, we are better able to take a non-judgemental attitude towards clients who have very different values from ours.

Being attentive, understanding and supportive

In our view, although the characteristics described previously are highly desirable, they are not of themselves sufficient to ensure that counselling is as effective as it can be. As will be discussed in this and the following paragraphs, we believe that the counsellor also needs to be active. One of the most important ways in which a counsellor can be active is to be attentive. This involves deliberately and intentionally listening to what the client is saying. The counsellor needs to get on the same wavelength as the client; not only to hear the words spoken but also to gain a deep understanding of the client's story and their view of their world. While actively listening, the counsellor needs to be able to let the client know that they are understood. Wherever possible and appropriate the counsellor needs to demonstrate and communicate their understanding and support for the client so that the client really does feel as though the counsellor has joined with them and is walking alongside them in their exploration.

Being collaborative while showing respect for the client's competence

When discussing this particular counsellor behaviour it is interesting to note that some theoretical models differ from others with regard to an emphasis on collaboration as compared with an emphasis on respect for the client's competence.

In the person-centred approach there is a strong emphasis on the ability of the client to find solutions from their own resources. The counsellor is a facilitator who enables the client to use their own inner processes in order to resolve issues and find solutions. Other approaches, including cognitive behavioural approaches and solution focused counselling, emphasise the need for the counsellor and client to work together as equal partners in finding solutions. In these approaches the counsellor will be active in making suggestions and in proposing and exploring possible solutions with the client. There is therefore a difference with some counsellors believing that we need to facilitate a process which relies on the client's ability to discover their own solutions, and others believing that it is more beneficial to engage in a collaborative process. As integrative counsellors we believe that we need to combine these processes rather then see them as incompatible. In our experience the needs of clients are best met if the counsellor has a high level of respect for the client's own competence while working collaboratively with the client.

> Integrative counselling is both respectful and collaborative

If a useful counselling relationship is to occur, the counsellor must respect and value the client as a capable person. It is extremely important for a counsellor to respect the client's competence and to hold the belief that the client has the inner resources needed to deal with troubling issues, find solutions to problems, make decisions to change behaviour, and put desired changes into action. Some clients come to counselling believing that they do not have the inner resources and capability to do such things. Their expectation is that the counsellor will help them by finding solutions for them. Such clients are clearly lacking in a sense of personal power and the self-confidence which they require to enable them to be self-reliant. If the counsellor maintains the belief that the client does have the required inner strength and competence required for self-reliance, then the counsellor will be in a position to enable the client to get in touch with their own strengths and resources, to become self-reliant, to make decisions which suit them, and consequently to gain in self-esteem. However, in facilitating this process the integrative counsellor may as a collaborative partner introduce new ideas which can be explored with the client. If this is done with sensitivity and respect the client will continue to be encouraged to explore their issues, make their own decisions, and find solutions which fit for them. Also, the counselling conversation will be enriched by the introduction of additional ideas by the counsellor. In this situation the client is likely to believe that the counsellor cares enough to be involved as an equal partner in the exploration of problems and the search for solutions thereby enhancing the client–counsellor relationship. Thus the counsellor is actively helpful and involved in a process which is purposeful while working collaboratively with the client as an equal partner but with different skills and attributes. During this collaborative process the counsellor shows respect for the client's competence and ability in exploring and choosing their own solutions and making personal decisions which fit for them.

Being proficient in using counselling skills purposefully

For the counselling relationship to be fully effective the counsellor needs to be proficient in the use of counselling skills. It is these skills which enable the counsellor to build a relationship encompassing the qualities described previously. The counsellor needs to know when it is appropriate to make use of individual skills, and also needs to have an understanding of the overall counselling process as it occurs in individual sessions and over a series of counselling sessions (see Chapter 12).

Importance of the counselling relationship

In this chapter we have discussed the counselling relationship, and have explained how that relationship is important in providing a trusting, caring environment in which the client will feel free to share with the counsellor in the most open way possible. The attributes of congruence, genuineness, warmth, empathy, unconditional positive regard, and trust in the client's competence are extremely important if a counsellor is to be fully effective. A counsellor needs to walk alongside the client and to be with them in a very real sense so that the client experiences a togetherness. The precise words the counsellor uses are less important than their ability to form a meaningful relationship with the client and to listen intently to what the client is saying. An effective counsellor listens more than talks, and what they do say gives the client a sense of being heard and understood. The counsellor's role involves helping clients to explore their world and thus to make sense out of inner confusion. It is not the counsellor's role to choose the direction in which a client moves, but rather to provide the environment in which the client can best decide where to go. The counsellor accompanies the client on their journey of exploration, working collaboratively with the client by purposefully making use of counselling skills within a process which facilitates change.

We suggest that as a counsellor, you allow your clients to go where their current energy is taking them rather than try to lead them in particular directions. When a client has learnt to trust you, and to know that you will listen to what may appear trivial, then that client will feel safe enough to venture towards the real source of their pain. In other words, *if you stay with what may appear trivial, the important will emerge.*

You may by now have come to the conclusion that counselling is a terribly serious process. It often is. It is also a process which can give a great deal of satisfaction to the counsellor, and there are even times when counselling can be fun. Do you have a sense of fun? We certainly do, so we enjoy bringing our sense of humour into the therapeutic environment when that is appropriate. Don't fall into the trap of thinking that counselling is always a deadpan, heavy and serious process. It may not be. As counsellors we are real people and need to be congruent. Each of us needs to be able to bring all of ourselves into the counselling relationship, and to use those parts of our personalities that can add richness to the therapeutic encounter whenever possible.

LEARNING SUMMARY

- Important qualities in a counsellor include congruence, empathy, warmth, sensitivity, rapport, unconditional positive regard, being active, attentive, understanding, supportive, having respect for the client's competence, and being proficient in the use of counselling skills.
- Congruence means being genuine, integrated, and a whole person.
- Being empathic means joining with the client so that there is a feeling of togetherness.
- Unconditional positive regard involves accepting the client

---

LEARNING SUMMARY (cont'd)

▪ non-judgementally as a person of value, regardless of strengths and weaknesses.

▪ Integrative counsellors respect the client's ability to explore and choose their own solutions within a collaborative process.

▪ Counselling is usually a serious process but can legitimately involve humour.

References and further reading

Agnew-Davies, R. (1999) Learning from research into the counselling relationship. In C. Feltham (ed.) *Understanding the Counselling Relationship* (pp. 200–36). London: Sage.

Egan, G. (1994) *The Skilled Helper: A Problem-management Approach to Helping*, fifth edition. Belmont, CA: Brooks/Cole.

Feltham, C. (ed.) (1999) *Understanding the Counselling Relationship*. London: Sage.

Horvath, A. O. and Symonds, B. D. (1991) Relationship between working alliance and outcome in psychotherapy: A meta-analysis. *Journal of Counseling Psychology, 38*: 139–49.

Howe, D. (1999) The main change agent in psychotherapy is the relationship between therapist and client. In C. Feltham (ed.) *Controversies in psychotherapy and counselling* (pp. 95–103). London: Sage.

Luborsky, L. (1994) Therapeutic alliances as predictors of psychotherapeutic outcomes: Factors explaining the predictive success. In A. O. Horvath and L. S. Greenberg (eds) *The Working Alliance: Theory, Research and Practice* (pp. 34–42). New York: John Wiley.

Mearns, D. (1994) *Developing Person-Centred Counselling*. London: Sage.

Rogers, C. R. (1955) *Client-Centered Therapy*. Boston: Houghton Mifflin.

Rogers, C. R. (1957) The necessary and sufficient conditions of psychotherapeutic personality change. *Journal of Consulting Psychology, 21*, 95–103.

Rogers, C. R. (1961) *On Becoming a Person*. London: Constable.

Part II

Basic Principles
and Skills

Chapter 3

Learning the Necessary Skills

When we started to write this chapter it was interesting for us to discover that we had some common ideas and beliefs about how to learn to be an effective counsellor, but we also had some differences in emphasis. We realised that it is important for us to recognise that we are all unique individuals and that we each have our own preferred ways of learning. For David, learning to become an effective counsellor was a long process. During this time he was exposed to and absorbed ideas about counselling by undertaking an approved course of study, participating in practical training, and by having regular and ongoing contact with supervisors who supervised his counselling practice. Additionally, he learnt through his own personal experience as a client in therapy, and through contact with other counsellors, clients and friends. Although he did read counselling textbooks he didn't find that this was the most useful way for him to learn. Instead he placed a much higher emphasis on experiential learning.

Kathryn's learning process was similar and also included a significant amount of experiential learning. However, a major difference was that she placed a high value on information obtained through reading and recognised that information obtained in this way had significantly influenced her counselling style and effectiveness.

After discussing the issues, we recognised that we are all different. Some people will find it easier to learn by reading, and others by experiential learning. Clearly, a combination of both methods is required.

An essential part of counsellor training involves learning the particular counselling skills appropriate for your preferred theoretical model. We both agree that the best way to learn counselling skills is by using a combination of three methods. These are to read about counselling skills, to see them demonstrated by experienced counsellors; and to practise them while being observed so that useful feedback can be obtained. We would like to remind the reader that learning counselling skills is only a part of the process required to become a counsellor. As explained in Chapter 1, becoming a counsellor involves fulfilling the requirements of the professional organisation of the country or state in which you reside. In some ways counsellor training is never finished; as counsellors ourselves, we both place a high value on ongoing supervision of our work by another counsellor. This is essential if we are to maintain the professional standards which are required of us (see Chapter 27).

Enhancing natural counselling skills

When learning to become a counsellor it can be useful to ask yourself whether you have in the past unconsciously made use of your natural ability to help people. Have you ever comforted a child who was crying? Have you ever spent time sitting quietly with a friend who was distressed? Have you ever listened to somebody who was faced with a dilemma, and did not know what to do? My guess is that you have done all of these things. If so, you have on some occasions in your life acted in a natural way to help a friend, a relative, a child, or maybe even someone you met in a casual setting.

What was the most important thing you did in these situations? Was it just to let the person know that you cared enough about them to listen to their problem and to be with them in their distress? It probably was. If it was, then you were taking the first step in the process of becoming a counsellor.

> The first step is to join with the person in distress and listen

Counselling can be seen as an extension of what we all do naturally in our relationships with others when they are experiencing emotional pain. However, counsellor training not only enhances natural counselling skills but also supplements these with additional skills and processes to enable the counsellor not only to listen, but also to be capable of facilitating change in the other person so that they can feel better and be better equipped to face future challenges (see Chapters 11 and 12).

Learning specific skills (micro-skills)

In Chapter 2, we considered the importance of the counselling relationship. Certainly the relationship is central in counselling, as it is the foundation on which the counselling process develops. The counselling process is also reliant on the use of a number of individual counselling skills. The new counsellor needs to become proficient in the use of these, as when used appropriately they greatly enhance the quality and effectiveness of the counselling process. Conversational skills used by counsellors have been analysed with the result that small elements of useful verbal counselling behaviour have been identified. These are known as counselling micro-skills.

> Counselling micro-skills are small elements of counsellor

Each of the micro-skills can be learnt individually. However, be warned: a trainee needs to remember that counselling competence seems initially to diminish after each input of micro-skill training. This is because the trainee inevitably concentrates on using the new skill, rather than on building and maintaining the relationship. Also, the trainee isn't able to behave naturally when using a new skill until that skill is fully mastered. Once a trainee becomes fully competent in using the a new skill is fully mastered it becomes a natural part of the counsellor's way of relating with a client, and counselling effectiveness is considerably increased.

Learning in triads

In the following chapters, each of the micro-skills will be explained. After reading each chapter, it will be best if you practise the relevant micro-skill in a group setting. The usual way to do this is in a triad or a group of three students. One student takes the role of counsellor, a second student takes the role of client and the third student takes the role of observer.

Here are some suggestions about how to work in triads. If you are training for face-to-face counselling, set the room up with the chairs facing each other as shown in Figure 3.1, so that the 'client' faces the 'counsellor' and the 'observer' watches both.

The use of genuine personal problems

If counsellor training is to be most effective, then the 'client' in the triad needs to present a current and real personal problem of their own. Sometimes we have met students who have told us quite emphatically that they did not have such a thing as a personal problem, and we have found that difficult to believe. We doubt whether there are any people in the world who have no personal problems of any sort. In our experience, whenever people have said to us that they don't have any personal problems, we have discovered later that there have been areas of their lives that they were unwilling to discuss, and/or that they had blocked off and were afraid to venture near. However, we can understand why many trainees worry about using real problems. There are a number of reasons for this, including the following:

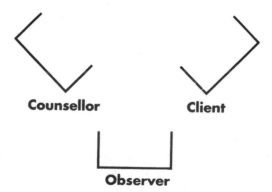

Counsellor   **Client**

Observer

Figure 3.1   Chair arrangement for counselling practice

1 The worry may be related to a lack of trust in other members of the triad, leading to feelings of vulnerability associated with self-disclosure. The trainee may think, 'They won't respect me if they find out about my problems.'
2 Unfortunately trainee counsellors frequently believe that they will not be accepted as counsellors if they disclose problems of their own. Our response to this is to say that as counsellor trainers we prefer to work with trainees who are able to own and address their problems. We are always worried by trainees who are not able to do this, because later, when they are trained, their disowned and unresolved issues may interfere with their ability to help others effectively.
3 Trainees may be justifiably afraid that they may become distressed if they use a real problem.
4 Trainees may fear that if they do become distressed they may not receive adequate counselling help from the trainee 'counsellor'. This is understandable. However, we believe that responsible trainers will inform trainees that follow-up counselling from experienced counsellors will always be available.

> Real problems make it easier for the trainee counsellor to recognise 'client' feelings

Trainees have often asked us whether they can use invented problems or other people's problems. Although this is better than not entering into a client role at all, in our view it is not very satisfactory. Most people who have been involved as trainers of counsellors would agree that it is much easier for the student counsellor to respond in a real and genuine way to what is being said if the problem is real, not invented or borrowed from someone else. Whenever a make-believe problem is used, it is difficult for the trainee counsellor to accurately pick up the 'client's' feelings and to appropriately practise counselling skills.

Tasks of triad members

The 'counsellor' in a counselling triad should listen, and practise only those micro-skills that have been taught up to that point; preferably, they should try not to use any other type of response at all. This may seem to be very limiting, but in fact it is possible to carry out an effective counselling session by exclusively using only one or two micro-skills. This is demonstrated in Chapter 5, which contains a transcript of a counselling session where only minimal responses and paraphrasing are used.

The observer's role in the triad is to take notes of anything significant they observe during the counselling practice session. The observer does not make judgements about what should have been done, but rather has the task of observing, as objectively as possible and without making interpretations, what actually happens during the practice session. For example, the observer may notice that when the 'counsellor' made a particular response, there was a change in the 'client's' verbal or non-verbal behaviour. The observer may also notice tones of voice used, pace of speaking, silences, and the use of particular skills. The observer does not interrupt, but the information noticed by the observer is fed back to the 'counsellor' and 'client' at the end of the session.

Length of triad practice sessions

Practice counselling sessions should typically be short, of about 10 minutes in length, and at the end of each session the observer should share their observations with the other two members of the triad. After that, the 'client' should be given the opportunity to talk about how they felt during the counselling session, and finally the 'counsellor' should explore their own feelings and share with the group how the session was for them. Preferably, in addition to the student observer, there should be an experienced trainer observing the triad throughout. Unfortunately, in large group counsellor training, it frequently happens that trainers have to go from triad to triad and are able to spend only a short time with each small group.

Learning through observation

Before practising micro-skills in a triad, the relevant micro-skill should be modelled by a competent counsellor. There are two ways in which this can be done. Either the demonstration can be performed live, or a video-recording may be used. Both options have advantages and disadvantages. Live demonstrations model the real life situation so that the trainee can see how the counsellor responds to whatever emerges. However, the conversation may not lead to a convincing demonstration of the micro-skill being taught. Video-taped demonstrations can be selected to powerfully demonstrate a particular micro-skill but may be less convincing as the counselling is not happening in real time in front of the trainees.

Modelling of the counselling process

In addition to learning by practising micro-skills in triads, and by observing those micro-skills being modelled by an experienced counsellor, it is very valuable for trainee counsellors to have the opportunity to observe experienced counsellors in real life counselling sessions. There are three ways in which this can happen:

1 An experienced counsellor may counsel a trainee who has volunteered to discuss a real problem in front of the training group.
2 An experienced counsellor may counsel a client with the trainee observing while sitting in the same room, watching over a video link, or observing through a one-way mirror equipped with a sound system. For this to occur, the permission of the client is essential.
3 The trainee may watch a videotape of a real counselling session where the client has given permission for this to happen.

Is the use of micro-skills sufficient?

In the previous chapter we discussed desirable qualities in a counsellor and necessary characteristics of the counselling relationship. In this chapter, we have provided an overview of skills training for beginners with no previous counselling experience. We would like to make it clear that learning the basic micro-skills and using them appropriately in the context of a suitable counselling relationship is necessary but not sufficient. As explained in Chapter 1, a counsellor needs to have an understanding of psychology, human development, and the processes of change. Additionally, a counsellor needs to have an understanding of the processes which occur during a counselling session, and needs to learn how to identify, respond to, and manage these processes for the benefit of the client. This can be learnt in a variety of ways: by learning from, and observing experienced counsellors, by reading, by practising counselling with other trainees as clients, and through practical experience under supervision as discussed in Chapter 27.

Sequential learning

The following chapters on micro-skills have been deliberately arranged in the most suitable sequence for training. By learning the skills in this sequence, the trainee can practise counselling by using only one or two micro-skills initially, and can then gradually incorporate additional skills into their repertoire. The sequence given is such that the most important basic skills are learnt first, with the consequence that more practice will be obtained in using these skills and the trainee counsellor will begin to rely on them as being those skills most appropriate for frequent use.

LEARNING SUMMARY

■ Learning to be a counsellor must involve completing an accredited course of study, practical training and supervision as required by the relevant counsellor accreditation body (BACP in the UK).

■ Counsellor training supplements and enhances natural counselling skills so that clients can feel better and lead more satisfying lives.

■ A micro-skill is a small element of counsellor conversational behaviour which can be learnt and practised.

■ Micro-skills are best learnt in a particular sequence so that the later skills build on the earlier ones.

References and further reading

Bor, R. and Watts, M. H. (eds) (1999) *The Trainee Handbook: A Guide for Counselling and Psychotherapy*. London: Sage.

Dryden, W., Horton, I. and Mearns, D. (1995) *Issues in Professional Counsellor Training*. London: Cassell.

Chapter 4

Joining and Listening

This chapter deals with both joining and listening because these two processes are interrelated. If we are to join with our clients, we need to listen to them and attend to what they are saying. We also need to use a range of behaviours to help them to feel at ease.

The first meeting

The initial meeting with a client is particularly important. The client's first impressions of the counsellor will influence their willingness to share openly. First impressions can be enduring and even if they aren't they are likely to influence the early part of the relationship. It is therefore very important that the climate of the relationship is established right from the beginning. However, it needs to be recognised that joining doesn't just occur at the initial meeting with the client but is an ongoing process. Throughout the counselling process the client needs to feel comfortable with their relationship with the counsellor.

Greeting the client

Imagine that you are meeting a client for the first time in your waiting room. What you do, as you move towards the client to greet them, will in some way affect their feelings towards you, and their confidence in you. It's important that the person you meet feels valued and at ease with you. As you meet the client, you need to be true to yourself rather than putting on an act. Remember that you are a person, like everybody else, so try to meet the client in a person-to-person encounter where you aren't intimidating, are neither expert nor inferior, but friendly, open and informal. Most importantly, help the client to feel at ease and welcome.

> Be yourself – relaxed and friendly

Be aware of cultural considerations when greeting clients. For example, although many people see shaking hands as a sign of welcome, in some cultures hand-shaking is seen as an intimate act, so offering your hand may be excessively intrusive (see Chapter 24).

Observing the client

As you greet the client you can, if you are observant, pick up a lot of information without asking any questions. Notice the way they are sitting or standing. The client's non-verbal behaviour will tell you something about the way they feel. Look at the clothes they are wearing, and how they are worn. By doing this you will learn something about how the client sees themself, and how they want to be seen. Don't jump to unverified conclusions, but use the information gleaned from your first meeting so that you can gradually build up a picture of the client's world and of their view of that world.

Putting the client at ease

When one of us meets a client for the first time, we introduce ourself and usually chat to the client as we walk to the counselling room. This helps the client to feel at ease. When we meet the client prior to subsequent interviews, although friendly in greeting them, we are usually less chatty and sometimes silent, unless the client initiates conversation. This enables the client to stay with any troubling thoughts rather than be taken away from them. Be aware that as a client leaves the waiting room and walks to the counselling room, they may well be putting their thoughts together, and may be experiencing the beginnings of heavy emotion as they get nearer to the issues they want to discuss. If the client is doing that, then it isn't helpful to be chatting about unimportant matters. It's better to be quiet.

Notice that we have differentiated between the first and subsequent sessions. We try to help the client to feel very much at ease during the first session, and are happy to use the first few minutes during that meeting to allow the client to settle in and feel comfortable. We allow the client to sit down, to look around, and maybe to comment on the pot-plants in the room or some other aspect of the room or the agency. We may even talk about some other casual topic. For example we may ask how the client travelled to the agency, and what the traffic was like, or we may share something of ourselves and our day with them. As a result we start to establish a relationship before moving forward into working on issues.

The invitation to talk

Clients sometimes find it difficult to know how to start to talk about their problems. There are obviously many different ways of inviting a client to talk about their problems. Here are some suggestions:

- 'What made you decide to come to see me today?'
- 'I'm wondering what's troubling you.'
- 'What is it that you would like to talk to me about?'

Some clients may respond to your invitation by talking quickly as a result of their anxiety and concern about taking up your time. Reassure them that it is OK to take time. Other clients may find it difficult to start to talk and may say that they don't know where to begin. When this happens, you might say something like:

> 'There's no need to hurry, just relax and take time. Sit quietly, and then if you can, tell me whatever it is that comes into your head even if it seems unimportant.'

This invitation may be helpful in enabling a nervous client to start talking. Once the client has started to talk it is important for them to know that you are listening and attending to what they are saying.

Tuning in

Have you ever talked about being on the same 'wavelength' as someone? Maybe you have sometimes noticed that a person has really 'tuned in' to what you are saying. Joining is about 'tuning in', or 'being on the same wavelength' as someone else. Thus, a harmonious connection is established between the person who is talking and the person who is listening. This is what we need to achieve as counsellors.

Whenever we listen to someone, we give out very subtle clues. These clues give an indication of how we are responding to what is being said, and give an indication of our feelings towards the person who is speaking. As helpers we therefore need to be careful to give out the right messages.

Listening with interest

People usually go to counsellors because they are troubled and don't know what to do to cope with their emotions. They will often expect that the counsellor will give them advice to enable them to change their situation. Because of this it is easy for new counsellors to feel pressured into trying, even early in the counselling process, to find solutions for clients. As a new counsellor, try to remember that the counsellor's primary task is to *listen to the client* and to use strategies which will enable them to find their own solutions. These solutions are likely to suit them because they have discovered them for themselves. The client will have also discovered that they are capable of making their own decisions.

> The most important counselling skill is to listen attentively

In our experience, before looking for solutions, the first thing most people want to do when they seek counselling help is to *talk about* the things that trouble them. They want to get things off their chest, to vent their feelings, and to say things which might be very difficult or maybe impossible to say to friends or family.

When you are with a client, try to remember that the client has come to talk to you and wants to feel free to unload what is troubling them. To do this, they need an invitation and opportunity to talk without unnecessary interruption. If you do a lot of talking, then you are likely to interfere with your client's ability to talk freely and the counselling process is likely to be compromised.

A counsellor is primarily a listener. By listening to what the client says, the counsellor is able to help them to sort through their confusion, identify their dilemmas, explore their options, and come away from the counselling session feeling that something useful has occurred. The counsellor therefore needs to attend very carefully to everything that the client is saying and to remember, as far as is possible, the details of the conversation. If you want to convince your client that you really are listening, then focus your concentration on the client and on what they are telling you. Try to remember, for example, the names of their relatives, what happened five years ago in their relationships, and even those things that are mentioned only briefly.

The first skill for the new counsellor to learn is to put deliberate effort into *listening with interest*. This needs to be done in such a way that the client recognises that you are totally focusing your attention on what is being said, and are completely understanding it. Listening with interest involves the use of the following:

1   minimal responses;
2   brief invitations to continue;
3   non-verbal behaviour;
4   voice; and
5   silence.

We will now discuss each of these.

Use of minimal responses

A good way to let a client know that they have your full attention and that you are listening to what they are saying is by use of minimal responses. The minimal response is something we naturally do in conversation when we are predominantly listening rather than talking. Minimal responses are sometimes non-verbal and include just a nod of the head. Also included among minimal responses are expressions like:

'Mm', 'Mm-hmm', 'Ah-ha', 'I see', 'Yes', 'OK', 'Sure', 'Right', 'Oh', *and* 'Really'

These expressions let clients know that they have been heard and also encourage them to continue talking. Some longer responses serve a similar function to the minimal response. For example, the counsellor might say:

'I hear what you say' *or* 'I understand'

While the client is talking continuously, the counsellor needs from time to time to reaffirm that they are listening to what the client is saying, and this can be done by inserting minimal responses at regular intervals. Space your minimal responses appropriately. If they are given too frequently, then they will become intrusive and will be distracting. Conversely, if they are not included often enough, the client may believe that you are not really attending to what is being said. It is also possible that the client will wonder whether you are silently making judgements or interpretations concerning what they are telling you.

Using the minimal response to convey a message

The minimal response is not just an acknowledgment that the client is being heard. It can also be a way, sometimes subtle, of communicating other messages. It may be used to signify that the counsellor agrees with the client, or to emphasise the importance of a client statement, to express surprise, or even to query what the client is saying. The way in which a minimal response is given – the tone and intensity of voice used, and the accompanying non-verbal behaviour such as eye movements, facial expressions and body posture – all combine to convey a message to the client.

Counsellors need to be careful in giving out messages of agreement or disagreement. Sometimes, despite the best of intentions, showing agreement with a client may be counterproductive. We remember being told by an acquaintance that she had discontinued going to see a counsellor because that counsellor had strongly agreed with her criticisms of her husband. Presumably the counsellor thought that by doing this he would join with the client. Unfortunately the counsellor's behaviour prevented the person concerned from talking further because she felt that by doing this she would be disloyal to her husband. By agreeing with her, the counsellor also blocked her from talking through her own feelings of guilt about her relationship with her husband. She wanted to be heard, understood, and valued, but did not want a stranger who didn't know her husband to be critical of him.

Being *empathic* involves hearing, understanding, and valuing the client. Can you see how this is different from *agreeing* with the client? Although there are times when agreeing with the client may be useful, generally it is more helpful to listen and understand without judgement.

Use of brief invitations to continue

Sometimes, a client will pause and it is important for the counsellor to allow the client time to think. However, once the client has finished thinking it may be useful to give a brief invitation to the client to continue. This can be done by using one of the following responses:

'Then . . .', 'And . . .', 'Tell me more', 'Can you tell me more?', 'Would you like to tell me more?', *or* 'Would you like to continue?'

Counselling involves the art of listening constructively, so appropriate use of minimal responses and brief invitations to continue is essential.

Use of non-verbal behaviour

There are a number of ways in which a counsellor can use non-verbal behaviour to join with the client and enhance the counselling process. These include:

- matching non-verbal behaviour;
- physical closeness;
- the use of movement;
- facial expression; and
- eye contact.

Matching non-verbal behaviour

Along with the use of minimal responses, another way in which counsellors can help clients to feel that they are really being listened to is to match their non-verbal behaviour. If a client is sitting on the edge of the seat, with their arms on their knees and looking forward, then it may be useful for the counsellor to sit in the same way and in effect to mirror the client's posture. By doing this, the client is likely to feel as though there is some intimacy between themself and the counsellor, rather than seeing the counsellor as a superior expert sitting back, listening and judging what is being said. Similarly, if the client leans back in their chair with legs crossed, and the counsellor casually matches that posture, the client may well feel more at ease. Clearly, matching needs to be done appropriately so that the counsellor is seen to be acting naturally rather than mimicking the client.

> Appropriate matching of non-verbal behaviour helps in the joining process

If a counsellor matches a client's non-verbal behaviour and posture for a while, then more often than not the client will match the counsellor's behaviour when the counsellor makes a change. In this way the counsellor can sometimes bring about some change in the client's emotional state. For example, a client may be so tense that they are sitting on the edge of the chair and are unable to relax into a more comfortable sitting position. If the counsellor matches this position initially and then moves back to sit more comfortably, the client is likely to follow the counsellor's example and consequently to experience a reduction in their level of tension.

Physical closeness

We all have different personal comfort levels with regard to physical closeness. Also, we need to recognise that there are major differences in comfort levels related to physical closeness for people from different cultures (see Chapter 24).

Think about how you would feel personally if someone you were talking to was to stand a long way from you, or was to move further away while you were talking. You might get the message that that person wasn't interested in what you were saying, or that they thought that you weren't a very nice person so they didn't want to be close to you. Also, consider what it's like when someone stands too close to you for your comfort. How does that feel?

Clearly, as a counsellor, it is best to sit at an appropriate distance from the person you are helping, so that they feel comfortable. Knowing the correct distance is a matter of judgement. Remember, you need to sense what is comfortable for the other person and to be careful not to intrude on their personal space.

The use of movement

Sometimes, at significant times in the counselling process or when a client is experiencing a high level of emotional distress it can be useful for the counsellor to lean forward. This can help the client to recognise that the counsellor is joining with them in an empathic way. However, a counsellor should be careful not to move too quickly during a counselling session, as this can distract the client and interrupt their train of thought. Clearly it is important for a counsellor to feel as relaxed as possible and feel free to move position in a natural way whenever that is more comfortable, but this should preferably be done slowly, not suddenly.

Facial expression

Facial expression usually has a significant impact on the joining process. Our facial expressions give very obvious clues about what we are thinking, and about our attitudes. Clearly, we want to show an expression of interest, care, and concern. Also, we want to try to avoid giving the impression that we are making negative judgements about the person or what the person is saying.

Eye contact

Eye contact is an important way in which we human beings make contact and join with each other. Not only do we use our eyes to make contact, but we also convey subtle messages by the way in which we use our eyes. We wonder what impression you would get if somebody was looking away from you while you were talking to them? Our guess is that you might believe that they weren't interested in what you were saying. However, if that person were to look at you directly, eye to eye, you might feel uncomfortable and think that their eyes were 'boring into you'. What is required is an appropriate level of eye contact where your eyes meet with the other person's eyes in a socially and culturally acceptable way. It is important to remember that different cultures have different social norms with regard to appropriate levels of eye contact (see Chapter 24). However, if your client is to believe that you are listening to what is being said, then eye contact at an appropriate level will give a clear message that you are attending to, and interested in, what is being said.

Use of voice

When we speak, it is not only the words that convey a message. Additionally, a message is conveyed through the way in which we use our voice. If we want to create an empathic relationship with our clients and to make it clear to them that we are concentrating on, and listening to, what they are saying, then we need to attend to our voice quality and be aware of the effects of:

- clarity and volume;
- speed of speaking; and
- tone of voice.

Over an extended period, David sought counselling help from a very capable and skilled counsellor. This counsellor helped him to address many painful issues and to experience satisfaction through personal growth. David very much appreciated the help given. However, the counsellor had one annoying fault. Sometimes, it was difficult to hear what he was saying because he mumbled. He didn't articulate words clearly and didn't talk loudly enough. At times this interfered with the counselling process as it was distracting. At other times it enabled David to deflect away from issues which he needed to address. It was also embarrassing for him to have to tell his counsellor from time to time that he couldn't hear him.

> **Speak clearly!**

When you are counselling, be careful to talk clearly and at a comfortable volume. Make sure that your tone of voice is one which will help to create an empathic relationship. Generally, it can be helpful if you match the speed of talking and tone of voice of your client. When the client talks rapidly respond similarly, and when they slow up be more leisurely yourself. If you match, to an appropriate degree, the speed and tone of speaking, and also the speed of breathing of an agitated client, you will be likely to join with them. Then, if you slow down your breathing and your speaking speed, and sit back comfortably in your chair, the client may follow your example, slow down and adopt a more relaxed posture.

Use of silence

When both of us were new counsellors, we remember that sometimes we did not focus fully on what the client was saying because we were too concerned with trying to decide what our next counselling response would be. This was detrimental to the counselling process. However, such behaviour is common among new counsellors as a result of nervousness and a desire to appear to be professional and competent, even though it is more important to be friendly and real. New counsellors are often uncomfortable with silence and feel that they have a responsibility to fill gaps in the conversation. Once you are comfortable with silence, there will be less pressure for you to give a response the instant the client stops talking. Instead you can feel relaxed enough to allow the client, if they want, to think in silence. Often a client who has just finished making a very powerful and personal statement will need time to sit silently and process what has been said.

When a client is silent, match that silence while continuing to pay attention by using appropriate eye contact, so that you are seen to be listening with a high level of interest. If you observe the client's eye movements and focusing, you may be able to tell when they are thinking and need to be left to think rather than be interrupted.

LEARNING SUMMARY

- Joining is an ongoing process.
- A counsellor's primary function is to deliberately and intentionally listen.
- Deliberate listening with interest involves use of minimal responses, brief invitations to continue, non-verbal behaviour, use of voice, and silence.
- Minimal responses can be verbal or non-verbal.
- Minimal responses let the client know that you are attending, and help create an empathic relationship. They can also give messages.
- Joining with the client is enhanced by matching non-verbal behaviour such as posture, matching verbal tone and speed, and making appropriate eye contact.
- Rapid movements by a counsellor can distract a client.
- Silence is important in giving the client time to think and process what has been said.
- A client's eyes may give you an indication of when they have stopped thinking.

Chapter 5

Paraphrasing of Content

As explained in the previous chapter, the primary function of a counsellor is to deliberately listen with interest so that clients believe with confidence that they are being both heard and understood. However, it's obvious that just attending to a client by matching non-verbal behaviour and giving minimal responses is not sufficient. The counsellor also needs to respond more actively, and by doing so to draw out the really important details of what the client is saying and to clarify those for the client. The most common and generally most effective way of doing this is by using the skill called *paraphrasing of content* or *reflection of content*. Using this skill, the counsellor paraphrases or reflects back to the client what the client has said to the counsellor. The counsellor does not just parrot or repeat word for word what the client has said. Instead, the counsellor picks out the most important content details of what the client has said and re-expresses them in the counsellor's own words rather than in the client's. The following are some examples of paraphrasing of content to illustrate how the skill is used.

Examples of paraphrasing or reflection of content

Example 1

Client Statement: *I'm fighting with my daughter, my husband's not speaking to me, at work the boss keeps picking on me, and what's more my best friend doesn't seem to understand me any more.*
Counsellor Response: You're having a lot of relationship problems.

48

Example 2

Client Statement: *I spent all day Saturday tidying up my girlfriend's garden but she was annoyed because she said I'd cut the shrubs too short, I'd over-pruned them. Then I went to a great deal of trouble repainting the back door. Once again she didn't like the colour. Finally I suggested that she might go out to eat with me and would you believe when she got to the restaurant she decided that she really didn't like that restaurant at all. I keep trying to think of things that she would like but whatever I do she never seems to be happy.*

Counsellor Response: It seems as though you just can't please your girlfriend.

Example 3

Client Statement: *Yesterday I rushed around, I seemed to have no time to myself, I went from one place to another and it was really hard to fit everything in.*

Counsellor Response: You had a very full day yesterday.

What the counsellor does when paraphrasing or reflecting content is literally to tell the client, in a clear, brief way, in the counsellor's own words, the most important things that the client has just told the counsellor. The counsellor tries to capture the essential ingredients of what the client is saying and reflect these back. This method alone, together with minimal responses, can be used successfully throughout a complete counselling session, if it is carried out by a skilful person who is capable of accurately and clearly reflecting content.

The following transcript of a short counselling conversation (using invented names) demonstrates the way in which paraphrasing alone can be used to bring a client to a sense of resolution.

Transcript of a counselling conversation using minimal responses and paraphrasing

Mary (the counsellor): Susan, you said that you would like to talk something over with me. Can you tell me what's troubling you? [Mary gives Susan an invitation to talk.]

Susan: Yes. I'm worried about what's happening at work. I'm getting very stressed when I'm there.

Mary: Mm-hmm.

Susan: *It seems as though I am continually at odds with some of the other workers and with my boss. I just don't seem to be on the same wavelength as them.*

Mary: You're not fitting in.

Susan: *No, I'm not. I don't agree with the policies which are being adopted by the top management because they don't fit in with the way I learnt to deal with customers. Over the years I've developed ways of working which I think work ...*

Mary: Right.

Susan: *And now I'm being expected to change my whole style of working.*

Mary: They want you to work in a way that doesn't suit you.

Susan: *Yes they do, and I'm beginning to think that I'll either have to resign or compromise my principles. I'm just not sure what to do.*

Mary: You have a difficult choice to make.

Susan: *Yes, I have ... [pause]*

Mary: [silent but attending]

Susan: *... but you know I don't see why I should resign. I need the job, it's convenient, the money's good, and there aren't many other jobs I could do that would suit me. They will just have to put up with me.*

Mary: You sound as though you've made a decision to stay.

Susan: *Yes, I have, but I'll need to think about the implications.*

Mary: Mm-hmm.

Susan: *I suppose that if I continue to work in the way I think is best I'll still get the outcomes the boss wants but she'll get annoyed because I'm not following policy ... Somehow, I've got to compromise so that I can satisfy the boss and still feel OK about what I'm doing myself.*

Mary: You'd like to please the boss and still feel OK yourself.

Susan: *Yes, I would. I would like to please the boss so that the atmosphere at work is more relaxed. I suppose I've been a bit stubborn in resisting change.*

Mary: Mmm.

Susan: *That's probably the issue. I don't like change. But then nobody does. I'd rather change and continue working where I am than move somewhere else.*

Mary: Accepting change is difficult for you.

Susan: *Yes it is. But that's what I need to do. I suppose that if I agree to do some in-service training I'd feel more confident about the new methods but I don't like other people believing that I need further training after all these years.*

Mary: Ah-ha.

Susan: *I suppose that the truth is that I do need further training and it's hard for me to accept that fact.*
Mary: You want other people to respect you as an experienced worker.
Susan: *Yes, and at the moment they see me as a dinosaur. Out of date and inflexible.*
Mary: Ah-ha, they don't see you as able to adapt.
Susan: *Well, I am out of date but I'm not inflexible. I can learn new ways of working. I'll show them that an old magician can learn new tricks!*
Mary: You're going to accept the challenge.
Susan: *Yes, I am. I don't want to be seen as an old fossil, because I'm not.*
Mary: You seem to have reached a firm conclusion.
Susan: *Yes, I have. Thank you for listening.*

If you look through the transcript above, you will notice that Mary has used no other responses except minimal responses and reflection of content. Once she combined a minimal response with paraphrasing by saying, 'Ah-ha, they don't see you as able to adapt.'

Did you notice as you read the transcript that there was a natural flow to the conversation? Each time Susan made a statement and Mary paraphrased it, her reflection of Susan's statement set off a train of thoughts for Susan so that she continued with the conversation in a natural way. Consequently, it would have seemed to Susan that Mary really was understanding what she was saying. Mary wasn't intruding on Susan's thoughts by adding in her own ideas.

By paraphrasing and reflecting back what Susan said, Mary was able to help Susan think clearly about what she had said. This enabled her to continue talking about the same issue, in a constructive way. It was as though she was walking along a path, in her thoughts, with Mary walking alongside her.

> Paraphrasing encourages the person to continue along their own path

You may have noticed that even though the conversation between Susan and Mary was short, Susan resolved her issue without Mary asking questions, putting in suggestions or giving advice. All she did was to skilfully reflect back to Susan what she was saying.

It's important for you to learn how to paraphrase. In order to help you to do this we have provided some more examples of paraphrasing below.

In each case we suggest that you might like to cover up the counsellor response with a sheet of paper, read the client statement and see whether you can work out a suitable counsellor response to the client's statement. Good paraphrasing doesn't intrude. It doesn't distract the client from the real issues that they are trying to resolve.

Further examples of paraphrasing

Example 4

Client Statement: *Within a week I've had a rates notice, an electricity bill, my car broke down and I've had to spend three hundred pounds having it fixed, there was a big dinner I had to attend as part of my work and it was very expensive, and in addition I've had to fork out money for my son's trip overseas and for my daughter's school fees.*
Counsellor Response: You've had a lot of expenses to meet in a very short time.

Example 5

Client Statement: *Now that my father has died I can't help thinking about him. I think about the good times I had with him when I was young and about the way he showed so much interest in me in the early days of my marriage. I remember the way he played with my children, his grandchildren. He always seemed to be enjoying himself.*
Counsellor Response: You have some good memories of your father.

Example 6

Client Statement: *The house is old and ramshackle, the rooms are very large, there isn't much in it and it needs redecorating. Parts of it are starting to fall down. Where you walk there are bare floorboards and they creak. It doesn't sound very much like home because it is such a big, open, old, barren sort of a place, but you know I really like living there.*
Counsellor Response: Even though the house is in poor condition, it's home to you.

Example 7

Client Statement: *I used to have a very bad drinking problem so I stopped drinking for a couple of years. Well last night I had a drink and now I'm just wondering how that's going to affect me in the future. I'm really surprised, though, because I was able to have just one drink and stop, whereas in the past I always used to carry on drinking once I'd started.*

Counsellor Response: Although you surprised yourself, you're not too sure how you'll cope with alcohol from now on.

Example 8

Client Statement: *My daughter's a very attractive girl, she's good looking and vivacious, she dresses very nicely, and she is a good-natured person. She often smiles and seems to be very happy.*
Counsellor Response: Your daughter has many positive qualities.

We need to remember that each counsellor will paraphrase in their own unique and personal way. Two counsellors hearing the same client statement will not necessarily pick up on the same detailed content as each other. The words they each use will be their own, so they will not express themselves in exactly the same way. The model answers which we have given above are not necessarily the best responses; they are our suggested responses, so yours might be different. We believe that we are good counsellors, but do not consider ourselves to be perfect when using any of the micro-skills. We have yet to find someone who is. It's really important to remember that it doesn't matter how perfect your responses are. What does matter is that you create a real, trusting, caring, empathic relationship with the client in which you are genuinely yourself. This may mean sometimes being a bungler, and occasionally saying something inappropriate. Both of us have at times given inappropriate responses. Although we try not to do that, there will always be times when we do.

Using inappropriate responses

Sometimes a counsellor's paraphrase will be inaccurate. More often than not when this happens the client will think more clearly about what they were trying to say, will say it again, and in the process clarify their thoughts. The counsellor can then check out that they have now understood correctly, thus making it clear that they do want to take the time to fully understand.

As we were writing this, we started to talk together about the inevitability of sometimes using inappropriate counselling responses. David explained that he used to think that it was a disaster to give an inappropriate response until he talked to an artist friend about pencil sketching. He told her how when he tried to sketch he very often had the sketch three-quarters complete and then ruined it by putting in a dark line in an inappropriate place. His artist friend laughed and said, 'You never draw lines in the wrong place, because whenever you put in a line you can use it

to create something different.' He learnt a lesson from what she said, and applied it to his counselling. Now, when he makes an inappropriate response, he uses that response. It will generate an interaction between the client and him which can be explored. He will encourage the client to talk about the effect of the inappropriate response. By doing this he uses the immediacy of the relationship between the client and himself. This will be discussed more fully in Chapter 19.

Parroting

Parroting is not the same as paraphrasing. Parroting involves repeating word for word what the client has said to you. Occasionally it can be useful to parrot the client's last few words to draw attention to the importance of those words, or to enable the client to continue a half-finished statement. As a general rule, paraphrasing is a much more helpful process. This is because paraphrasing picks out the most important and salient parts of the content rather than just repeating the words the client has used. Continually repeating part or all of what the client has said would be likely to annoy the client rather then create a good relationship. Skilful paraphrasing in the counsellor's own words does the reverse. It makes the client feel valued, listened to, and heard, and is useful in helping the client to move forward in their exploration.

In conclusion

In this chapter we have discussed paraphrasing or reflection of content. Paraphrasing is a very useful basic skill to use. To paraphrase you have to listen carefully and to repeat back in your own words the essence of what the client has said. By doing this, the client believes that you have heard them and also becomes more fully aware of what they have said. They are then able to really savour the importance of what they are talking about and to sort out their confusion.

LEARNING SUMMARY

- Paraphrasing involves reflecting back to the client the important content of what the client has said, but in a clearer way and using the counsellor's words.
- Parroting involves repetition of some of the client's words.
- Occasional parroting can be useful either to emphasise the importance of what the client has said or to help a client to complete a half-finished statement.
- Paraphrasing, together with the use of minimal responses, helps the client to follow through on a train of thoughts and continue talking.

Practice examples: Practice examples to help in learning to paraphrase are provided in Part VI.

Chapter 6

Reflection of Feelings

As explained in the previous chapter, one of the best ways to help clients to feel as though you are listening to them and understanding what they are telling you is to reflect back to them the content of what they are saying. Reflection of feelings is useful in a different way. When we reflect feelings we let the person know that we are empathising with them and are in touch with the way they are feeling. In our opinion, reflection of feelings is one of the most useful micro-skills when used correctly at appropriate times in the counselling process.

Reflection of feelings is similar to but also different from paraphrasing. It is similar because it involves reflecting back to the client information provided by the client. However, it is different because it involves reflecting back emotional feelings, whereas paraphrasing involves reflecting back the information and thoughts that make up the content of what the client is saying.

How are feelings different from thoughts?

Feelings are quite different from thoughts. Thoughts are at a 'head' level, they are continually running around in our brains. In contrast with this, feelings are at a gut level, not a head level. They are emotional in character and are linked to our bodily sensations. For example, a person who is feeling tense emotionally may experience the tension in their muscles, often in the neck or shoulders, and an anxious person may have sweaty palms, an increased heart rate, or the sensation of 'butterflies in the stomach'.

> Feelings are at a gut level – thoughts at a head level

Avoiding feelings

Frequently, clients try to avoid exploring their feelings because they want to avoid the pain associated with strong emotions such as sadness, despair, anger, and anxiety. We ourselves recognise that it's much less painful for us to philosophise about our problems, and to discuss them as though they were 'out there' and don't really belong to us, than for us to get in touch with the related emotions. Unfortunately when we avoid our feelings, philosophise, and talk in a general way about our problems rather than fully experiencing the effect they have on us emotionally, we rarely feel better or reach a resolution. Instead, we tend to go round in circles and get nowhere. However, if we get in touch with our feelings, own them, and experience them fully, then we usually move forward, to feel better emotionally and maybe then to make sensible decisions.

Experiencing feelings

It can be tempting for a new counsellor to help their client to avoid painful feelings rather than to face them. This is understandable because most of us learn from childhood to comfort people by encouraging them to run away from their feelings. We are taught to say, 'Don't cry, it'll be all right', when it quite probably won't be all right, and the person really needs to cry in order to release their emotional pain.

To be an effective counsellor you will need to unlearn some of what you learnt as a child. You will generally need to encourage your clients to experience their emotions, to be sad, to cry, to be angry, overwhelmed, amused, frightened or whatever. By doing this you will help them to gain from emotional release and to move forward. This healing process of emotional release is called *catharsis*.

> Catharsis involves releasing troubling emotional feelings

There are exceptions to this approach. A small minority of people are so continually in touch with and overwhelmed by their emotions, that to encourage them to do more of the same is unlikely to be useful. These people may find it more helpful to make use of their thinking processes in order to control their emotions. For them a more cognitive behavioural approach may be preferred (see Chapter 11).

Distinguishing between thoughts and feelings

New counsellors often have problems in distinguishing between thoughts and feelings because people often use the word 'feel' when they are describing a thought. For example if someone were to say, 'I feel angry', then they would be expressing a feeling, but if they were to say, 'I feel that counsellors learn best through practical experience', they would not be expressing a feeling, they would be describing a thought. It would have been more accurate to say, 'I think that counsellors learn best through practical experience.' The words 'feel that' followed by a string of words generally mean that a thought is being expressed and not a feeling. Feelings are usually expressed by one word. For example, a person can feel 'angry', 'sad', 'depressed', 'frustrated', 'miserable', 'tense', 'relaxed', 'happy' or 'frantic'. Each of these feelings is expressed by one word, whereas thoughts can only be expressed by using a string of words.

> Most feelings are described by using only one word

How to reflect feelings

When a counsellor reflects back a feeling to a client it is not essential to use the word 'feel'. Here are some options for reflecting feelings of anger and happiness:

- *'You're feeling angry'* or *'You feel angry'* or *'You're angry'*
- *'You're feeling happy'* or *'You feel happy'* or *'You're happy'*

As counsellors, we need to continually identify the client's feelings and to reflect them back at appropriate times. Sometimes a client will tell you directly how they are feeling and at other times you will need to be able to assess what they are feeling by listening to the content of what they are saying or by noting their non-verbal behaviour or by listening to their tone of voice.

Sometimes we will be uncertain about whether or not we are accurately identifying a feeling but may think that it is important to help the client to get more fully in touch with the feeling. In this case we might say something like:

- I am wondering whether you are feeling ... (angry, sad, etc)
- If I were you I think I might feel ...
- If that had happened to me I think I would feel ...

Feeling words

Table 6.1 provides a list of commonly used 'feeling' words. Notice that all of the words in the table could be used as counsellor responses by prefacing them with 'You're feeling ...', or 'You feel ...', or 'You're ...'. Clearly we have to use our personal judgement in deciding which option to use.

The words in Table 6.1 have been arranged so that the words on each line relate to each other over a continuum from strong feelings to mild feelings. Some of the cells in the table are white and contain question marks. You may wish to choose suitable words for insertion in these white cells and then look at Table 6.2 at the end of this chapter for our suggestions. Can you see how by choosing our words carefully we may be able to accurately reflect back a client's feelings?

With practice it becomes easier to identify feelings such as tension, distress and sadness from a person's body posture, facial expressions and movements. Tears starting to well up in your client's eyes might let you know about their sadness.

Permission to cry

Sometimes people need permission to cry because in our culture crying, particularly by men, is often considered to be unacceptable. If you say to a client, 'I can see the tears in your eyes' or 'For me, it's OK if you cry' or just 'It's OK to cry' in a gentle, accepting tone of voice, then the tears may start to flow. This can be helpful as it will enable the person to release their emotions more fully then just talking about them. If a client does start to cry, allow them to continue without unnecessary interruption until the emotion subsides naturally. Try not to intrude on their internal processes while they are crying because if you do they may withdraw from fully experiencing their feelings, and the healing effects of emotional release may be diminished.

Table 6.1 Some commonly used feeling words

Line	Strong feelings	Medium level feelings	Mild feelings
1	honoured cherished treasured	valued appreciated	accepted
2	powerful energetic	strong determined	positive certain
3	powerless	weak	tired
4	thrilled	very pleased	pleased
5	???	loved	liked respected
6	optimistic confident	???	uncertain
7	paranoid	suspicious	curious
8	hated	alienated	disliked
9	proud	self-satisfied	contented
10	perplexed	puzzled confused	uncertain doubtful
11	frantic agitated	???	concerned
12	relaxed	calm	indifferent
13	jealous	envious	discontented
14	???	surprised	pleased
15	terrified	???	worried anxious
16	distraught	distressed miserable	unhappy
17	secure	safe	OK
18	vulnerable	???	uncertain
19	appalled	dismayed	disappointed
20	humiliated ashamed	embarrassed	stupid

Table 6.1 Continued

Line	Strong feelings	Medium level feelings	Mild feelings
21	???	worn out	tired
22	intolerant	impatient	uneasy
23	betrayed	cheated	misled
24	ready to snap	tense	???
25	bewildered	puzzled	uncertain
26	horrified appalled shocked	dismayed taken aback	surprised
27	???	delighted	happy
28	devastated shattered broken-hearted	sad miserable depressed	disappointed troubled
29	grieving	shocked lost empty	alone
30	furious mad	angry resentful	???
31	abused victimised attacked	threatened	blamed

Response to reflection of feelings

If you reflect feelings accurately it is likely that the person you are helping will get more fully in touch with their emotional feelings. As a counsellor you do need to be prepared for a variety of possible responses when you reflect feelings. Sometimes a new counsellor will experience high levels of anxiety or heightened emotional feelings themselves, as a consequence of a client's response to reflection of feelings. For example, if you correctly say to your client, 'I get the impression that you are really hurting inside', then the client may get in touch with their painful feelings and start to cry. In this case, you will need to deal with your own emotional feelings that will be generated by being in the presence of someone who is crying.

> We need to be able to deal with our own feelings

As a counsellor you also need to be prepared to respond appropriately to unexpected responses to reflection of feelings. For example, you may correctly reflect back anger by saying, 'You're angry' or perhaps, 'You sound very angry.' Instead of owning the anger and recognising its true source, the client may respond by angrily snapping back with, 'I'm not angry', followed by an angry tirade, possibly directed at you. If this happens, while sensibly defusing the situation, recognise that you have been accurate in reflecting the person's feelings and that this may have been useful. You have enabled the client to indirectly express anger which they are not ready to own. They have been able to express some of their anger by directing it onto you, and it may be that they will feel better for that. However, dealing with angry clients can have its dangers, so be careful to ensure your own safety.

> Take action to ensure your own safety at all times

Another way in which an angry client may disown feelings of anger is to say, 'I'm not angry, I'm just frustrated.' In this case it may be helpful for the counsellor to respond by saying, 'My guess is that if I were you, I would feel angry.' By saying this, the counsellor effectively gives the client permission to get more fully in touch with angry feelings.

Being ready to burst!

Human beings can be likened in some ways to party balloons. When we are functioning effectively, we have sufficient emotional energy inside us to keep us motivated to live our daily lives adaptively and creatively: the balloon has sufficient air inside it to be robust and float through the air. At crisis times in our lives, the emotional pressure builds up until we are ready to burst. In this state our thought processes are often blocked or distorted and we are unable to cope. We feel out of control of ourselves. To regain control we first need to release some of the emotional pressure.

This may be difficult as many of us have been taught from childhood to hold our emotions in, not to cry, and not to be angry.

An effective counsellor can help a client to fully experience their emotions and thus to feel better as a result of releasing those emotions. With cathartic release the pressure in the balloon drops back to normal. Rational thinking can start to take place again so that constructive decision making can occur.

Reflection of feelings is therefore, as stated previously, one of the most important counselling micro-skills.

Examples of reflection of feelings

The following are examples of client statements, followed by suitable reflections of feeling. Before reading the suggested counsellor response for each example, you may wish to think about the response you would give.

Example 1
Client Statement: I keep expecting my mother to show more interest in me. Time and again I've asked her to come over to see me but she never does. Yesterday it was my birthday and she did come to visit me, but do you know she didn't even remember that it was my birthday. I just don't think she cares about me at all. [Said slowly in a flat tone of voice.]
Counsellor Response: You're disappointed *or* You feel hurt.

Example 2
Client Statement: First of all, my brother broke my electric drill. He didn't bother to tell me that he'd broken it, he just left it lying there. Then what do you think he did, he borrowed my motorbike without asking me. I feel like thumping him.
Counsellor Response: You're very angry *or* You're furious.

Example 3
Client Statement: I got a new job recently. It's quite different from the old one. The boss is nice to me, I've got a good office to work in, the whole atmosphere in the firm is really positive. I can't believe that I'm so lucky.
Counsellor Response: You feel really happy *or* You're really happy.

Example 4

Client Statement: Young people nowadays aren't like they used to be in my day, dressed smartly; they're dirty, they're rude, they don't stand for you in buses, I don't know what's become of the new generation!
Counsellor Response: You're disgusted.

Example 5

Client Statement: My boyfriend just rang me from his hotel overseas. He's a reporter and is in a real trouble spot. While I was talking to him on the phone I could hear angry voices in the background, and then there was an incredible crash, and the line went dead, and I don't know what's happened to him! [Said very quickly and breathlessly.]
Counsellor Response: You're terribly worried *or* You're panicking.

These examples probably gave you an idea of how difficult it is to assess the feelings underlying a client statement when non-verbal cues including facial expression and body posture are not available. When you are actively engaged in a counselling interaction with a client, it will be easier for you to identify what the client is feeling because you will have the use of all your senses. If you are attending closely to your client your own feelings may start to match theirs. When they are hurting, you may experience something of the hurt, at a less intense level, and this will be useful in helping you to reflect feelings accurately.

With experience at reflecting feelings you will be able to use a variety of expressions so that your responses sound natural rather than stereotyped and somewhat mechanical. Sometimes a short response such as 'You're sad' is appropriate. But at other times you might use expressions such as the following:

- *'I get the impression that you are very sad.'*
- *'From what you are saying, my guess is that you are feeling very sad.'*
- *'Right now you're sad.'*

As a general rule, try to keep your counselling responses short. Remember that it is desirable for the client to do most of the talking and that your job is to listen and hear. Long counsellor responses intrude on the client's own inner processes and prevent the client from freely and openly exploring their issues.

When you have fully mastered reflection of feelings, move ahead to the next chapter to discover how to combine reflection of *content* with reflection of *feelings*.

LEARNING SUMMARY

- Feelings are emotions, not thoughts. They are experienced at a gut level and not at a head level.
- Feelings are usually expressed by one word, for example, 'sad', 'happy', 'lonely' or 'bewildered'.
- Reflecting feelings back to clients is helpful in promoting emotional release with consequent healing.
- Clients sometimes need permission to cry.
- Counsellors need to ensure their own safety when dealing with angry clients.

Practice examples: Practice examples to help in learning to reflect feelings are provided in Part IV.

Table 6.2   Suggested solutions for Table 6.1

Line	Suggested solutions	Line	Suggested solutions
5	adored worshipped idolised	18	insecure
6	hopeful	21	exhausted
11	worried	24	nervous worried
14	amazed astonished	27	ecstatic
15	frightened scared	30	annoyed

Chapter 7

Paraphrasing Content and Reflection of Feelings

In previous chapters we have discussed the skills involved in listening, using minimal responses and encouragers, in reflecting content, and in reflecting feelings. These skills are commonly known as Rogerian counselling skills because they were initially identified and extensively used by Carl Rogers. We believe that these skills are the most basic and important ones, because they provide a foundation onto which other skills can be added. Remembering this can be particularly useful for counsellors who use an integrative approach.

> Rogerian counselling skills provide a foundation onto which other skills can be added

In addition to using reflection of content and reflection of feelings as separate skills, we can combine these skills to reflect content and feeling in single counsellor responses. With experience you will find that it is often convenient to combine these two types of reflection. For example, the statement 'You feel disappointed because your brother didn't do as he promised' includes both feeling and content. The feeling is disappointment, the content is to do with the reasons for being disappointed – because the brother didn't do as he promised. So that the idea of combining reflection of feeling and content becomes clearer, let us look at a few examples. First, we will take another look at the examples given in Chapter 6, but this time the counsellor responses will include reflection of both feeling and content, whereas in Chapter 6 reflection of feeling alone was used. Notice that the responses are short and not wordy.

Examples of reflection of content and feeling

Example 1

Client Statement: I keep expecting my mother to show more interest in me. Time and again I've asked her to come over to see me, but she never does. Yesterday it was my birthday and she did come to visit me, but do you know she didn't even remember that it was my birthday. I just don't think she cares about me at all. [Said slowly in a flat tone of voice.]

Counsellor Response: You're disappointed by your mother's behaviour *or* You feel hurt by your mother's apparent lack of caring.

Example 2

Client Statement: First of all, my brother broke my electric drill. He didn't bother to tell me that he'd broken it, he just left it lying there. Then what do you think he did, he went and borrowed my motorbike without telling me. I feel like thumping him.

Counsellor Response: You're very angry with your brother because he doesn't respect your possessions *or* You're furious with your brother because he doesn't respect your possessions.

Example 3

Client Statement: I got a new job recently. It's quite different from the old one. The boss is nice to me, I've got a good office to work in, the whole atmosphere in the firm is really positive. I can't believe that I'm so lucky.

Counsellor Response: You feel really happy with your new job *or* You're delighted to have a pleasant work environment.

Example 4

Client Statement: Young people nowadays aren't like they used to be in my day, dressed smartly; they're dirty, they're rude, they don't stand for you in buses, I don't know what's become of the new generation!

Counsellor Response: Young people disgust you *or* You feel disgusted by the younger generation's behaviour.

Example 5

Client Statement: My boyfriend just rang me from his hotel overseas. He's a reporter and is in a real trouble spot. While I was talking to him on the

phone I could hear angry voices in the background, and then there was an incredible crash, and the line went dead, and I don't know what's happened to him! [Said very quickly and breathlessly.]
Counsellor Response: You sound really worried about what might have happened to your boyfriend.

Further examples of reflection of feeling and content

Here are some more client statements for you to use for practice if you wish. In each case, you might like to invent a suitable counsellor response and then compare your response with the one supplied at the end of this chapter.

Example 6
Client Statement: I'm getting very worn out, whenever anything goes wrong I get blamed. I spend my time running around looking after other people's needs and in return I get no thanks and lots of criticism. It's just not fair. The more I do, the less I'm appreciated.

Example 7
Client Statement: You just wouldn't believe, the dishwasher has broken down, the washing machine still hasn't been fixed, my husband ran the car into a post, my daughter's bike has a puncture, I just can't believe it, so much is going wrong. What's going to go wrong next? I just can't take any more.

Example 8
Client Statement: I just can't understand my son and daughter. They always want to be together, but whenever they are together they fight. It doesn't seem to matter what I suggest they do when they're together, they always start an argument. It's incessant, it never stops, and now I'm starting to get like them, I'm starting to get angry and irritable too. Sometimes I'm so angry that I could knock their heads together.

Example 9
Client Statement: I've done everything I can to get her back. I've given her presents, I've phoned her, I've written her letters, sent messages through her friends, I've said I'm sorry, and I've even offered to go and get counselling with her, but whatever I do I just can't get through to her and she just won't come back to me. I just can't live without her!

Example 10

Client Statement: I can't understand why my landlord won't give me my bond back but he won't. I cleaned the flat, I left it in good condition, I know he doesn't like me and he just won't give me the bond back. I know I really ought to go and confront him and say to him that this isn't fair. It's not fair. I even got my friends to come round and help me clean up. I spent two days trying to make the place decent, and it was beautiful when I walked out, but he still won't give me the money back. I really ought to go and confront him, but he's a big man and he tends to get very angry at times and you never know – if there was an argument he might hit me!

Example 11

Client Statement: I went next door to ask my neighbour if he would drive me over to my boyfriend's place because I'm worried about him. I know it's a long way, but I'm sure my neighbour could do it. All he said was, 'No, I can't afford the petrol, and in any case I don't want to go out in this bad weather.' I can't understand how he can be so callous because my boyfriend could be seriously ill for all I know. I just can't understand how my neighbour can sit and do nothing, and I'm sure that if it was one of his friends, someone he cared about, that he would go out tonight.

The use of short responses

As stated previously, it is usually desirable for a counsellor to keep responses short so as not to intrude on the client's inner processes. The problem with using long statements is that they may take the client away from what they are currently experiencing and may bring them out of their own world and into the counsellor's world.

Deciding whether to reflect content or feeling or both

We have just been explaining how it is easy to combine the skills of reflection of content and reflection of feelings. There are times when it is appropriate to use this combined type of response. However, at other times it will be more appropriate, in the interests of brevity, to use either reflection of content, or reflection of feeling, but not both. This is particularly true when using reflection of feeling. Sometimes reflecting the feeling alone, without mention of content, can be more powerful in helping the client to own a feeling that they may be trying to avoid owning. If a counsellor says, 'You're really hurting' the statement focuses on the client's pain rather than encouraging the client to escape from experiencing pain by latching onto 'content' words and moving into a cognitive rather than a feeling level of experiencing.

> Using reflection of feeling alone directly focuses on the emotional feeling

Generally, it is desirable for counsellors to help clients to experience their emotional feelings rather than to suppress feelings by working at a head or cognitive level. Experiencing feelings fully is often painful, but is cathartic and consequently therapeutically desirable for most clients. However, as discussed in Chapter 6, there are a minority of clients who have difficulty living adaptive lives because they are not able to deal with and control continually high levels of emotional expression. For such clients, it may be more useful to focus on content than feelings.

The use of lead-in words when reflecting

Generally, it is sufficient to use the reflection statements as given in the previous examples in this chapter and in Chapters 5 and 6. However, sometimes it can be helpful to preface a reflection statement by using words such as those suggested below.

When reflecting content

- *'I've heard you say ...'*
- *'What I've heard you say is ...'*
- *'I get the impression that ...'*
- *'I'm getting the idea that ...'*

When reflecting feelings or content and feelings

- *'If I'm hearing you correctly you are (disappointed etc.) ...'*
- *'I'm sensing that you feel ...'*
- *'I get the impression that you feel ...'*

These suggestions should be used sparingly otherwise they are likely to sound repetitive and trite. Usually, a reflection such as 'You're angry because ...' is sufficient.

Learning the skills already discussed

We have now discussed the use of the basic skills of *listening, the use of minimal responses and encouragers, reflection of content, reflection of feelings*, and *reflection of both content and feelings*. We believe that it is sensible to practise these skills until they are fully mastered before proceeding to learn any of the other micro-skills. This is because, in our view, these skills provide a foundation onto which other skills can be added. Use of these skills is also extremely helpful in enhancing the quality of the counselling relationship.

Initially, during the learning process, you may feel awkward in using counselling skills. This is normal, because it is always difficult to learn new ways of relating. However we suggest that you keep practising until you can use the skills in a natural way which does not seem to be contrived or artificial. Once this has been achieved, the counselling interaction will flow smoothly and you will not feel pressured to think of 'smart' responses. Instead, your listening skills will be enhanced and you will feel more relaxed and spontaneous. Interestingly, if the skills are used competently, the client will not realise that you are primarily using reflection, but will feel as though you are listening and commenting in a sensible way on what is being said.

> With practice the skills learnt will fit naturally into your normal conversational style

Many experienced counsellors use the basic skills which we have already discussed more frequently than other skills, because these skills enable the client to explore their world fully in their own way without interference by the counsellor, but with the certain knowledge that the counsellor is actively listening.

Focusing on the counselling relationship

Remember that counselling is about walking alongside a person as they explore their world. Some people say that a counsellor should, metaphorically speaking, walk in the shoes of the other person. Certainly it is important that the counsellor attempts to see the world in the way the client sees the world. Thus, at times, an experienced counsellor will almost get into the client's shoes, so that they can better understand what it feels like to be the client, and how it might be to look at the world from the client's viewpoint. By doing this a trusting relationship is developed which enables the client to risk exploring the most painful issues of their life, and so to move forward out of confusion.

Suggested counsellor responses for further examples of reflection of content and feeling

Example 6

Counsellor Response: You feel resentful because other people don't appreciate your efforts.

Example 7

'You're feeling overwhelmed by so many negative experiences' *or* 'So many things have gone wrong that you're starting to feel pressured and unable to cope.'

Example 8

'The continual fighting between your son and daughter infuriates you.'

Example 9

'You're despairing because you can't get your wife to come back to you.'

Example 10

'Even though you believe the landlord is being unfair you're too scared to confront him.'

Example 11

'You're disgusted by your neighbour's unwillingness to help.'

LEARNING SUMMARY

- Reflection of content and feeling can be combined into one statement.
- There are times when it is more effective to reflect back only feelings, or only content, and not both.
- Effective counsellors try to see the world as their client sees it.

Practice examples: Practice examples to help in learning to reflect content and feelings are provided in Part VI.

Chapter 8

Use and Abuse
of Questions

You may be surprised that a chapter on asking questions hasn't come earlier in this book. Certainly, we believe that many people in the general community assume that counselling necessarily requires a counsellor to ask questions throughout a counselling session. Additionally, in some therapeutic approaches there is a stronger emphasis on the use of questions than in others. For example, in narrative therapy (White and Epston, 1990) there is an emphasis on exploring and understanding the client's story through an enquiry process involving the use of a particular style of questioning. In brief solution-focused counselling (O'Connell, 1998), although the exploration of the client's problem and possible solutions are collaborative, questions are extensively used in order to explore past successes and search for possible solutions. Similarly, in Cognitive and Cognitive Behavioural Counselling significant use is made of questions in helping the counsellor to understand the problem, thoughts related to the problem, and their origins.

> Integrative counsellors use questions sparingly
> but effectively

As integrative counsellors we recognise that knowing how to use questions effectively can be of great use in the counselling process. In Chapter 12 we will examine a complete counselling process and explain how questions can be especially useful at particular times in that process. However, as integrative counsellors, we have found that it is usually not necessary to ask many questions at all in most counselling sessions. Certainly this is generally true when counselling people who need help in dealing with emotional issues rather than behavioural problems. Most of the information the counsellor needs to know will emerge naturally without asking questions if the counsellor actively listens to the client, uses the skills which have already been learnt, and skilfully reflects back the content and feeling of what the client is saying.

Although questions are certainly useful, there is often a temptation, particularly for new counsellors, to use them when they are not required. If this is done, the counselling process is likely to be compromised. Consequently, before discussing the use of questions we will consider the abuse of questions.

The abuse of questions

There are a number of problems associated with using too many questions when counselling. These relate to:

- being intrusive;
- interrogating the client;
- creating unnecessary inequality;
- compromising the counselling process;
- controlling what the client explores;
- using 'Why?' questions; and
- satisfying the counsellor's needs.

Being intrusive

Often, people who come to see us as counsellors have never met us before. We are strangers to them, and yet we hope that they will feel free to talk to us about things that are troubling them which are very personal. Many people who come to see us have been unable to talk about their problems to family or friends because they have felt unable to disclose their innermost thoughts to them. As counsellors, our first job is to join with the person who has come to see us in a way which will allow them to trust us. We need to be aware of the difficulty they may have in disclosing personal information. We need to give them time without rushing them so that gradually they are able to start trusting us with what is likely to be sensitive and private information. If we ask questions to obtain information before trust is established, the client is likely to withdraw and withhold information from us. This is generally true, and is especially true when working with people from particular family or ethnic cultures. Many people grow up in a cultural environment which precludes disclosing private information to people outside the immediate family. Asking questions of such people may be seen as intrusive and damage their ability to join with and learn to trust us.

Interrogating the client

If a counsellor asks one question after another the counselling session will become more like an interrogation than a counselling session. The person who has come for help may start to feel pressured and overwhelmed by the questioning, and may be worried by the intrusiveness of the process. Have you ever felt uncomfortable yourself when someone has asked you a number of personal questions? We have. Our natural reaction is to withdraw and to say very little. This is what is likely to happen in a counselling session when a counsellor relies on asking questions rather than using reflective listening to help the client to feel free to talk. It is obvious that it is not helpful to use a counselling process which results in the client becoming less open and communicative.

Interrogating is NOT counselling

Creating unnecessary inequality

As counsellors it is important that we don't set ourselves up as experts who are superior to or different from the people we're trying to help. As we have discussed earlier, it is inevitable in a counselling relationship that there will be a level of inequality because the roles of the client and counsellor are clearly different. The client has come for help and the counsellor is the helper. As a result of the difference in roles, we need to be careful to avoid creating an undesirable power imbalance resulting in disempowerment of the client. While recognising the essential difference in roles, what we want to do is to join in a collaborative process with our clients in a relationship where any power imbalance is minimised. When they are talking to us, the conversation needs to be as natural as possible. If we ask too many questions, the conversation will become very one-sided. This will interfere with our ability to join with the client in a person-to-person relationship so that we can enable them to share, explore, and find solutions to their problems.

> If we value and respect the person, they will not be disempowered

Compromising the counselling process

Have you ever noticed what happens in a conversation when one person continually asks questions of another? In our experience when this happens, the person who is being questioned will often start to withdraw and wait for the next question to be asked before continuing. Similarly in counselling, asking too many questions will interrupt the normal conversational flow. The client may start to feel pressured and withdraw, and instead of thinking about what they want to tell the counsellor may wait for the next question before continuing. If during a counselling session you recognise that this process is occurring, then it is usually advisable to reflect back content or feeling, or to summarise what you have learnt instead of following up with another question.

Controlling what the client explores

A major problem with relying on the use of questions is that the counsellor may end up controlling the direction in which the conversation will go.

This is, as a general rule, unfortunate, because it is desirable for the client to go in whatever direction their energy leads them. It is important for the client to fully explore the area in which their problem lies. Often a client won't zero in on their real problem until they have spent some time meandering around the general problem area. If the counsellor tries to find out what is really troubling a person by predominantly asking questions, the client may never move towards the most painful things that are causing trouble, but may in fact just go off on a tangent in a direction of the counsellor's choosing. Once again, the solution is to use a reflective active listening approach instead of relying on questions.

Using 'Why?' questions

There is one particular type of question that we recommend counsellors try to avoid using unless absolutely necessary. Try to avoid asking questions beginning with 'Why?'. The problem with asking 'Why?' questions is that in response to such questions clients tend to look for an intellectually thought-out response, rather than centring on what is happening to them internally. 'Why?' questions tend to generate answers that are 'out there' – answers that don't seem to come from inside the client and often aren't convincing. They frequently fall into the category of 'excuses' or 'rationalisations'. In comparison to 'Why?' questions, questions beginning with 'What', 'How', and 'When' are generally more useful. Open questions often begin with these words as will be discussed later in this chapter.

Satisfying the counsellor's needs

It is very easy for new counsellors to fall into the habit of asking questions at inappropriate times instead of using other more useful micro-skills. If you find yourself doing this, ask yourself what your goal is; why are you asking questions?

> Asking unnecessary questions is unhelpful

Are you just curious and seeking information to satisfy your own curiosity? If so, this is not a legitimate reason for asking questions. By asking questions to satisfy your own needs you might interrupt the natural flow of the client's conversation and may be seen as intrusive. If your goal is to stimulate the client into talking, then you are probably using the wrong approach. More often than not, simply reflecting back what has already been said will stimulate the client into further sharing of important and relevant personal information without the need for you to ask a question.

The use of questions

From the previous discussion it is obvious that there can be problems with asking unnecessary questions and in asking questions at inappropriate times. Having said this, we would like to make it clear that at times in the counselling process, as will be discussed in Chapter 12, the appropriate use of questions can considerably enhance the counselling process.

Questions broadly fall into two categories: open questions and closed questions. Additionally, there are a number of types of question which are useful for specific purposes. Open questions and closed questions can both be useful in the counselling process and it is necessary for you to fully understand the difference between the two types. Then it will be clear when it is more appropriate to use closed questions, and when it is more appropriate to use open questions.

Closed questions

Closed questions are questions that lead to a specific answer. Usually the answer to a closed question is very short. It may be an answer like 'Yes' or 'No'. Consider for example the closed question, 'Did you come here by bus today?' Obviously the most probable answer is either 'Yes' or 'No'. The client may choose to expand on the answer but is unlikely to do so. Closed questions such as 'Do you love your wife?' and 'Are you angry?' usually lead to the answer 'Yes' or 'No'. If I ask the closed question, 'How many years have you lived in Manchester?' the answer might be 'Twenty-four', and it is a specific answer.

> Responses to closed questions are usually short

There are times in a counselling session when you will need to ask closed questions because you require an answer to a specific question. There are also other important reasons for asking closed questions, as we shall see later. However, there are some problems with asking closed questions and these will probably be apparent to you already. If you ask a closed question, it is possible that the client may continue to talk to you and to enlarge on the answer given, but it is not necessary for the client to do that. Moreover, if they directly answer your question, they may feel restricted in the type of answer they can give. Another problem is that closed questions can be leading questions and sometimes suggest to the client that the counsellor has a specific agenda or point of view. The client may then feel constrained with regard to what they may say, and may believe that it is important for them to respect what they perceive to be the perceived agenda of the counsellor. For example, if a counsellor were to ask the question, 'Do you think that you did that because your mother is a domineering person?', the client might feel restricted in what they would be able to say, believing that the counsellor sees their mother as domineering and their behaviour as a result of that. Thus, the counsellor's implied suggestion might constrain the client from thinking and talking freely. Lawyers in a court like to ask closed questions so that witnesses are restricted in the range of answers that can be given. Counsellors are not lawyers, and generally the counsellor's intention is to free the client up so they can speak more freely.

Open questions

The open question is very different in its effect from the closed question. It gives the client lots of scope, allows the client to explore any relevant area, and in fact encourages the client to freely divulge additional material. If I ask the closed question, 'Did you come here by bus?', the answer is likely to be 'Yes' or 'No'. Contrast this with the open question, 'How did you travel here?' The client is freer to answer the open question and the answer is likely to be richer in information. For example, the client might explain the difficulties involved in the journey, might describe the type of transport used, might talk about having travelled with someone else, or might talk about experiences during the journey.

Examples of open and closed questions

Examples to illustrate the difference between closed and open questions are presented below. In each case we suggest that you might like to read the closed question and try to replace it by an equivalent open question yourself before reading the suggested alternative.

Example 1

Closed Question: Do you feel angry?
Open Question: How do you feel?

Example 2

Closed Question: How many children do you have?
Open Question: What can you tell me about your children?
(An alternative to this open question is to use a statement requesting information such as: 'Tell me about your children.')

Example 3

Closed Question: Do you argue with your wife often?
Open Question: What is your relationship like with your wife?

Example 4

Closed Question: Did you punish your son when he misbehaved?
Open Question: What did you do when your son misbehaved?

Example 5

Closed Question: Do you love your husband?
Open Question: Can you tell me about your feelings towards your husband?

Example 6

Closed Question: Is the atmosphere tense at home?
Open Question: What's the atmosphere like at home?

The closed questions above give the client little room to use their own imagination when giving an answer. The sort of answer given to a closed question will usually be direct and probably short. A closed question doesn't encourage the client to be creative and share new information, but tends to confine the client to a limited response.

> An open question extends an invitation to expand on the answer

The open question is quite different as you can see from the above examples. In each case, by asking an open question, the counsellor might get unexpected additional information. If you look at the open question,

'What can you tell me about your children?', you will realise that the client could give a number of quite different answers. For example, the client might say, 'My children are beautiful and very happy' or, 'I have two sons and a daughter' or, 'My children are all grown up and my husband and I live happily together on our own.' It is clear from this example that by asking an open question the counsellor may get a variety of answers and may get an answer quite different from the one which might have been expected. This is an advantage, because counsellors are not mind-readers, and cannot know what the client is thinking unless the client verbalises their thoughts. Also, it is sensible for counsellors to use questions that will encourage the client to talk about those things that are of most interest to the client, rather than those things that are of most interest to the counsellor.

When to use closed questions

As explained previously, it is generally preferable to use open questions rather than closed questions. Exceptions are when helping a client to be more specific, or when specific information is required. In such cases closed questions are very appropriate. In order to make sense of the client's story a counsellor may need to know whether the client is married, whether they have children, how old they are. If a counsellor needs to know this information, then it may be appropriate to ask directly by using closed questions.

Practice examples

Below are some more examples of closed questions. You may wish to practise framing open questions to replace them. Suggested open questions for each example are given at the end of this chapter.

Example 7
Would you like fish for dinner tonight?

Example 8
Do you like it when your husband praises you?

Example 9
Was your mother a dominating person?

Example 10
Did your father make you come to see me?

Example 11
Did the change disrupt your life?

Questions for specific purposes

In the previous discussion, we have strongly suggested that questions are best used sparingly. However, it is important to recognise that when questions are used creatively and appropriately, they can be extremely powerful in achieving specific purposes. We will now consider a number of questions which are useful for specific purposes. In addition to the types of question described below, Chapter 18 includes examples of several other types of question which are specifically useful in enabling a client to make use of their strengths.

Questions to invite the client to talk freely

When a client first comes to see a counsellor they need to be put at ease. Particularly if they are not familiar with the counselling process, they are likely to expect the counsellor to start the conversation. Obviously, as part of the joining process, the counsellor needs to introduce themselves. It is also important for the counsellor to give the client an invitation which will help them to feel free to talk about anything they want. This can be done by asking questions such as:

- *'Would you like to tell me why you have come to see me?'*
- *'What is it that you would like to talk to me about?'*
- *'Are you able to tell me what's troubling you?'*

When asking questions such as these it is important for the counsellor to be patient and not to hurry the client. It is quite common for a person coming to a counsellor for the first time to find it difficult to start talking and to say, 'I don't know where to start'. In this case it can be useful to say to the client *'Take your time, there is no hurry. When you're ready, tell me whatever it is that you would like to talk about.'* By doing this you give the person permission to take their time, to sort out their thoughts, and then to start talking.

Sometimes it is useful to ask a client, *'Would you like to tell me more?'*. This can be particularly useful when the client has given a very brief summary of the problem and is uncertain about whether or not it is appropriate for them to go into more detail.

General information-seeking questions

We use general information-seeking questions in everyday conversation in order to find out information which may be useful, or of interest to us. In counselling, when such questions are framed in a way which indicates the counsellor's genuine curiosity and interest, the client is likely to feel valued and to respond positively. Requests for information should be made with caution. As a counsellor, before you ask for information, ask yourself whether you really need it. If you didn't have the information, would you still be able to help the client? If the answer to that question is 'Yes', then asking a question may be unnecessary, and the desire to ask the question may stem from your own needs. In our opinion, there is no justification for a counsellor seeking information solely in order to satisfy their own curiosity. As explained previously, to do so would be to pry unnecessarily into the client's affairs. Such prying is likely to intrude into the counselling process and interrupt the natural flow of the counselling interaction.

Questions which clarify what the client has said, or help the client to be more specific

Clients frequently make very general, vague statements, and this is unhelpful to both the client and the counsellor because it is impossible to think clearly about a problem if it is expressed in vague, woolly, non-specific language. Consequently, when clients make such statements, it is often useful for the counsellor to ask a question to help the client to clarify their thinking, be more specific and to focus more clearly on what is troubling them. For instance, if a client makes a vague statement like, 'That sort of thing always makes me annoyed', it may not be at all clear to either the client or the counsellor what is really meant by the words 'that sort of thing'. It is then appropriate for the counsellor to ask the client, '*What sort of thing?*'. Similarly, a client might say, 'I just can't stand it any more.' The word 'it' is non-specific and to help the client to be more specific the counsellor might ask, '*What is it that you can't stand any more?*' Similarly, consider the client statement, 'I'm fed up with him.' This is a very general statement and may need clarification, in which case the counsellor might well respond by asking, '*Can you tell me in what ways you are fed up with him?*'

Questions to heighten the client's awareness

These questions are commonly used in Gestalt therapy (Clarkson 2000). The aim of these questions is to help the client to become more fully aware of what is happening within them, either somatically or emotionally, so that they can intensify those bodily or emotional feelings, deal with them, and move on to discussing associated thoughts. Typical questions in this category are:

- *'What are you feeling emotionally right now?'*
- *'Where in your body do you experience that emotional feeling?'*
- *'Can you tell me what's happening inside you right now?'*
- *'What's happening inside you right now?'*

If a client is starting to cry, the counsellor might ask, *'Can you put words to your tears?'*. This may enable the person to verbalise thoughts related to the internal experience. By doing this, these thoughts can be processed, the counsellor is aware of them, and can achieve empathic joining and help the client move ahead. Similarly, if a client seems to be stuck and unable to speak, the counsellor might ask, *'Can you tell me what is happening inside you right now? What are you experiencing in your body?*

Transitional questions

Generally, as we have discussed previously, it is important to allow the client to travel in their own direction at their own pace in the counselling conversation. However, sometimes the client will deflect away from discussing important issues. One way of addressing this is to give the client feedback about the process that you have noticed, and to say something such as, 'I notice that you have moved away from talking about ...' An alternative is to use a transitional question.

The transitional question effectively returns the focus to an earlier part of the discussion. Transitional questions generally start with a statement about an earlier part of the conversation, and then raise a question about that earlier discussion. Examples of transitional questions are:

- *'Earlier you talked about the option of leaving your job. I'm wondering about how you're feeling about that option now?'*
- *'A few minutes ago you mentioned the possibility that you might consider killing yourself. I'm wondering how you're feeling about the possibility right now?'*
- *'Earlier today you mentioned that you are extremely troubled by your relationship with your neighbour. Would you like to spend some time talking about that relationship now?'*

■ *'I've noticed that several times you've alluded to your fear of the future. Would you like to tell me more about that fear?'*

When using transitional questions the counsellor makes a clear decision to be an active participant in the conversation, and to take responsibility for introducing a possible change in the direction of the counselling process.

Choice questions

Choice questions have their origin in reality therapy (Glasser & Wubbolding 2000). They are especially popular for use by counsellors who work with young people. These questions provide a way for a counsellor to help the client recognise that they have choice about the way they think and behave, and that there are consequences associated with their choices. Choice questions specifically invite the client to think about and consider alternative choices. Examples of choice questions are:

■ *'What would have been a better choice for you to have made at that time?'*
■ *'In what other ways could you respond to that?'*
■ *'If the same situation arises during the coming weeks, what do you think you will do? (Will you do this, or will you do that?)'*
■ *'What would you like to do now, would you like to continue talking about this issue or would you like to leave it there for now?'*

Such questions about the past, present, or future, enable the client to look at the likely consequences of different behaviours. By exploring choices and consequences, the person is likely to be better prepared for future situations.

The guru question

Guru questions have their origin in gestalt therapy (Clarkson, 2000). When using this type of question, the counsellor first invites the client to imagine that they can stand aside and look at themselves from a distance, and then to give themselves some advice. For example, the counsellor might say, *'Imagine for a minute that you were a very wise guru and that you could give advice to someone just like you. What advice would you give them?'* With some people this approach can be extremely helpful as human beings often find that it is easier to give advice to other people than to recognise and own what is the most sensible thing for them to do themselves.

Career questions

Career questions are questions which exaggerate and extrapolate beyond the client's present behaviour. They help the client to recognise that they have a choice about the direction in which they are heading and that this choice might lead to extremes of lifestyle. An example of a career question is: *'What would it be like for you to make a career out of being an extremely high achiever who set an example for everybody else by giving up everything except hard work?'* This question raises the client's awareness of a path or journey along which they can progress, if they wish. It enhances their ability to make choices, at the current point in time, to bring about change which might have long-term positive consequences for them.

Career questions have a level of paradoxical intent. They are asked in the hope that the ensuing discussion will lead the client to make a sensible choice which will result in their choosing satisfying behaviours that are not extreme. However, we need to be careful to use these questions with discretion or they may become self-fulfilling prophecies. Consider the question: *'Would you like to continue your shoplifting behaviour, take more risks, and move on to becoming a career criminal?'* While this question might be useful for some clients, for others it might encourage them to follow the 'suggested' career.

Circular questions

Circular questions come from the Milan model of family therapy (Palazzoli et al. 1980). They are most useful when working with couples or families. However circular questions can also be useful when working with individual clients who are having difficulty in getting in touch with their own feelings, attitudes, thoughts, or beliefs. Instead of asking the client directly about how they feel or what they think, or what their attitude is, the counsellor asks them how someone else feels or thinks, or asks what the other person's attitude might be. Examples of circular questions are:

- *'I wonder how your brother feels now that your father has gone to jail?'*
- *'If your wife was here, what do you think she would say about your need to come for counselling?'*
- *'How do think your colleague feels about the possibility that you might both be retrenched?'*
- *'If you had to guess, what do think your wife's attitude is to your loss of mobility?'*

By asking circular questions such as these, the counsellor effectively invites the client to speculate about someone else's feelings, thoughts, beliefs, or attitudes. This can be less threatening than asking the client to talk directly about themselves. Often, having answered a circular question, the client will continue by talking about their own feelings, beliefs, or thoughts, because they want to make it clear whether they agree or disagree with the person who was mentioned in the circular question.

Miracle questions

Miracle questions are used to help the client begin to find hypothetical solutions to the problems they are experiencing. Typical miracle questions are:

- *'If a miracle happened and the problem was solved what would you be doing differently?'*
- *'If things changed miraculously, what would life be like?'*
- *'If you waved a magic wand what would be different?'*

This sort of question appeals to people who have a good imagination. Such questions enable them to explore what would be different if their situation changed for the better. As a result of thinking about ways in which things might change, they are likely to explore new ideas which might be useful in helping them to make changes.

Goal-oriented questions

Goal-oriented questions are direct questions that invite exploration of ways in which things could be different. They help the client to identify broad changes which they might like to make. In exploring how things could be different, goal-oriented questions invite the client to look ahead to the future. Examples of goal-oriented questions are:

- *'What do you think your life would be like if you didn't get angry?'*
- *'How would you know that you had resolved this problem?'*
- *'Can you tell me what your life would be like, and what sort of thing you would be doing, if you were no longer feeling miserable?'*
- *'If you had a particular goal which you wanted to achieve with regard to ..., what would it be?'*
- *'How would you like things to be?'*
- *'When you think about ..., can you identify any particular goals?'*

Other goal-oriented questions identify perceived restraints, which in the client's mind interfere with their ability to achieve particular goals. They help the client to identify ways to overcome these restraints. Examples are:

- *'What stops you from achieving your goal?'*
- *'What would you need to do to achieve your goal?'*

Scaling questions

Scaling questions often lead into goal-oriented questions as they are related to goals. They help the client to be specific when identifying and discussing goals. Examples of scaling questions are:

- *'On a scale of 1–10, 1 being hopelessly incompetent and 10 being really competent, where do you think you fit right now?'*
- *'On the scale of 1–10, where would you like to be in the future?'*
- *'If 1 corresponded to being an honest and upright citizen, and 10 corresponded to being a hardened criminal, where would you like to be?'*

In conclusion

In this chapter we have looked at the usefulness of closed and open questions and have discussed the differences between the two. We have also considered the use of a number of questions that are useful for particular purposes. Now is the time for you to practise using questions. There is a risk that through practising asking questions, you may quickly become reliant on using them excessively. If that were to happen, it would be unfortunate because, as explained previously, instead of clients feeling that you were travelling beside them as they explored their thoughts and feelings, they would feel more as though they were being interrogated. This would greatly diminish the quality of the counselling relationship and would inhibit clients from opening up freely. When a person is continually questioned, that person tends to withdraw rather than to open up.

> A counselling conversation should flow freely and naturally

Remember that paraphrasing and reflection of feelings are more likely to motivate the client to talk freely than asking questions. Because of this, we suggest that when you are practising asking questions you try to ask only one question in every three or four responses, with the other responses being reflection of content or feelings or minimal responses. There is no need to be rigid when doing this, because counselling needs to be a natural free-flowing process rather than one conforming to rigid rules. However, if you use fewer questions than other responses in practice sessions, then your continued practice of the most important basic reflective responses will be ensured. Consequently, when you start counselling real clients you will be skilled in reflection of feelings and content, and will use questions only when it is advantageous to do so because reflection is not appropriate.

Suggested open questions to replace closed questions in practice examples

Example 7

What would you like for dinner tonight?

Example 8

How do you feel when your husband praises you?

Example 9

What was your mother like? *or* How did your mother behave in her relationships with other people?

Example 10

What brought you here?

Example 11

How did the change affect your life?

LEARNING SUMMARY

■ Dangers in asking too many questions relate to a number of factors including:
   – The counselling session may become more like an interrogation.
   – The counsellor may deflect the client from the real issue by controlling the direction of the session.
   – The client may stop exploring their own world and instead wait for the counsellor to ask more questions.

LEARNING SUMMARY (cont'd)

- Closed questions:
  - lead to a specific answer
  - confine the client to a limited response
  - help the client to be more precise
  - are useful in eliciting specific information.
- Open questions encourage the client:
  - to share new information
  - to speak freely and openly
  - to bring out those things that are of most importance.
- There are a wide variety of questions which are useful for specific purposes at particular points in a counselling session.
- Counsellors are not justified in asking questions merely to satisfy their own curiosity.

Practice examples: Practice examples to help in learning the use of open questions are provided in Part VI.

References and further reading

Boscolo, L., Cecchin, G., Hoffman, L. and Penn, P. (1987) *Milan Systemic Family Therapy: Conversations in Theory and Practice*. New York: Basic Books.

Clarkson, P. (2000) *Gestalt Counselling in Action*, second edition. London: Sage.

Glasser, W. and Wubbolding, R. (2000) Reality therapy. In R. Corsini & D. Wedding (eds), *Current Psychotherapies*, sixth edition (pp. 293–321). Itasca, IL: Peacock.

Jones, E. (1993) *Family Systems Therapy: Developments in Milan-Systemic Therapies*. Chichester: Wiley.

O'Connell, B. (1998) *Solution-Focused Therapy*. London: Sage.

Palazzoli, S. N., Boscolo, L., Cecchin, F. G. and Prata, G. (1980) Hypothesising circularity and neutrality: Three guidelines for the conductor of the session. *Family Process, 19*, 3–12.

White, M. and Epston, D. (1990) *Narrative Means to Therapeutic Ends*. New York: Norton.

Chapter 9

Summarising

The skills we have previously discussed have been those designed to create a good counselling relationship so that the client will feel free to talk openly, sharing with the counsellor issues that are causing emotional distress. If we use the analogy of the counsellor walking alongside the client on a journey, then the skills we have described encourage the client to continue exploring. As this journey of exploration occurs, the client moves in a direction of their own choice with the counsellor walking alongside. From time to time it is important for the client to stop and review the ground that has recently been traversed. This review can be encouraged if the counsellor uses the skill of *summarising*.

Summarising is rather like paraphrasing. When a counsellor paraphrases, they reflect back whatever has been said in a single client statement. Similarly, when a counsellor summarises, what the counsellor does is to reflect back to the client what has been said in a number of client statements. The summary draws together the main points from the content, and may also take into account the feelings the client has described. A summary does not involve a complete re-run of the ground covered, but rather picks out the salient points, the important things that the client has been talking about, and presents them in such a way that the client is provided with an overview of what they have been discussing. By doing this, the counsellor enables the client to absorb and to ponder over what they have been sharing. Summarising clarifies what the client has been saying and puts it into an organised format so that the client is better able to see a clear picture of the situation.

> Summarising involves reflecting back the
> essence of the conversation

Frequently when a client comes to counselling they are confused. It is as though they are walking through a forest and can see nothing clearly. They are lost in a confusing jungle of overgrowth and trees. By summarising, the counsellor assists the client to see the trees more clearly and to find a path among them.

The following is a short transcript of part of a practice counselling session to illustrate the use of summarising.

Transcript to illustrate summarising

Client: *You know ... [pause] ... I really believe in people taking responsibility for themselves ... [pause] ... and so I can't really understand why it is that I do so much worrying about my brothers.*

Counsellor: You sound puzzled by your concern for your brothers. (Reflection of feeling and content.)

Client: *Yes, I am concerned. I'm not too sure what it's all about because I even seem to be worrying about them when I'm at work and yet I know that they are adults and are quite capable of looking after themselves.*

Counsellor: Even though you know they're adults, you still worry. (Reflection of content and feeling.)

Client: *Yes, I do. Incessantly. I'm always thinking the worst, you know. That maybe Bill has had an accident in that crazy car which he will insist on driving around, and I'm afraid that as far as Sidney is concerned, he's just not in very good health and I'd hate anything to happen to either of them.*

Counsellor: Even as you speak now you sound anxious. (Reflection of feeling.)

Client: *Yes, I am anxious, I'm really anxious ... [pause]*

Counsellor: As you experience that anxiety, can you tell me more about it? (Open question.)

Client: *Yes, yes I think I can, I'm just, uh-mm, becoming aware of some very painful memories that I have of my elder sister. [Said slowly and with hesitation.]*

Counsellor: I get the impression that you're finding it difficult to talk about your memories. (Reflection of feeling.)

Client: *Yes, it's really painful for me to remember what happened to her. I was really very fond of her and I hurt inside when I think about the way she finished her life. [Voice quivering.]*
Counsellor: It distresses you to think about her death. (Reflection of feeling and content.)
Client: *Yes, it does. You see she killed herself. She took an overdose and it was too late when we found her.*
Counsellor: I can understand you feeling very sad. (Joining statement, bringing closeness between client and counsellor.)
Client: *[Sobs] ... yeah, it was very sad for me and it still is. I just wished I could have done something to have changed the way she saw her life.*
Counsellor: You wish that you could have helped her. (Reflection of feeling and content.)
Client: *Yes, I do. I would love to have been able to put my arms around her and to tell her that I really loved her. I couldn't have told her that her life was good because it wasn't, but I could have told her that she mattered to me.*
Counsellor: You'd have liked to have told her how much you cared about her. (Reflection of content.)
Client: *Yes I would, and I guess that if I had, I would feel a lot better now, even if she had still killed herself. I suppose it would have been much better for me if I could have told her how I felt when she was alive and now it's too late.*
Counsellor: You're sad because you missed an opportunity. (Reflection of feeling and content.)
Client: *Yes, I did, and I suppose I'm starting to realise something about the way I feel anxious when I think about my two brothers. You see, I would really like to be able to tell them how much I care about them, but somehow I just can't.*
Counsellor: You've told me how you worry about your brothers and how your sister killed herself. It seems as though you're really sad because you weren't able to tell your sister that you really cared for her when she was alive and now you'd like to be able to tell your brothers that you care about them, but somehow you can't. (Summary.)
Client: *You're right. That's what my problem is. I think what I need to do is to go and talk to them, and then maybe I'll stop worrying about them.*

What the summary does

If you look at the above transcript you will see that in summarising the counsellor tied together the elements of what the client had said during the previous statements. This enabled the client to put the whole package together and, as a result, to get some resolution. The resolution was the client's own and as such was fitting for the client. It wasn't suggested by the counsellor.

When to summarise

Summarising is something that needs to be done from time to time during a counselling session so that the client is able to clarify their ideas and combine the various elements of what they are saying into an understandable form. In particular, towards the end of the counselling session it is often sensible for the counsellor to summarise the main issues that were dealt with during the session. By doing this, the counsellor ties together the thoughts, ideas and feelings that were expressed in the session, leaving the client feeling less confused and better able to deal with their life situation. This tying together enables the counsellor to move towards closing the session as explained in Chapter 10.

LEARNING SUMMARY

Summarising does the following:

- picks out salient points;
- draws these together; and
- presents them to the client in a clear and precise way.

Practice exercise: A transcript to help when learning to summarise is provided in Part VI.

Chapter 10

Creating Comfortable Closure

It is often very hard for new counsellors to know when to terminate a counselling session or when to terminate a series of counselling sessions. In this chapter we will discuss the following aspects of termination:

1 the termination of an individual counselling session;
2 the need for ongoing appointments;
3 client and counsellor dependency; and
4 the termination of a series of counselling sessions.

The termination of an individual counselling session

Most counselling agencies and private practice counsellors schedule a particular length of time for each counselling session, and it is fairly common for this to be one hour. In our experience, this is a suitable time for most individual counselling sessions although a longer time may be required for marital or family counselling. Of course, there are exceptions. Sometimes it will be clear after a shorter time that an interview can be terminated because the client has resolved their issues and there is little point in sitting around chatting unnecessarily. At other times it may be apparent that a client is in a highly distressed emotional state at the end of a one-hour session and it may be necessary to continue the interview for longer.

Work to be done between sessions

Between counselling sessions, the counsellor may need to make another appointment for the client who is leaving, to show the client out, and to write up notes on the interview. They may also need to debrief, as otherwise there may be emotional consequences for them as a result of listening to the client's painful story. When a counsellor is not able to do this, they may not be emotionally ready to meet a new client and are setting themselves up for burnout (see Chapter 28, entitled 'Looking after yourself'). Debriefing can sometimes be achieved just by writing up case notes, or having a cup of tea, or by chatting informally with someone. However, in cases where a counselling session has been particularly stressful for the counsellor it may be necessary for them to talk through their issues with a supervisor or another counsellor. After debriefing, the counsellor needs to prepare for the next client by reading case notes, if they are available.

> All counsellors need to debrief after counselling sessions

Because of the counsellor's own needs and the work that is preferably done between appointments, we believe that it is wise for agencies to schedule in at least a quarter of an hour between the end of one counselling session and the beginning of the next, particularly where counsellors are dealing with very distressed clients. For new counsellors a longer gap between the end of one appointment and the start of another is recommended. We recognise that not all agencies are willing to permit this, but think that this is unfortunate because it may compromise the effectiveness of counselling and may lead to counsellor burnout.

Keeping the counselling experience dynamic

In our experience clients often deal with important issues in the first three-quarters of an hour of a counselling session, and then begin to lose energy. It is important that each counselling session is dynamic and that the client is working actively throughout the session. Once a client becomes used to sessions being of fixed length, they will tend to work comfortably within that time frame. During a one-hour interview, a client will be likely to have raised important issues and to have explored them. The client then needs time in which to process the work done. It may therefore be appropriate to terminate the session at that point and to leave a few days, or maybe a week or two, before making another appointment, if that is needed.

Client anxiety about time constraints

If the matter is raised, let the client know that you, the counsellor, are in control of the length of the counselling session. Frequently clients show anxiety by looking at a clock in the room, because they are worried about taking up too much of a counsellor's time. In such cases, it is important for the counsellor to say that they will control the length of the session, and that the session will probably last about 60 minutes, or whatever is appropriate. If a client is told this, their anxiety regarding timekeeping is likely to be reduced.

Preparing for the end of a session

Where a counsellor is working within a set time frame, and knows that there is a time limit to the counselling session, the counsellor needs to prepare for terminating the session. This preparation should be commenced about ten minutes before the end of the session. If the counselling session is to last an hour, then after about 50 minutes it is sensible for the counsellor to assess the progress of the session. The counsellor can then decide how to use the remaining time in order to close the session in a way that is satisfactory for the client. Sometimes it can be useful for the counsellor to say to the client: '*I am conscious of the need for us to finish talking in about 10 minutes time and it seems to me that you may wish to explore ... (a particular area) ... that we have been talking about.*' Alternatively, the counsellor might say, '*We only have a few minutes left*

and I am wondering if there's anything in particular that you would like to talk about before we finish.'

By giving the client a warning that the counselling session must end within a few minutes, the client is given an opportunity to deal with, or at least mention, any pressing unfinished business.

Closing the session

Near the finishing time, it is sometimes appropriate for the counsellor to provide a summary of the material discussed by the client during the session. The counsellor might also add a statement regarding goals for the future and the possibility or probability of future counselling sessions being required. When finishing, it's useful if you can give the client some positive feedback, especially as clients usually come to see counsellors at times when their self-esteem is low. For example, the counsellor might say, *'It's clear to me that you have been having a very difficult time. I'm impressed by the way that you have explored your problem and then thought about possible solutions'*, or, *'Having heard your story, I am impressed by the way that you have coped with a very difficult situation.'*

> Affirm your client's strengths!

As a counsellor, you need to take control of the termination of the session. If you are to do this successfully, you need to be very careful not to compromise your decision to end the session by:

1 asking a question;
2 reflecting feelings; or
3 reflecting content.

If you do any of these things, the session is almost certain to continue because the client has an implied invitation to respond! However, unless they are careful, skilled counsellors can easily fall into the trap of doing one of these three things at a time when they want to finish.

You may need to be assertive with those clients who want to linger on and chat rather than do useful work. In such a case, be direct. You may even find it necessary to interrupt and say something like: *'We do need to finish the session right now.'* Then stand up and lead the way firmly out of the room without stopping to linger, even if the client wishes to do so. Many counsellors find this difficult to do, because it is hard to do politely and respectfully. However, if you are direct and firm, you will still be able to give your client a positive message by saying, '*Goodbye, Jim*' (or whatever their name is) in a friendly way as you turn away to leave their company.

The need for ongoing appointments

Inexperienced counsellors are often apprehensive about asking clients to come back for further appointments. If you feel apprehensive about doing this, explore your feelings. You may be afraid that the client will not want to come back and will reject your offer of another appointment. If the client does that, would it be a disaster? If you think that it would, then you need to discuss the issue with your supervisor. Remember that it is hard for clients to make appointments. It is much easier for them to cancel. If you don't make another appointment for the client, then they are likely to assume that you don't think that it is necessary for them to come back. They may wonder whether you would consider it to be a nuisance if they were to do so. It is therefore important, if you do not make another appointment, that you say to your client: '*I won't make another appointment for you now, because I am not sure that it's necessary for you to come back to see me as you seem to have resolved your current issues. However, I would like you to know that if you decide that it would be useful for you to come back, then you are welcome to ring up and make an appointment.*'

Making a contract for ongoing appointments

For clients who need ongoing appointments, it may be desirable for the counsellor to spell out an ongoing contract. It may be sufficient to say, '*I think it would be useful for you to come back to see me again next week – would you like to do this?*' Alternatively, it may be appropriate to say: '*It seems to me that you have a number of issues which need to be resolved, and this is likely to take several counselling sessions. Would you like to come to see me on a weekly basis for the next three or four weeks and then review the situation?*' In this way, the client can be made aware of the counsellor's willingness to continue seeing them.

Clients often feel insecure about the counselling relationship and are afraid that the counsellor will terminate the counselling process before important issues have been explored. It is therefore important to ensure that the client has some clear expectation regarding the possible duration of the counselling relationship.

Client and counsellor dependency

Sometimes it's desirable to terminate a series of counselling sessions sooner than the client would wish. This raises the issue of dependency. We ourselves have noticed that often some degree of dependency will occur in ongoing counselling relationships.

Dependency on the relationship

It is easy for clients to become dependent on counsellors for a number of reasons. Firstly, it is inevitable that a meaningful relationship will develop if the counsellor is genuine, warm and accepting. Of course, there are necessary and appropriate limits to the counselling relationship (see Chapter 26, regarding ethical issues). However, the quality of a counselling relationship is such that it is natural for some clients to wish that the counselling relationship could continue after its usefulness for legitimate counselling purposes has ended.

> Dependency is inevitable, particularly when counselling is ongoing

Clients tell counsellors their innermost secrets, whereas generally, from childhood, people learn to share such private material only with someone they are close to, or love. Consequently, as a result of the client's past experiences, because they have shared intimate personal information with you, they might wish or expect that they will have an ongoing relationship with you.

Some people who come to counsellors are very alone in the world, and do not have a close relative or friend with whom to share the problems and stresses which arise in their daily lives. It is perfectly understandable why such people might want to become dependent on the counselling relationship. We all have a need for closeness and affection, and the counselling relationship may, for a while, provide this for the lonely. They may then become dependent on the relationship unless the counsellor is careful to address the issue in a way which is acceptable for the client.

Dependency on the counselling process

After the initial trauma of a crisis has passed, it is often very comfortable for a client to be able to continue to discuss and work through less important life issues in the caring counselling environment. Most of us like comfort, but to continue to provide counselling to clients who no longer need it does them a disservice. It effectively interferes with the desirable tendency for people to become self-sufficient. We believe that effective counselling helps clients to learn strategies they can use to work through most of their troubling issues, and helps them to recognise when they really do need counselling help.

Counsellors can become dependent too

Dependency can occur in two directions. The client may become dependent on the counsellor, and equally the counsellor may become dependent on the client. Counsellors are not emotionless robots, but are human beings with emotions and needs. As described above and in Chapter 26, the counselling relationship often involves an unusual degree of intimate sharing, and by its very nature involves a degree of closeness. Consequently, it is easy to understand how a counsellor can get hooked into a dependency relationship. Clearly, a counsellor needs to stay vigilant to ensure that they do not encourage their clients to continue with counselling merely to satisfy their own needs.

It is inevitable that dependency issues will arise from time to time for counsellors. Sometimes counsellors will be unaware that such dependency is occurring. It is here that regular supervision is essential to help counsellors identify dependency issues and to reduce the likelihood of inappropriate transgression of professional boundaries (see Chapter 27).

The termination of a series of counselling sessions

The decision about when to terminate a series of counselling sessions is often fairly clear, and will frequently be made by the client in discussion with the counsellor. However, there will be times when the decision is more difficult, particularly if either client or counsellor dependency is occurring. Counsellors therefore need to regularly review the progress that is being made in counselling sessions, and the goals that are being achieved, to ensure that counselling is continuing for the client's wellbeing, rather than in order to satisfy dependency needs. Where progress is not being made and goals are not being achieved, it is essential for the counsellor to discuss the case with their supervisor in order to make a sensible decision about what action to take. It may be that as a consequence of supervision the counsellor will be able to identify why the counselling process is failing to enable the client to change. This might be as a consequence of the counsellor's own unresolved personal issues interfering with the counselling process. Alternatively, it may be because the counsellor lacks the required skills to help a particular client. We do need to recognise, of course, that we cannot help every client to change so that they feel better and engage in more helpful behaviours. However, as a consequence of supervision, a counsellor may be able to use a different strategy or approach with a client who appears to be stuck and is unable to change, so that change does occur. Another possibility is that a client may require a different approach which is not within the counsellor's current repertoire of skills. In this case the counsellor might say to the client, *'I've noticed that although you have been coming to talk with me for several weeks, you still seem to be experiencing the same difficulties. This makes me wonder whether it might be more useful for you to seek help in some other way.'* The counsellor might then invite the client to think of possible alternatives, and/or may make some suggestions of alternatives which might be useful.

Confronting dependency

If client dependency is identified, then the issue should be brought into the open to let the client know what the counsellor believes is happening. This needs to be done with sensitivity, because it would be easy for a client to feel hurt and rejected as a consequence of inept confrontation regarding dependency. However, if the dependency is reframed positively, as a normal occurrence which involves both counsellor and client, then progress can be made towards termination.

Dealing with the loss of the relationship

With clients who are terminating a long counselling relationship, there will be some grief associated with the loss of that relationship. Particularly where a long relationship has been established, counsellors need to help their clients prepare for the feelings of loss that will occur when the relationship ends. In order to minimise this pain, it may be advisable for a counsellor to make one or two appointments at longer intervals than previously, at the end of a series of counselling sessions. For example, when we have seen clients on a weekly basis for several weeks, we have often made remaining appointments at fortnightly and monthly intervals.

With some clients, it can be useful to have a follow-up session after a three-month break. A three-monthly follow-up session serves three purposes. Firstly, it helps the client to adjust to the idea of being independent and not dependent on the counsellor; secondly, it enables the client to deal with the loss of the counselling relationship in a gentle way; and thirdly, it enables the counsellor to review the progress that the client continues to make after regular counselling has ceased. Also, it sometimes happens that after a series of counselling sessions has been completed, a three-monthly follow-up session will reveal that there is a 'loose end' that needs to be tied up before final termination.

> Saying 'Goodbye' can be difficult

Termination of both single sessions and a series of sessions is often slightly painful. It is usually difficult to say 'Goodbye' and accept the loss of a meaningful relationship. As a counsellor, be aware of this, both for the client and for yourself. As discussed previously, it is important to address this issue openly and to help the client to adjust to termination. Termination needs to be done sensitively and caringly.

LEARNING SUMMARY

- Let the client know that you are in control of the length of the session.
- Warn the client when the session is coming to an end.
- Negotiate a contract with the client with regard to future appointments.
- Finish each session by summarising, outlining future goals if appropriate, and giving some positive feedback where possible.
- Take control when finishing a session.
- During a series of ongoing counselling sessions, review progress and be aware of dependency.
- Deal with dependency by openly discussing it.
- If necessary, deal with grief associated with closure of a series of sessions.
- When terminating, don't ask questions or reflect content or feelings.

Part III

Promoting Change through the use of an Integrative Approach

Chapter 11

An Integrative Approach to Helping People Change

There are a number of different therapeutic models of counselling practice in use today. These are each based on particular theoretical foundations. Models of practice can broadly be grouped as follows:

1 Psychodynamic
2 Humanistic/existentialist counselling
3 Cognitive-behavioural
4 Behavioural
5 Integrative-eclectic approaches.

The various approaches to counselling which fit into the above groupings are described in some detail by Dryden (2002) and Feltham and Horton (2000). We, the authors of this book, prefer to use an approach which fits into the last group. This is an integrative approach. This approach integrates and makes use of theoretical concepts, skills, and strategies, taken from a number of the different counselling approaches which belong in groups 1 to 4 in the above list.

As a new counsellor, or a counsellor in training, you may be curious about our reasons for choosing to use an integrative approach; so we will consider this now.

Why use an integrative approach?

We have noticed that there is currently a strong movement among many practitioners within the counselling profession towards the use of integrative or eclectic approaches in preference to single theory approaches. There is a considerable body of literature supporting an integrative approach (Alford, 1995; Davison, 1995; Goldfried and Castonguay, 1992; Greenberg, 2002; Hillman and Stricker, 2002; Jacobson, 1994; Nuttall, 2002; O'Brien and Houston, 2000; Pinsoff, 1994; Scaturo, 1994; Steenbarger, 1992; Stricker and Gold, 1993; Tierney, 2003; Watkins and Watts, 1995). It is clear that integrative counselling is now recognised as useful by many practising counsellors. An important reason for this is because none of the individual counselling approaches has sufficient explanatory, technical, or conceptual power to help all clients (Beitman, 1994). Further, in our experience the individual approaches are often insufficient when used exclusively to effectively help some clients to address emotional issues, to make useful changes to their thinking, and to start to use new behaviours which are more adaptive.

> There are advantages in using an integrative approach

Prochaska and DiClemente (1992) point out that both in the research literature and in clinical experience it has become clear that no single system of therapy adequately addresses what to do, when to do it, with whom, in what way, and with which problem. We believe that this problem can be minimised by using an integrative approach which involves a systematic but flexible process, as described in the next chapter. Such an integrative approach enables a skilled counsellor, in each stage of the counselling process, to choose from particular skills and strategies which are relevant to the stage of the process, and are most suitable for addressing client needs at that stage. Additionally, when selecting skills within a particular stage of the counselling process, the counsellor can choose those skills which best suit the client's specific problems and personal presentation.

When using an integrative approach we need to recognise that the strategies that we use come from various models of counselling and that these depend on differing theoretical frameworks. However, this does not need to be a problem. As pointed out by O'Brien and Houston (2000) what the integrative therapist does is to call on the practical wisdom that has evolved in whatever theoretical camp that seems relevant to the work at hand.

The difference between an integrative approach and an eclectic approach

In an eclectic approach skills from various therapeutic approaches are selected in an ad hoc fashion with the intention of addressing particular client issues. In the integrative process described in this book and explained in detail in the next chapter, skills are sequentially selected from particular therapeutic approaches at particular stages of the counselling process. This sequential use of particular skills enables a counsellor to help the client move from a position of emotional disturbance, to fully explain their situation and be understood, to deal with their emotions, and to change their thinking and behaviour so that they are able to move forward into the future with more confidence.

Helping people change

As we have stated previously, a major goal of counselling is to help people change. People come to counsellors at times of crisis and are usually emotionally distressed and do not know how to change so that they can feel better and be able to live more comfortable, satisfying, and adaptive lives. If we are to be effective as counsellors in helping our clients to change, then we need to have some understanding of the change processes which can occur as a consequence of counselling.

We need to recognise that people with emotional, psychological, and behavioural problems often do change as part of a natural process without the benefit of counselling. This raises the question, 'What is the value of counselling?' Beitman (1994) suggests that rather than seeing counselling as a specific agent of change we need to recognise that counselling can be seen to be a facilitator or accelerator of the self-change process which occurs naturally within people. In our experience this is true. When people come to see us as counsellors we notice that they are often confused and overwhelmed by their problems and cannot recognise ways to change which would be helpful for them. By coming to counselling they are usually able to engage in a process which relatively quickly helps them deal with their emotions, change their thinking, and make decisions regarding future behaviours. The facilitative nature of the counselling process speeds up what might occur naturally over time without counselling.

Prochaska (1999) draws on research findings to conclude that positive change occurs regardless of the model of counselling used. Further, research suggests that the relationship between the client and counsellor may be a more important factor in producing change than the model of counselling (Howe, 1999). While we recognise that this may be true, in our experience the effectiveness of counselling in producing change can be maximised if we recognise differences in the ways in which changes in the client's emotional state, thinking processes and behaviours can be achieved. Additionally, we believe that we need to recognise that it is important to match the skills we use with the particular stages of the counselling process.

> Skills and strategies should meet the client's needs at each stage in the counselling process

In order to lead satisfying and comfortable lives we human beings need to feel good emotionally, to be free from troubling thoughts, and to engage in behaviours which lead to positive outcomes. Many clients come for counselling because they are experiencing troubling emotions and thoughts and are engaged in behaviours which are unhelpful for them. It therefore follows that to be most useful counselling should address emotions, thoughts, and behaviours. Now it is true that most, if not all, single theory counselling approaches do have the goal of bringing about change in a client's emotions, thoughts and behaviours. However, when we examine the strategies used in specific counselling approaches we find that most approaches tend to focus more heavily on either emotions, or thoughts, or behaviours. Additionally, in our view, most single theory counselling approaches do not significantly adjust their strategies to match stages in the counselling process, or to match the particular needs of individual clients.

In most single theory approaches there is an assumption that if change occurs in one of either emotional feelings, or thinking processes, or behaviour, then change will spontaneously occur in the others. Although we recognise that this may often happen to some extent, it will not necessarily occur. We therefore think that it is advantageous for counsellors to sequentially make use of strategies which firstly address emotions, then thoughts, and finally behaviours. Strategies which are most effective in directly addressing each of these are different from each other and come from different theoretical models of counselling.

> Ideally change should influence emotions, thoughts, and behaviours

In order to help in the understanding of change processes, we will discuss methods counsellors use to promote emotional change, changes in thinking (cognitive change), and changes in behaviour. While pointing out differences in the ways in which these three attributes can be addressed, we recognise that changing one of them may sometimes spontaneously produce change in the others.

Facilitating emotional change

As we know, most clients come for counselling help when they are experiencing a level of emotional distress. For some clients, their emotions are clearly expressed, either verbally or non-verbally. For other clients, although they may exhibit some level of emotional distress, their emotional expression is more contained. Many clients are unable to identify with clarity the emotions they are experiencing. Sometimes a client's emotions are so repressed that in the early stages of counselling it may be impossible for them to get in touch with their emotions.

As human beings our experience is that when we release our emotions we tend to feel better and to enter into a calmer state. For example, if we are grieving and very sad, our experience is that if we let our emotions out by crying, afterwards we will feel better. We may not feel happy, but we are likely to be less distressed and more comfortable. Clearly, one way in which a counsellor may help a client to feel better is to help the client to achieve catharsis through emotional release.

Many counsellors who use person-centred counselling place a significant emphasis on reflection of emotional feelings. As a consequence of this, clients are likely to get in touch with strong emotions. When this occurs, usually the counsellor will allow the client to fully experience the emerging emotion (subject to safety when dealing with clients who are very angry). Generally, if a client starts to cry, the counsellor will allow the crying to continue until it naturally abates. Consequently emotions are released and catharsis occurs. With regard to other emotions, such as frustration, anger, and despair, the person-centred counsellor will usually encourage the client, through reflection of content and feelings, to verbally express the emotions rather than to avoid dealing with them. The reflective skills used by these counsellors are clearly very useful in helping a person to get in touch with, and release, emotional feelings.

> Reflection of feelings can facilitate emotional release

You might ask, 'Is emotional release sufficient in itself?' Pierce, Nichols and Du Brin (1983) in their book, *Emotional Expression in Psychotherapy*, are clear in their belief that when feelings are expressed fully they lead to new ways for clients to view themselves and the world. In other words the client's thinking changes. They go on to say that the new ways of thinking and viewing the world then lead to more satisfying behaviours. However, they do recognise that this process does not happen automatically. Unfortunately, it does not necessarily happen at all. Although we believe that emotional release is a very important component of the change process, we do not believe that it is sufficient in itself. In our experience many clients who release emotions in counselling are unable to make significant changes to their thinking and behaviour without receiving more direct help to deal with their thoughts and behaviours. Unfortunately, clients who are unable to make changes in their thinking and behaviours are quite likely to re-experience ongoing problems in the future as troubling situations arise.

> Releasing emotions is necessary, but not sufficient

Facilitating cognitive change (changes in thinking)

There are usually two stages in helping a client make changes to their thinking. The first stage is to help the client to clarify their problem. Commonly, people who come to see counsellors are highly confused and are unable to sort out their confused thoughts so that they can see their problem clearly. Consequently, a task for the counsellor is to help the person to see their situation more clearly. The second stage involves helping the client to restructure their thoughts, or to think differently about their problem so that they can make sensible choices to enable them to feel more comfortable.

Clarifying the problem

Several different counselling skills can be used to help the client to clarify their problem. These include paraphrasing content, summarising, the use of questions, and confronting.

Paraphrasing, summarising, and the use of questions have been described in previous chapters. These skills enable the client to explore their problem in collaboration with the counsellor. While doing this, they are likely to start sorting out their thoughts so that they can see their problem more clearly. Additionally, the client may be helped to clarify their thoughts through the use of confrontation.

Confronting

Confronting is described more fully in Chapter 13. Confronting is particularly useful in helping the client to clarify their problem when there are inconsistencies in what they are saying or believing. If they are confronted by these inconsistencies they may be able to clarify their thinking so that it is more congruent, with the result that they can move towards restructuring their thoughts and finding a solution to their problem.

Restructuring thoughts

The counselling skills most useful in helping a client to restructure thoughts include normalising, reframing, challenging self-destructive beliefs, exploring polarities, making use of strengths, and using the 'here and now' experience. We will now discuss their origins, and their usefulness in promoting change.

Normalising

Normalising, as will be explained in Chapter 14, involves giving the client information which helps them to understand that their feelings, reactions, and/or situation are normal and to be expected rather than unusual. After normalising the client will usually be able to think about their situation differently. This is likely to affect not only their thinking but also their emotional state, enabling them to move forward and make useful decisions. Although normalising may have an effect on behaviour, it does not directly target behaviour, so behavioural change may not occur.

Reframing

This skill has its origins in the neuro-linguistic programming (Bandler, Grinder and Andreas, 1989). This skill is particularly useful for those clients who think within the constraints of a very narrow and negative view of their world. By using reframing, the counsellor may be able to help them to take a wider and more positive view, thus changing the way they think about their situation as described in Chapter 15.

Challenging self-destructive beliefs

The idea of directly challenging a client's self-destructive beliefs comes from rational emotive behaviour therapy as developed by Albert Ellis (Ellis, 1995; Dryden, 1995). Ellis believes that clients can be helped if what he called 'irrational beliefs' were challenged and replaced by more 'rational beliefs'. As will be discussed in Chapter 16, rational emotive behaviour therapy theory suggests that changing thoughts automatically results in changing emotions and behaviours. Although this may sometimes happen, we don't believe that it will necessarily occur because, as pointed out by Greenberg (2002), the interactions between emotions, cognitions, and behaviour are complex and do not follow a simple linear sequence. In other words, changing one of these attributes will not necessarily change the others. However, strategies from rational emotive behaviour therapy can be extremely useful in helping to change self-destructive thoughts.

Exploring polarities

As will be explained in Chapter 17, exploring polarities is a gestalt therapy strategy. While the intention is to target the client's experience as a whole, we believe that this particular strategy is most useful in changing the way the client thinks about, values, and manages particular personal attributes. This strategy is most useful in helping to change the thinking of clients who are focusing on what they perceive as negative aspects of themselves.

Making use of the client strengths

Focusing on the client strengths will be discussed more fully in Chapter 18. This approach helps the person to think more positively, and start to recognise that they have the ability to cope with difficult situations. This strategy has its origins in solution-focused counselling (De Jong and Berg, 1998; De Shazer, 1988), and in Narrative Therapy (White and Epston, 1990).

Using the 'here and now' experience

Using the immediacy of the 'here and now' experience is a gestalt therapy approach. This approach is explained more fully in Chapter 19. The aim in using this approach is to raise the client's awareness of what is happening in the interaction between the client and the counsellor. By doing this, the client is likely to get more fully in touch with what is happening within themselves, and what may be happening in their relationships with others. The gestalt therapy aim is to bring about change in the whole of the client's experience including emotions, thoughts, and behaviours. However, we believe that focusing on the immediacy of the counselling process is initially most likely to impact on the client's thoughts, particularly with regard to the way they relate to others.

Can you see how we can use a number of different strategies, taken from different therapeutic approaches, for different purposes in addressing the way a client thinks? Some theorists from single model counselling approaches such as rational emotive behaviour therapy (Ellis, 1995) believe that changing thoughts automatically leads to emotional and behavioural change. Although we agree that changing thought processes may to varying extents influence the emotions and behaviours of people, as integrative therapists we believe that it is more useful to target emotions and behaviours by using specific strategies which address these.

Facilitating behaviour change

Up to now, we have discussed ways of helping a client by using methods which involve emotional release and changes in thinking. For some clients, this may be sufficient to produce behavioural change, but for others the counselling process needs to be more strongly directed towards behaviours.

> By changing our behaviours, we can avoid repeating mistakes we have made previously

As will be explained in Chapters 20 and 21, we can help a client to explore their options for the future, to make decisions about their future behaviour, and to take action so that change occurs.

Change in counselling is related to a process of exploration and self-discovery

A good model to illustrate the usefulness of the process of self-discovery in counselling is the Johari window. The Johari window was devised by Joseph Luft and Harry Ingham at a workshop in 1955 and is shown in Figure 11.1. According to Luft (1969), the name 'Johari' is pronounced as if it were 'Joe' and 'Harry', which is where the name comes from: Joe–Harry. The window has four panes as shown. Each pane in the window contains information about the person represented by the window. The two panes on the left-hand side contain information which is known to the person, whereas the two panes on the right-hand side contain information which is unknown to the person. The two panes at the top contain information which is known to others and the two panes at the bottom contain information which is unknown to others.

Information in the top left-hand pane (the *open* pane) is openly recognised by both the person and other people. For example, if David were to use his own personal Johari window as an example, he would be likely to tell you that other people know that he tends to be a workaholic, gets satisfaction from writing textbooks, enjoys counselling and training counsellors, likes to walk on the beach near our home; enjoys playing golf, even

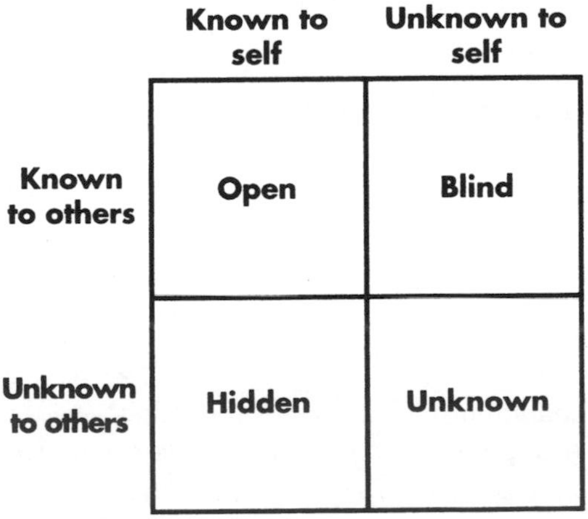

	Known to self	**Unknown to self**
Known to others	Open	Blind
Unknown to others	Hidden	Unknown

Figure 11.1 The Johari Window

Source: Group Processes: An Introduction to Group Dynamics, 3rd edn, by Joseph Luft © 1984, Mayfield Publishing Company. Reprinted by permission of The McGraw-Hill Companies.

though he is not good at the game; is a father and grandfather; and has a serious side with a social conscience, but can also let his hair down and have fun. Because this information is known to others, it is in his *open* pane. Information in the bottom left-hand pane, labelled *hidden*, is known to David alone and unknown to others. Some of the information which was in David's hidden pane is now in his open pane. For example, until the last few years he kept to himself the trauma he experienced while growing up in South London as a child during the blitz near the end of the Second World War. He can now talk freely to other people about this, so this information is now in his open pane. However, there will almost certainly be other information which is still in David's hidden pane. Because David knows about this information but doesn't talk about it, it remains hidden. Information in the top right-hand pane labelled *blind* is known to other people but not to David. For example, other people may know that he has certain behaviours or attributes which he may not recognise himself. Information in the bottom right-hand pane labelled *unknown* is totally unseen and unrecognised by David himself as it is locked in his subconscious.

The influence of counselling on the Johari window

The likely influence of successful counselling on the Johari window is shown in Figure 11.2. When a person comes to talk with a counsellor, it is quite likely that at first they will talk about information in the *open* pane. However, if a trusting relationship develops, the person may take the counsellor into their confidence and self-disclose information from the *hidden* pane, thus enlarging the open pane. Additionally, as counselling proceeds, the counsellor may give the client feedback or ask questions. As a result of the feedback and questioning, the client may discover information which was unknown to them but may, or may not, have been recognised by the counsellor. Once again the open pane is enlarged. As a consequence of the counselling process the client may gain in insight (to use a psychoanalytic term), or gain in awareness (to use a gestalt therapy term), or discover previously unknown possibilities (to use a solution-focused or narrative therapy description). As shown in Figure 11.2, the person's self-knowledge is likely to increase during an effective counselling process, allowing for personal growth which will inevitably result in some level of change in either emotional affect, thinking processes, or behaviours. We believe that this change process is enhanced when an integrated approach is used which specifically includes skills to address emotions, thoughts, and behaviours as explained in the next chapter.

Figure 11.2 The effect of counselling on the Johari window

In conclusion

As discussed at the beginning of this chapter, the counselling style described in this book is integrative, that is, it describes a counselling process which sequentially draws on strategies and skills taken from a number of differing counselling models.

As counsellors, if we are to be effective in helping clients we need to be skilled in enabling them to make changes. If we help them to release emotions, they will feel better in the short-term. However, if our counselling help is to be of long-term value, after emotions have been released we also need to help clients to change their thoughts and behaviours. If we do this, it is likely that they will be able to deal with future problems in more adaptive ways.

LEARNING SUMMARY

- Many counsellors now prefer to use an integrative approach, drawing theories, strategies, and skills from individual counselling approaches to suit the immediate needs of the client.

LEARNING SUMMARY (cont'd)

■ Changing one of either emotions, or thoughts, or behaviours does not necessarily change the others because the interaction between emotions, thoughts and behaviours is complex.

■ Integrative counselling can directly address emotions, thoughts, and behaviours.

■ Counselling facilitates and accelerates the natural processes of change.

■ Clients will generally feel better if they are able to talk about and express their emotions.

■ A number of approaches can be used to facilitate changes in thinking. These include: using the 'here and now' experience; normalising; confronting; challenging self-destructive beliefs, focusing on the client strengths; exploring polarities; and reframing.

■ Human beings naturally have information about themselves, some of which is hidden from others and some of which is hidden from themselves, as described by the Johari window.

■ If clients can accept the hidden parts of themselves, then they are likely to be better able to deal with these parts, and consequently to be able to lead more adaptive and satisfying lives.

References and further reading

Alford, B. A. (1995) Introduction to the special issue: Psychotherapy integration and cognitive psychotherapy, *Journal of Cognitive Psychotherapy*, 9, 147–51.

Bandler, R., Grinder, J. and Andreas, C. (1989) *Reframing: Neurolinguistic Programming and the Transformation of Meaning*. Moab: Real People Press.

Beitman, B. D. (1994) Stop exploring! Start defining the principles of psychotherapy integration: Call for a consensus conference. *Journal of Psychotherapy Integrations*, 4(3), 203–228.

Davison, G. C. (1995) Special Issue: What can we learn from failures in psychotherapy. *Journal of Psychotherapy Integration*, 5, 107–112.

De Jong, P. and Berg, I. (1998) *Interviewing for solutions*. Pacific Grove, CA: Brooks/ Cole.

De Shazer, S. (1988) *Clues: Investigating Solutions in Brief Therapy*, New York: Norton.

Dryden, W. (1995) *Brief Rational Emotive Behaviour Therapy*. London: Sage.

Dryden, W. (ed) (2002) *Handbook of individual therapy*, fourth edition. London: Sage.

Ellis, A. (1995) *Better, Deeper, and More Enduring Brief Therapy: The Rational Emotive Behavior Therapy Approach*. New York: Bruner/Mazel.

Feltham, C. and Horton, I. (eds) (2000) *Handbook of Counselling and Psychotherapy*. London: Sage.

Goldfried, M. R. and Castonguay, L. G. (1992) The future of psychotherapy integration. Special Issue: The future of psychotherapy. *Psychotherapy*. 29, 4–10.

Greenberg, L. S. (2002) Integrating an emotion-focused approach to treatment in psychotherapy integration. *Journal of psychotherapy integration*, 12(2), 154–189.

Hillman, J. and Stricker, G. (2002) A call for psychotherapy integration in work with older adult patients. *Journal of psychotherapy integration*, 12(4) 395–405.

Howe, D. (1999) The main change agent in psychotherapy is the relationship between therapist and client. In C. Feltham (ed), *Controversies in psychotherapy and counselling* (pp. 95–103). London: Sage.

Jacobson, N. S. (1994) Behaviour therapy and psychotherapy integration. Society for the Exploration Psychotherapy Integration. *Journal of Psychotherapy Integration*, 4, 105–119.

Luft, J. (1969) *Of Human Interaction*. California: Mayfield.

Nuttall, J. (2002) Imperatives and perspectives of psychotherapy integration. *International Journal of Psychotherapy*, 7(3), 249–265.

O'Brien, M. and Houston, G. (2000) *Integrative Therapy: A Practitioner's Guide*. London: Sage.

Pierce, R. A., Nichols, M. P. and Du Brin, M. A. (1983) *Emotional Expression in Psychotherapy*, New York: Gardner.

Pinsoff, W. M. (1994) An overview of Integrative Problem Centered Therapy: A synthesis of family and individual psychotherapies. Special Issue: Developments in family therapy in the USA. *Journal of Family Therapy*, 16, 103–120.

Prochaska, J. O. (1999) How do people change, and how can we change to help many more people? In M. A. Hubble, B. L. Duncan and S. D. Miller (eds) *The Heart & Soul of Change: What Works in Therapy* (pp. 227–255). Washington DC: American Psychological Association.

Prochaska, J. O. and DiClemente, C. C. (1992) The Transtheoretical Approach. In J. C. Norcross and M. R. Goldfried (eds), *Handbook of Psychotherapy Integration* (pp. 300–334). New York: Basic Books.

Scaturo, D. J. (1994) Integrative psychotherapy for panic disorder and agoraphobia in clinical practice. *Journal of Psychotherapy Integration*, 4, 253–72.

Steenbarger, B. N. (1992) Toward science-practice integration in brief counselling and therapy. *Counselling Psychologist*, 20, 403–450.

Stricker, G. and Gold, J. R. (eds) (1993) *Comprehensive handbook of psychotherapy integration*. New York: Plenum.

Tierney, G. T. (2003) Psychotherapy integration: Examination of clinical utilization. *Dissertation Abstracts International: Section B: The Sciences & Engineering*, 63(8-B), 39–43.

Watkins, C. E. and Watts R. E. (1995) Psychotherapy survey research studies: Some consistent findings and integrative conclusions. *Psychotherapy in Private Practice*, *13*, 49–68.

White, M. and Epston, D. (1990) *Narrative means to therapeutic ends*. New York: Norton.

Chapter 12

Combining Skills to Facilitate the Change Process

In Chapters 4 to 10, we described a number of basic counselling skills. In Chapters 13 to 21, we will discuss additional skills which can be used in conjuction with the basic skills. In this chapter, we will look at the way in which we can combine and integrate all of these counselling skills into a sequential process which optimises the possibility of producing change. In looking at this process we do need to recognise that each counselling session will be different – no two counselling interventions are going to be the same. However, after counselling for a long time, many counsellors recognise a common pattern in the processes that occur during counselling sessions. The flow chart in Figure 12.1 illustrates this pattern in diagrammatic form. Although this flow chart is useful in creating a general understanding of the stages of counselling processes which commonly occur in counselling, please be aware that the various stages described by the chart will often overlap each other, repeat themselves and occur in a different order from that shown.

> The stages of a counselling process often overlap, and earlier stages may be repeated

122

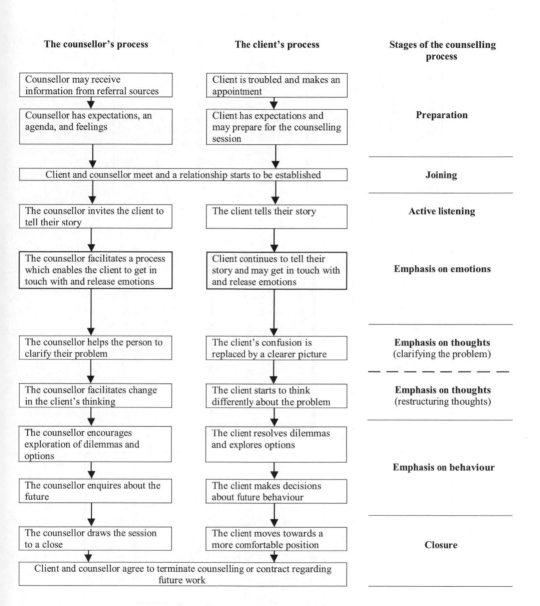

Figure 12.1 Stages of the counselling process

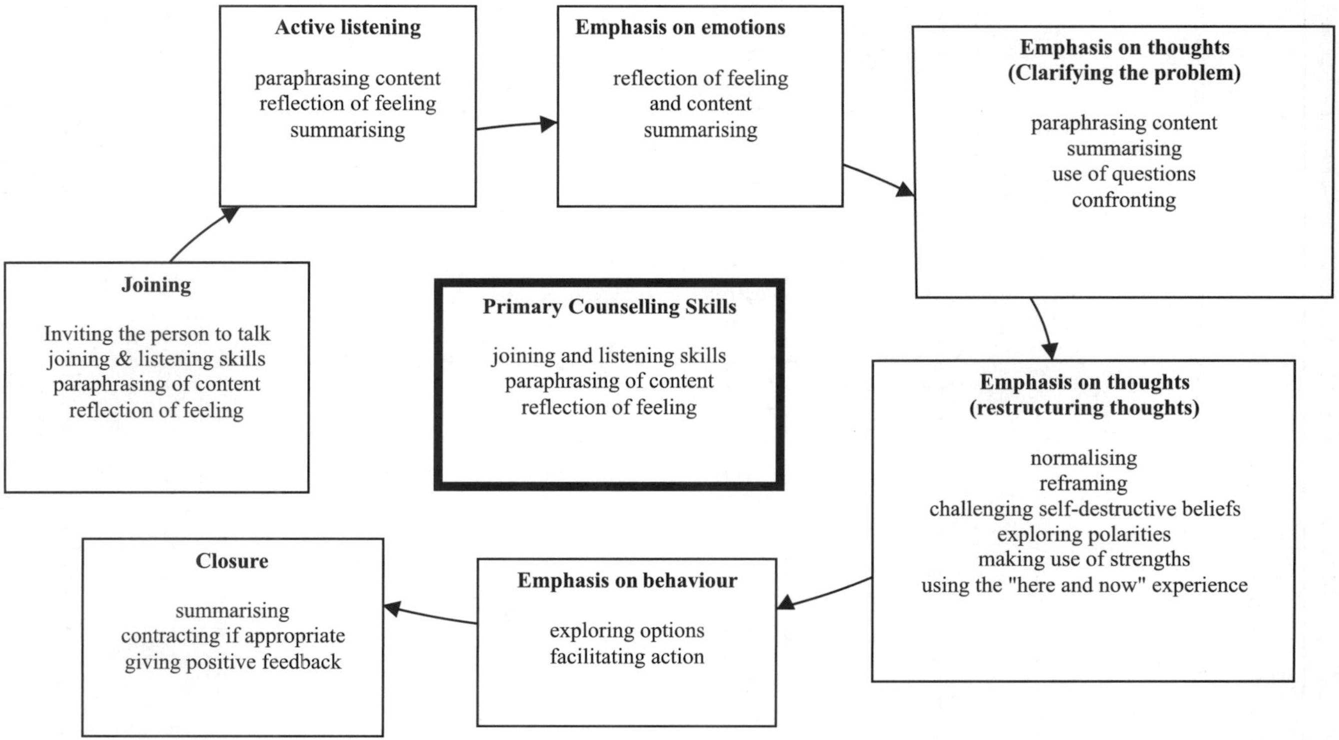
Active listening
paraphrasing content
reflection of feeling
summarising
Emphasis on emotions
reflection of feeling
and content
summarising
Emphasis on thoughts
(Clarifying the problem)
paraphrasing content
summarising
use of questions
confronting
Joining
Inviting the person to talk
joining & listening skills
paraphrasing of content
reflection of feeling
Primary Counselling Skills
joining and listening skills
paraphrasing of content
reflection of feeling
Emphasis on thoughts
(restructuring thoughts)
normalising
reframing
challenging self-destructive beliefs
exploring polarities
making use of strengths
using the "here and now" experience
Closure
summarising
contracting if appropriate
giving positive feedback
Emphasis on behaviour
exploring options
facilitating action

Figure 12.2 Relevance of skills to the stages of the counselling process

Primary counselling skills

Figure 12.2 shows how particular counselling skills fit into an integrative process which starts with the 'joining' stage and ends with the 'closure' stage. You may notice that in the centre of the figure we have a frame entitled 'Primary Counselling Skills'. We consider the skills of joining and listening, paraphrasing content, and reflection of feeling to be primary counselling skills. We believe that these skills are the most important and useful of all the counselling skills because they can be used with effect at any point within a counselling session. Consequently, we have placed the 'Primary Counselling Skills' frame in the centre of Figure 12.2 to emphasise the way that these skills are applicable in all stages of the counselling process. These primary counselling skills have been described in Chapters 4 to 6. They should be used almost exclusively in the early stages of counselling, and should also be used at other times throughout the counselling process. We have to remember that joining does not just happen at the start of a relationship. If we are not diligent in attending to the way we join with the person we are trying to help, our connection with them may be impaired. We need to continually attend to the joining process. Also, it is essential that at all stages during counselling the client feels heard and understood. The best way to ensure this is through paraphrasing and reflection of feeling.

> Primary conselling skills can be used at any stage

The stages of a counselling process as listed in the left-hand column of Figure 12.1 will be discussed in the following paragraphs. While reading this discussion it might be helpful to refer to both Figure 12.1 and Figure 12.2.

Preparation

The counselling process starts even before the client and counsellor meet. Clients on the way to counselling sessions will often rehearse what they intend to say. They are likely to bring with them preconceived ideas about what's going to happen in the counselling session. They will have not only expectations, but probably considerable apprehension too. Coming to a counselling session can be quite difficult for a client because it is painful to talk about deep inner feelings, and it can be quite threatening to do this with a stranger.

The counsellor's own experience

Counsellors also bring their own expectations, agenda, and personal feelings to counselling sessions. The counsellor's expectations and agenda may be inappropriate for the client, and the counsellor's personal feelings may intrude on the counselling process to the detriment of the client. The counsellor's own attitudes, beliefs, and feelings are certain to influence what happens in the session. If counsellors have personal problems of their own that are unresolved and currently troubling them, these are certain to affect their counselling. Obviously, it is very important for counsellors to try to minimise the intrusion of their own issues into the counselling process. One of the best ways for counsellors to achieve this is for them to become as aware as possible of their own personal troubling issues, and as aware as possible of what they are experiencing internally during each counselling session. We believe that if when counselling, you deliberately try to stay aware of what is happening within yourself, then you will be better able to deal appropriately with what is yours, and to separate that from what is the client's. In this way your own issues will be less likely to intrude on the counselling process. When you do notice that your own issues have intruded, it is essential to talk through these with your supervisor.

Information gained prior to counselling

Before a counsellor has met with the client, it is possible for them to have some preconceived ideas about the client. Often the counsellor will have information about a client before the session starts. This information may have come from the person or agency that referred the client for counselling. As a new counsellor, David has admitted that he believed that such material often distorted his own understanding of the client. Consequently, he went through a stage of trying not to listen to what referral sources told him. He would make an appointment and say to the referral source: 'I'll find it all out from the client.' Fortunately, he has changed that approach because he discovered that quite often a referral source will have factual information which may take time to come out in the counselling session, and which is useful in enabling him to understand the client better. Additionally, some clients may have an expectation that a referral source will have given him information.

Joining

During the joining stage the relevant counselling micro-skills are the primary counselling skills: the joining and listening skills decribed in Chapter 4, paraphrasing content; and reflection of feeling. Although one or two questions may be needed, the use of questions should be kept to a minimum.

This is the stage where the client and counsellor meet and a relationship is established, as discussed in Chapter 4, so that the client feels at ease. Also, at this time, the counsellor may be able to check out and adjust some of their preconceptions about the client.

After the initial settling-in period, it may be useful to start the working part of the session by enquiring about how the client is feeling. This brings the focus onto the client's current awareness and enables them to get in touch with their own anxiety or tension about coming for counselling. By helping the client to get in touch with these feelings, they may change so that the client feels more at ease as they start to talk about troubling issues.

Sometimes a client will come with a 'shopping list' of things which they wish to talk about, and may even produce lengthy handwritten notes. When a client of ours does this, we try to help them feel that what they have done is useful and valuable preparation. However, we avoid getting trapped into working through the shopping list item by item, but instead use the list to generate energy in the client. For example, we might say, 'This list is really important. When you think about it, what do you think about first?' Thus the client finds a starting-point from which to proceed naturally, in whatever direction their energy takes them. More often than not, the shopping list will become irrelevant as more important underlying issues emerge.

Clarifying the counsellor's role

Unfortunately, clients often perceive counsellors as 'experts', with almost magical skills, who are capable of using clever psychological techniques to solve other people's problems. Consequently, there may be a need for you, the counsellor, to explain to the client exactly how you *do* see yourself. For example, you might say to the client:

> 'Look, I don't see myself as an expert who can solve your problems for you. In fact, I believe that you will always know and understand yourself better than I will know and understand you. However, I hope that in this session you and I together can explore what's troubling you so that you can make some progress towards feeling more comfortable.'

> Counsellors are not experts or magicians who can solve other people's problems

Alternatively, you might say something like:

'It would be great if I were a magician who could wave a wand over you to solve your problems. I can't do that, but I can offer you the opportunity to come here and explore your problems with me in a safe and confidential setting. Hopefully, by doing that, you will start to feel more comfortable.'

Active listening

During the active listening stage a counsellor will usually rely mainly on paraphrasing, reflection of feeling, and summarising. Once again, although it may be necessary to ask one or two questions, these should be kept to a minimum.

During this stage of a counselling session, as the client starts to talk about their issues, the counsellor can respond by using minimal responses, paraphrasing, and reflecting feelings. By the counsellor's doing this the client is encouraged to disclose what is troubling them, in their own way and at their own pace, and without unnecessary intrusion into that process by the counsellor. Consequently the client's story unfolds and the relationship between client and counsellor develops as the client feels valued by the counsellor's active listening. By the counsellor's paraphrasing and reflecting, the client can gain an assurance that the counsellor has both heard and understood them.

During the active listening stage, while keeping a check on their own inner experiences, counsellors need to focus their energy by concentrating as fully as they can on what is happening inside the counselling room. In particular, they need to fully attend to the client, to concentrate on listening to and observing the client; and to sense what the client is experiencing. This is not always easy and there will inevitably be occasions when a counsellor's attention does wander through an intrusion in the counselling environment, the presence of intrusive thoughts, over-tiredness, or for some other reason. If this does happen, it may be best to be open and honest with the client and then to re-focus on the counselling process. Remember that no one is perfect. If you are starting to become over-tired, you might like to read Chapter 28, entitled 'Looking After Yourself'.

Emphasis on emotions

During this stage, the counsellor will use reflection of feelings in order to help the person get in touch with their emotions. Clearly, this needs to be done in the context of the information which is being disclosed. It follows that in addition to using reflection of feelings the counsellor needs to make use of paraphrasing and summarising. New counsellors need to be aware that during this stage of the counselling process it is likely that clients who are experiencing high levels of distress will get in touch with, and express, strong emotional feelings. While continuing to be empathic, the counsellor needs to remain grounded because inevitably, if they are joined with the client, they will experience emotional feelings them-selves. Although some counsellors believe that it is useful for them to fully experience the emotional feelings of the client, we think that there are dangers in doing this. For example, imagine that a client starts to cry. If the counsellor also were to start to cry, the client might become concerned and believe that what they were telling the counsellor was too hard for the counsellor to hear. Rather than focusing on their own problem, the client might become more concerned about the counsellor and want to nurture them. Clearly, this would not be useful. We think that when a client starts to cry it is important not to interrupt that process, but to allow the client to cry and express the emotion so that cathartic release can occur. In our view, it is most useful if the client believes that they can share their innermost thoughts and feelings with a counsellor who is able to listen calmly and dispassionately, but empathically. Some people will find this difficult to do, as they believe that being dispassionate is incompatible with being empathic. We don't see it that way. We think that when we are able to remain grounded so that our own emotions are contained we are able to show the client warmth and empathy without interrupting their need to fully express their emotions in the absence of unnecessary constraint.

> Counsellors need to be in control of their own emotions

It certainly can be difficult at times for counsellors to contain their own emotions during counselling sessions when they are listening to clients who are very distressed. We ourselves find that at times we leave a counselling session feeling strong emotions of our own as a result of what we have heard. When this happens, we are careful to make sure that we debrief by talking with another counsellor and/or with our supervisor (see Chapter 27).

Respecting the client's pace

In the early stages of counselling, it is common for clients to be unable to recognise and talk about their emotional feelings. Clients often want to talk about things 'out there' rather than get in touch with their inner experiences. They want to talk about other people's behaviour, and about other people's fears. They want to focus on what happened in the past rather than on the present, and to focus on events instead of on their own inner feelings. It is useful to encourage a client, in this situation, to focus on their inner feelings and thoughts, as they are, in the present. However, it is also important not to pressure the client, but to allow them to move at their own pace. At first, allow your client to talk about the 'out there' things, if it is too painful for them to focus on their own inner processes. With time, as they deal with the 'out there' problems and with the 'out there' situations, they are likely to move slowly towards recognising and talking about their own feelings from the past. This is because past feelings will probably not be as threatening as present feelings. Later, the client may feel more able to own current feelings and move towards experiencing them. Take time in helping the client to experience their own thoughts and feelings in the present. It is important to do this sensitively because the client needs to be able to gradually approach the painful parts of their life, rather than to be pushed too quickly, and then to run away from fully exploring the emotional feelings that are troubling them.

Emphasis on thoughts – clarifying the problem

During this stage of the counselling process, as explained previously, the counsellor needs to continue using the primary counselling skills as at all other times during the process. However, a number of additional skills are now needed. As the client's trust develops, the counsellor will be able to ask appropriate questions where necessary, in order to help the client move forward and identify the most pressing problem. The counsellor needs to be active in both using questions and in summarising to help the person to clarify the problem. Important parts of what the client has said need to be drawn together by summarising these to help the client to focus more clearly.

Sometimes, when helping the client to clarify the problem, it will be apparent to the counsellor that there are inconsistencies in the client's story, thoughts, or beliefs. These inconsistencies are likely to be confusing for the client and to make it difficult for the client to clarify the problem. In such a situation it is advisable for the counsellor to use the skill of confronting as described in Chapter 13.

Emphasis on thoughts – restructuring thoughts

During this stage of the counselling process, there are some additional skills that are particularly useful in promoting change by helping the client to think differently. These are the skills described in Chapters 14 to 19. They are: normalising, reframing, challenging self-destructive beliefs, exploring polarities, enabling the client make use of their strengths, and using the 'here and now' experience. One or more of these skills can be selected and used to encourage the client to choose more constructive beliefs and ways of thinking about their problem.

Emphasis on behaviour

The counsellor may now be able to assist the client to move forward into exploring options, resolving dilemmas, and planning for action using the skills discussed in Chapters 20 and 21. However, it is important to ensure, as stated previously, that the client does not feel pressured. It is important to focus on raising the client's awareness of their present situation rather than pushing for choice or action as explained in Chapters 21 and 22. To encourage a client to make a choice prematurely will pressure them and will make it harder for them to reach a decision. If the client is not ready to make a choice, they must be allowed to feel that it is acceptable to be unable to make a decision and to feel that it is acceptable to remain stuck for the present.

Closure

A good way to close a counselling session is to summarise important personal discoveries for the client that have emerged during the session. Generally, it is better to pick out what was important in a session rather than to attempt to summarise everything covered in the session. At the close of a session you might wish to imagine that when the session began the client brought into the room an awkward bundle of thoughts and feelings. The client then dropped the bundle onto the floor and started to examine the contents one at a time. After examining each item, some were retained, some were thrown away, and others were exchanged. After that, the client needed help to tie up the bundle into a neater, more manageable package. A counsellor can provide such help by using a summary to tie together important themes which have emerged during the counselling process. It is important to remember, using the metaphor of the bundle, that the bundle belongs to the client, so it must be their decision about how and when they complete their repackaging.

Respecting the client's process

Sometimes a client will not be ready to tie up the package. Sometimes the client will be left in a very uncomfortable space, either feeling stuck or fairly unhappy or distressed about what they have discovered during the counselling process. Many counsellors, especially new ones, want clients to leave sessions feeling happy. It is important to remember that often it is useful for a client to be able to spend time between counselling sessions mulling over what has been discussed in the counselling session so that they can absorb and make sense of it before coming back again if they need to.

> Clients often change by processing what they have discovered in counselling later

It can be distressing for a new counsellor when a client who arrived for a counselling session looking composed leaves the session showing signs of emotion. This will inevitably happen at times because if a counsellor is effective, the client may move into areas that previously had not been openly explored. Consequently, the client may feel the pain of experiencing emotions that had been suppressed and leave the counselling session exhausted and sad. Sometimes allowing the client to do this can be therapeutic, and the positive results of this process may be seen when the client returns for a subsequent session. However, if the counsellor suspects that the client may engage in self-harming behaviour as a consequence of raised emotions, then appropriate action needs to be taken (see Chapter 26).

In conclusion

The process of a counselling session described in this chapter gives an overview of the way in which various counselling micro-skills can be used at different stages of the counselling process. However, as a counsellor, we hope that you won't attempt to follow this process rigidly, but rather will allow the process to emerge naturally. As explained previously, the stages of the counselling process described in this chapter and illustrated in Figures 12.1 and 12.2 do not necessarily occur sequentially – not only may they overlap, but at times the process will return to an earlier stage before continuing. Consequently, it is sensible to do as described in Chapter 2: allow the client to go at their own pace, in their own direction and to feel as though they are going on a journey with you, the counsellor, walking alongside. In this process, you will at times use your skills to enable the person you're helping to continue on the journey in a useful way. If you do this, the counselling process will occur naturally, smoothly, and without great effort on your part. Most importantly, the client will be undergoing a process of growth which may enable them to lead a more fulfilling and less painful life.

LEARNING SUMMARY

- The typical stages in a counselling session are described schematically in Figure 12.1.
- Skills used at each stage in the counselling process are illustrated in Figure 12.2.
- Client and counsellor expectations, agenda, and personal feelings will affect the helpfulness of a counselling intervention.
- Counsellors don't pretend to have magic wands!
- Initially, clients often want to talk about things 'out there', including other people and past events.
- After the client has talked about their problem allow them to explore and express their emotions, then help them to clarify the problem and restructure their thoughts. Finally, help them to explore their options and make decisions regarding their future actions.

Part IV

Additional Skills for Promoting Change

Chapter 13

Confrontation

What do you feel emotionally when you decide to confront someone? Many people feel apprehensive and worry about the outcome of confrontation.

What is it like for you when someone confronts you? Is it sometimes threatening? It may be.

Generally, when we use the word 'confrontation', we think in terms of opposing parties and of people disagreeing as they confront each other. In such a situation, the person being confronted is likely to feel threatened and may become defensive, while the person doing the confronting is likely to feel anxious.

Confrontation in counselling

Confrontation as a counselling skill is different from the generally perceived view of confrontation. The micro-skill of confrontation involves raising the awareness of clients by presenting to them information that in some way they are overlooking or failing to identify. Correct use of this skill involves bringing into a client's awareness, in an acceptable way, information that the client may consider to be unpalatable and which is either being avoided or is just not being noticed.

How do you help a child to swallow medicine which doesn't taste nice? You can either force it down the child's throat, or use a more gentle, persuasive approach. The problem with trying to force the medicine down is that the child may well vomit it up and your relationship with the young person will not be improved. Respecting the child's feelings is likely to have a more positive outcome than ignoring them. Similarly, clients deserve a high degree of respect, and they usually don't like being told painful truths. Metaphorically speaking, the art of good confrontation is to help the client to swallow 'bad medicine' voluntarily, so that they can incorporate it into their bodily system and digest it.

Confrontation is clearly a difficult skill to master, and should not be attempted until the skills previously described in this book have become a natural part of your counselling style. The skills you have learnt already, together with the skills described in Chapters 14 to 21, are often sufficient in themselves, making confrontation unnecessary. Additionally, it is important to avoid using confrontation until a trusting relationship has been established with the client, as otherwise the client is likely to feel threatened and may withdraw from the counselling process without receiving the help they need.

> Inappropriate confrontation is likely to damage the counselling relationship

Self-examination before confrontation

Before using confrontation look within yourself to examine your feelings, motives, and goals. Ask yourself, 'Do I want to confront because I am impatient and not prepared to allow the client to move at their own pace; do I want to confront because I enjoy confrontation; am I wanting to use confrontation to put my own values onto the client; or am I feeling angry with the client and wanting to express my anger through confrontation?' If the answer to any of these questions is 'Yes', then confrontation is inappropriate. Satisfying the counsellor's own needs is no justification for confrontation. Confrontation is most appropriately used after the use of other micro-skills has failed to sufficiently increase the client's awareness.

When to confront

There are a number of situations in which confrontation is appropriate. For example, confrontation is appropriate where:

1 the client is avoiding a basic issue that appears to be troubling them;
2 the client is failing to recognise their own self-destructive or self-defeating behaviour;

3   the client is failing to recognise possible serious consequences of their behaviour;
4   the client is making self-contradictory statements;
5   the client is excessively and inappropriately locked into talking about the past or the future and is unable to focus on the present;
6   the client is going around in circles by repeating the same story over and over;
7   the client's non-verbal behaviour does not match their verbal behaviour; or
8   attention needs to be given to what is going on in the relationship between the client and counsellor, for example, where dependency is occurring, or where a client withdraws or shows anger or some other emotion towards the counsellor.

> Good confrontation is respectful

In situations such as these, the counsellor may decide to confront the client by sharing with the client what they feel, notice, or observe. Good confrontation usually includes elements of some or all of the following:

1   a reflection or brief summary of what the client has said, so that the client feels heard and understood;
2   a statement of the counsellor's present feelings
3   a concrete statement of what the counsellor has noticed or observed, given without interpretation.

In addition to the above, good confrontation is presented in such a way that the client can feel OK rather than attacked or put down. These points are best explained by means of examples.

Examples to illustrate the use of confrontation

Example 1
The client had been referring obliquely to her concerns about her sexuality. She mentioned the sexual problem briefly several times and then immediately deflected away from it by talking about seemingly irrelevant trivia.

Counsellor Confrontation: I'm puzzled because I've noticed that several times you've briefly mentioned your sexual problem, and then have started talking about something quite different.

Notice how the counsellor first expressed her feelings by saying, 'I'm puzzled', and then gave a concrete statement of what she had noticed occurring. This response is minimally threatening as it merely feeds back to the client what the counsellor has observed, without judgement.

Example 2
An angry separated husband who had been denied custody of his children was threatening to burn down the matrimonial home when his wife and children were out. Even though he had been asked about possible consequences, he failed to recognise the serious consequences of his threat. The counsellor had reflected back the client's anger and attitude towards his wife. This had reduced the client's anger level, but he still felt excessively vindictive and admitted to this.

Counsellor Confrontation: You are so furious with your wife that you want to hurt her by destroying the family home. I'm very concerned when I hear you threatening to do this because you would hurt your wife, your children, and yourself. Clearly, if you were to burn down the house your children would lose their home and possessions, and you might end up in jail.

Notice how the counsellor first reflected back the feelings and content of the client's message, followed this by a statement of his own feelings, and completed the confrontation by giving a factual statement of likely consequences. This latter statement was not a statement of the counsellor's opinion, but was an accurate statement of the likely consequences.

There is also an ethical issue here. Where people or property could be injured or damaged the counsellor has a clear responsibility to take action to prevent this from occurring (see Chapter 26). You may wish to discuss the issue of confidentiality in a situation such as this with your training group or supervisor.

Example 3
The client had come to the counsellor as a result of a crisis in her current relationship with a longstanding close friend. The counsellor helped her to explore past events at length, as she chose to do that. It seemed to the counsellor that nothing further would be achieved by continuing to focus

on the past. However, although the client said that she wanted to talk about her present crisis, she continually recounted past events.

Counsellor Confrontation: I am puzzled. My impression is that you want to resolve your present crisis and yet you continually talk about past events. Unfortunately, the past can't be changed, but what you can change is what is happening in the present.

The response started with a statement of the counsellor's feelings – 'I'm puzzled' – followed by a reflection of the client's desire to talk about her present crisis, and then a concrete statement of what the counsellor had observed: 'You continually talk about past events.' In this example, the counsellor adds another factual statement which might be useful for the client: 'Unfortunately the past can't be changed, but what you can change is what is happening in the present.'

Remember that it is appropriate for clients to deal with past events in a constructive way where those events are significantly influencing present thoughts and feelings. However, the suggested confrontation would be appropriate where a client was inappropriately and excessively using past history to avoid facing present problems.

Example 4

Here is an example of a counsellor response that addresses repetitive behaviour by a client, who kept repeating herself by going over and over the same ground.

Counsellor Confrontation: I've noticed that we seem to be going round in circles, so I'll summarise what we've talked about … (the end of this statement is a summary).

This example demonstrates how the client was confronted with her repetitive behaviour. The counsellor first told the client what she had noticed happening, and then gave a summary. By confronting in this way, a counsellor can increase the client's awareness of what is happening. With increased awareness, the client may be able to move out of the rut in which she is stuck. However, sometimes, even after confrontation, the client will persist in going around the track again and repeating the same details. It is here that stronger confrontation is needed and the counsellor might say, 'I'm starting to feel frustrated, because once again we are going around the same track.'

Example 5

The client said, 'I feel really happy in my marriage', using a very depressed tone of voice and slumping down in her chair as she spoke.

Counsellor Confrontation: I noticed that your voice sounded very flat and you slumped down in your chair when you said that you felt really happy in your marriage.

Here the counsellor confronted by reflecting back what he observed without putting an interpretation on his observation. The client was then free to make her own interpretation of the feedback given.

In summary, confrontation increases the client's awareness by providing the client with information which the client may have been unaware of. Confrontation is best done caringly, sparingly, and skilfully!

LEARNING SUMMARY

- Confrontation involves bringing into the client's awareness information which:
  - may be unpalatable to the client; or
  - may have been ignored or missed and needs to be considered by the client if the counselling is to be optimally helpful.
- Good confrontation often includes a summary, followed by a statement of the counsellor's feelings and a concrete statement given without interpretation.
- Good confrontation leaves the client feeling OK and not attacked.

Practice examples: Practice examples to help when learning to use appropriate confrontation are provided in Part VI.

Chapter 14

Normalising

As we sat down to discuss writing this chapter David told me this story about a client who came to see him:

'Some time ago a person came to me in deep distress. "I think I'm going crazy", she said. "My head is buzzing with thoughts that flit in and out, I can't concentrate on anything for even a minute or two, and I'm getting nothing done in my daily life."

'I was concerned. Was this person really going crazy? Did she need medication or specialist psychiatric help?'

'I listened to her story using the basic skills and processes of counselling as described in this book. As the counselling session proceeded she sobbed as she got in touch with her sadness, and I began to understand. Once again she asked me, "Do you think I'm going crazy?" and this time I was able to say, "No, I don't think you are going crazy. If I had suffered the trauma you've just described, I think that I would also feel the way you do." I continued: "I think that what is happening to you is inevitable and normal for someone who has had your recent experiences." I also said that maybe if she was finding the emotional pain too severe she could ask her doctor to consider prescribing medication. However, she chose not to do so, and I was pleased to notice that when she came back to see me a week later she was slowly and naturally moving into a more comfortable emotional space.'

That story illustrates the use of the skill called 'normalising'. David told the client that in his judgement what was happening to her was inevitable and normal. He noticed that she looked relieved and less tense as soon as he was able to tell her that he did not think that she was going crazy, but saw her emotional distress as normal for the situation.

> A client can feel relieved if the skill of normalising is used correctly

The skill of 'normalising' is a particularly useful and powerful one if used correctly. Often a person's anxiety can be considerably reduced if they can recognise that their emotional state is normal and appropriate for the situation.

The example given above involved normalising a person's emotional response to trauma. However, the skill can also be used to normalise behaviour and relationship changes which occur as part of life's normal developmental crises. Readers who are interested in learning more about the types of problem which often occur as a result of developmental crises at various stages in life may be interested in reading Chapter 8 of our book *Counselling Skills in Everyday Life* (Geldard and Geldard, 2003).

The need for care

Clearly we need to be careful in using the skill of 'normalising' because it would be irresponsible, unethical and possibly dangerous to tell someone who was experiencing severe problems of a psychiatric nature that they were OK and did not need specialist treatment. A counsellor who is in doubt about a person's psychological condition should consult with their supervisor and refer the client to a professional who is competent to make a proper assessment.

Uses of normalising

Normalising can be used:

1   to normalise emotional states; and
2   to normalise changes in behaviours, roles, and relationships due to developmental crises.

Normalising emotional states

The goal in normalising a client's emotional state is to help the client to reduce anxiety by letting them know that their emotional response is a normal one. Time and again, clients become frightened by their intense emotions in times of crisis. Fear of their highly charged emotional experiences leads them to wonder whether they are going to fall apart completely and end up in a psychiatric ward. As we know, the reality is that this could happen to any one of us. A high percentage of the general population require psychiatric help at some point in their lives, so it is not realistic to deny a client's fear of what could happen. Instead, recognition of the fear with a response such as, 'You're frightened that you're going crazy' is sensible. However, if, as a counsellor, you think that the client's emotional response is appropriate for the situation, then it will probably be helpful if you tell the client that. If you are unsure about the need for more specialist help, it is sensible to give your client the option of seeking further assistance. You might say: *'The emotional state you are experiencing and describing seems to me to be a normal response to your situation, but if you are unsure about your ability to cope then you may want to look for more specialist help. What are your options in that regard?'* It might then be possible for you to make suggestions with regard to referral for assessment or treatment. If in doubt, the appropriate thing to do is to consult your supervisor.

Normalising changes in behaviours, roles, and relationships due to developmental crises

We all go through normal developmental stages in our lives. An example of a developmental stage is when a child takes its first few steps. Previously the child had been unable to walk, and then their lifestyle changes as they learn to walk. The time when those first few steps are taken involves anxious moments, so in some sense it is a crisis time. However, it is inevitable and normal for a child to learn to walk and for there to be associated anxiety.

There are many developmental stages in our lives. These stages are generally inevitable and normal, but usually involve anxiety. Unfortunately, most people do not recognise the normal developmental processes and tend to respond to them inappropriately with panic and sometimes despair.

Consider some examples of common developmental changes. Happily married couples frequently run into trouble when a second or third child comes on the scene. With the first child things are usually fine, because both partners are delighted and proud as new parents and lavish time and affection on the new member of the family. However, things naturally and inevitably change with subsequent children. Often, although not always in our contemporary society, it's the mother who has most responsibility for parenting young children and much of her energy is taken up in doing this. Consequently, she does not have so much time or energy for her husband when the second or third child appears. She may feel resentful if she has interrupted her career by temporarily giving up her job with its associated social life. Her husband may feel resentful because his wife, due to the demands placed on her by the children, is no longer able to give him the attention and affection he previously enjoyed. Both partners may therefore be unhappy and may come to the conclusion that there is something terribly wrong with their relationship. However, this is a normal developmental crisis due to the changing nature of the family. It is to be expected and is almost inevitable. It can be a great relief to the partners in such a situation if the nature of the developmental crisis is explained. A counsellor might say, 'What is happening to you could almost have been predicted, because you have reached this developmental stage in your family life.'

> A level of stress and/or anxiety is inevitable at times of developmental change

Often, as counsellors, we find that it is useful to use the word inevitable when we are 'normalising' a client's situation, even though using this word may result in an overstatement. For example, we might say to the couple we have been discussing, 'It's inevitable that you would feel this way.' By our saying this, the couple are likely to feel relieved, because if they believe that what is happening to them is inevitable, they are likely to lose their feelings of failure. Thus, they may be able to recognise where they have succeeded, rather than focus on their disappointments. They may realise that there is nothing fundamentally wrong with their marital relationship, but that there is a need for both of them to look for new ways to deal with this developmental crisis. Without blaming themselves or each other, they can then take action to make changes so that they are both more comfortable. As you can see, normalising is a way for a counsellor to instill hope and optimism into the counselling process. This has been shown to be useful by Frank and Frank (1991), who identified that a counsellor who is hopeful contributes to a client's sense of relief and optimism about the future.

Another common time for distress due to a developmental crisis is when children grow to an age where they require very little parenting as they become more independent. This is a time when parents can feel a sense of worthlessness as one of their central life roles, that of 'parent', is diminished. Some people find considerable satisfaction in life through parenting and when this role diminishes they feel empty and lost unless they can find satisfaction in other ways. Additionally, they may feel rejected by their children who, in their search for individuation and independence, may naturally and appropriately distance themselves physically and emotionally from their parents.

Once again, 'normalising' the situation, by explaining to the client that what is happening is part of an inevitable and normal developmental stage in life, can help the client to feel better and to look for constructive ways in which to gain an increased sense of satisfaction.

If you stop to think, you will probably be able to identify a number of examples of times in your own life when feelings, behaviours, roles, or relationships have changed due to normal developmental processes. It is often easier to recognise these for what they are when they happen to other people rather than to ourselves. This is why the skill of 'normalising' is so useful because it brings emotional relief as it raises awareness of the inevitable and normal characteristics of a situation.

Warning!

Normalising does not and must not involve minimising or devaluing the client's problem and pain. Normalising does not involve saying to the client, 'This situation is normal and inevitable, it's really no big deal, everybody has to go through the same process!' To do that would fail to address the client's genuine pain. What normalising does do is to give the client a better understanding of their situation by putting it in its developmental context. By doing this, they may see their situation differently and understand why they are experiencing emotional distress, but also recognise that they are going through a normal process. This recognition may enable them to deal more effectively with their pain and to move forward rather than to think that they are a failure and should somehow have been able to avoid the crisis. It is much better for them to be able to say, 'I couldn't have avoided this crisis, it is a normal and inevitable crisis that couldn't be avoided. Now I can look for ways to respond to this crisis constructively.'

LEARNING SUMMARY

- Normalising involves:
  - letting a client know that their emotional feelings are a normal response to their crisis; or
  - explaining to a client that they are experiencing an inevitable and normal developmental crisis that could not be avoided.
- Normalising needs to be carried out appropriately with attention to the possible need for onward referral if the client is at risk psychologically.
- Appropriate normalising does not minimise the client's problem or devalue their pain.
- Appropriate normalising may help the client to feel better and to respond more constructively to their situation.

Practice examples: Practice examples to help in learning the skill of normalising are provided in Part VI.

References and further reading

Frank, J. D. and Frank, J. B. (1991) *Persuasion and Healing*, 3rd edn. Baltimore: Johns Hopkins University Press.
Geldard, K. and Geldard, D. (2003) *Counselling Skills in Everyday Life*. Basingstoke: Palgrave Macmillan.

Chapter 15

Reframing

Have you ever noticed how two people who observe the same event, such as a game of football, will give different descriptions of what happened? We all have individual perspectives, and the way in which another person sees things may well be different from the way in which you see things. Sometimes people who come for counselling have a very negative view of the world. They interpret events as they see them, but often view such events from a position of depression or of low self-esteem. The counsellor needs to listen very carefully to their description of the events or situation, and then try to look from the client's viewpoint and picture what the client has described. The client's picture, painted from the client's own perspective, will have a frame that is appropriate for them because it fits with their own particular mood and viewpoint.

> The picture I see may be different from the picture you see

The process of reframing

Sometimes a skilful counsellor can change the way a client perceives events or situations by 'reframing' the picture they have described. The counsellor, metaphorically speaking, puts a new frame around the picture so that the picture looks different. The idea behind reframing is not to deny the way the client sees the world, but to present them with an expanded view of the world. Thus, if the client wishes, they may choose to see things in a new way.

149

It would be quite useless to say to a client, 'Things are not really as bad as you think; cheer up!', if the client really sees the world in a very negative way. However, it may be possible to describe what the client sees in such a way that the client has a broader vision of what has occurred and thus is able to think less negatively.

Examples of reframing

Example 1

The client has explained that she seems to be unable to relax, because as soon as she turns her back her young son misbehaves and she has to chase after him and punish him. The counsellor has reflected back her feelings about this and now the client is calmer. At this point the counsellor decides to offer the client a reframe concerning the behaviour of her son.

Counsellor Reframe: I get the impression that you are really important to your son and that he wants lots of attention from you.

By making this statement, the counsellor has reframed the son's behaviour in a positive way, so that the mother may, if she accepts the reframe, feel important and needed. Maybe she will start to believe that her son is really crying out for more attention and will see his behaviour not as designed to annoy her, but as designed to attract her attention so that he can get more of her time. By reframing the child's behaviour in this way, there is a possibility that the mother may feel more positive towards her son and that this change in relationship could bring about a change in behaviour.

Example 2

The client has explained that he is continually getting angry with his daughter who will not study and attend to her school work but instead prefers to play around with what he describes as 'yobbos'. He explains how he can hardly cope with his anger and is getting uptight and feeling very miserable.

Counsellor Reframe: It seems as though you care so much about your daughter, you care so much about her turning out to be the sort of person that you want her to be, that you are prepared to sacrifice your own needs for a relaxed and enjoyable life, and instead to put a great deal of energy into trying to correct her behaviour.

This reframe allows the father to feel positive about himself instead of feeling negative and angry. He may now be able to see himself as caring about his daughter, and also may be able to see that he is putting his daughter's needs ahead of his own. He is reminded of his need to be relaxed and enjoy his own life. The reframe might take some of the tension out of the situation by removing the focus from the daughter, and putting it onto the client himself.

Example 3

The client has separated from her husband against her will. Her husband is now pushing her away and hurting her badly by refusing to talk to her or to see her. The client has shared her pain and suffering and the counsellor has reflected her feelings and allowed her to explore them fully. However, the counsellor now reframes the husband's behaviour.

Counsellor Reframe: You've described the way you see your husband pushing you away and not being prepared to talk to you, and that hurts you terribly. I'm wondering whether it is possible that what he is doing is really a result of his own inadequacy. Maybe your husband can't cope with the emotional pressure of talking to you, feels guilty when he sees you, and it's easier for him to avoid seeing you altogether, rather than to face his own emotional pain. Do you think that's possible?

By tentatively putting up this alternative the client may see that there could be other reasons for her husband refusing to have anything to do with her, and that it may be that he is also hurting and can't face the experience of seeing her. The counsellor's goal is to try to make it easier for the client to accept her husband's rejection.

Example 4

A senior executive has described to the counsellor how terrified he is of having to stand up and address a large meeting of professionals the following week, even though he wants to have the opportunity to tell them about the work he has done. The counsellor has reflected his feelings and allowed him, to some extent, to work through them. The counsellor then offers the following reframe.

Counsellor Reframe: It seems to me that you have mixed feelings about giving the talk. At times I almost get the impression that you are looking forward to it, and yet you say that you are very anxious about it. I am wondering if it would be possible for you to think of your anxiety as blocked excitement. Sometimes anxiety takes over when a person stops themselves from being excited. If they can let go and allow themselves to be enthusiastic and excited, then the anxiety reduces or even disappears as it is displaced by excitement.

The counsellor here is using a useful reframe from gestalt therapy by reframing 'anxiety' as 'blocked excitement'. Very often, holding our emotional selves in and putting restraints on ourselves prevents us from enjoying the exciting parts of our lives as we negatively reframe exciting events as anxious moments. A good example of this is the way a bride may prepare for her wedding. One way of thinking about going through the wedding ceremony and the reception is to say, 'Wow, that's a really anxiety-producing situation.' Another way of looking at it, a reframe, is to say, 'Wow, this is going to be a really exciting day and it's going to be fun.'

Example 5

The client explains how he is frequently being hurt by the boss who ignores him. The boss doesn't even look at him and she doesn't say 'Hello' when she meets him in the morning. She walks straight past him.

Counsellor Reframe: You've explained to me how your boss walks straight past you without noticing you, and I'm wondering if there is an alternative explanation for what's happening. Sure, it may be that she really does intend to snub you. On the other hand, is it possible that she gets terribly preoccupied and really isn't on this planet half the time?

In this reframe, the counsellor is presenting an alternative that may be partly true. It's quite likely that the boss is sometimes preoccupied, and that may be a partial explanation. By putting this possible explanation up as an alternative, some of the sting is taken out of the boss ignoring the client, and the client may then feel less uptight in his relationship with her.

Example 6

The client explained to the counsellor his feelings of inadequacy and failure. He knew that he was intellectually bright and that made him feel worse because he never completed any project he started. He would start enthusiastically and soon lose interest. He was deeply depressed by a long string of past 'failures', things that he had started and then left half-finished.

Counsellor Reframe: You seem to be a very intelligent person who is quite capable of completing any of the projects you have started. My guess is that you are excited by new projects because they present a challenge, and that you lose interest only when you believe that the challenge is easy for you to meet. Because you are highly intelligent you very quickly get bored and look for new stimulation.

This reframe enables the client to feel good about himself instead of perceiving himself as a failure. He is then left with the possibility that he can decide to do the boring thing and complete a project if he wishes, or he can choose to continue looking for excitement and stimulation without feeling so guilty.

As you can see, reframing needs to be done carefully, sensitively, and tentatively. If it is done in this way, it is likely to be accepted by the client, but may be rejected if it does not fit. Sometimes, though, the client may not think that your reframe fits. However, by being offered an alternative way of viewing things the client may be able to broaden their perspective with a resulting reduction in their distressing feelings.

Before reading the next chapter, you may wish to practise reframing by using the following examples of client statements. If you are in a training group, it might be useful to discuss and compare your reframes with those of other group members.

Client statements for reframing

Example 7

Client Statement: I can't believe something so terrible should happen. My husband has been granted custody of my children and I'm only allowed to see them on alternate weekends. He claims that I can't cope with them, and I feel like a total failure because in some ways he's right. They used to drive me crazy. But I love them and want to have a good relationship with them. Now I'll have so little contact with them, they'll hardly know me.

Example 8

Client Statement: I crave a long-term relationship with someone, and all I get is short relationship after short relationship. I just don't seem to be able to hold on to my lady friends. They always criticise me for being so restless and for never relaxing, and none of them want to stay with me.

Example 9

Client Statement: My father hates me, I'm sure. He picks on me for everything I do. All the time he follows me around and complains about my behaviour. He wants me to behave like a toffy-nosed snob instead of a normal human being. Not only that but he's always nagging me to study more!

Example 10

Client Statement: I've got so much that I have to do in a day and I get so angry with myself because I keep making mistakes. Sure, I get lots done, but I keep forgetting things and mixing arrangements up. I'm hopeless. When will I learn?

Example 11

Client Statement: I'm furious with my mother. She lets my sister, Annette, manipulate her with suicide threats and her refusal to eat properly. Mum rushes around attending to her every need. It's just not fair on Mum and I wish she'd stop doing it.

Example 12

Client Statement: My son's unemployed again, and I resent having to support him financially. Why should I spend my money on a person who's mean and nasty to me? It would serve him right if I let him starve. What annoys me is that he knows that he can treat me badly and then twist me around his little finger and I will support him. I'm angry at myself for being so stupid as to be manipulated so easily.

Suggested reframes for examples 7 to 12

Example 7

This reframe would be used only after fully reflecting and working through the client's distress in the usual way:

I'm wondering whether when the children are not with you, you will be able to do things for yourself to enable you to recharge, and regain your energy. Then when you do see the children you will feel good and be able to have some quality time in which to create a good relationship with them.

Example 8

You must be attractive to the opposite sex to be able to start so many new relationships. By the sound of it, you have plenty of energy, and I wonder whether the woman friends you've had would have been able to satisfy you for very long.

Example 9

Do you think it's possible that your father doesn't hate you but just worries excessively about you? Maybe he desperately wants you to be a success and worries in case you fail in life.

Example 10

People who do nothing never make mistakes. Making mistakes could be a sign that you are, to use your words, 'getting lots done'. You could feel good about that.

Example 11

Your mother must care a great deal about Annette to choose to do what she does.

Example 12

You must be a very caring person to choose to support your son, especially as you don't like his behaviour much.

Practice examples: Practice examples to help in learning reframing are provided in Part VI.

LEARNING SUMMARY

- ▪ Reframing provides clients with an expanded picture of their world which may enable them to perceive their situation differently and more constructively.
- ▪ Reframing needs to be done sensitively and carefully.
- ▪ Reframes should be offered in such a way that clients can feel comfortable in either choosing to accept them or in choosing to reject them.

References and further reading

Bandler, R., Grinder, J. and Andreas, C. (1989) *Reframing: Neurolinguistic Programming and the Transformation of Meaning.* Moab: Real People Press.

Chapter 16

Challenging
Self-Destructive Beliefs

Albert Ellis introduced the idea of challenging what he called irrational beliefs and developed a model of counselling which is now called rational emotive behaviour therapy. We will briefly describe the basis of rational emotive behaviour therapy and then discuss the usefulness of challenging self-destructive beliefs when using an integrative counselling approach.

Rational emotive behaviour therapy (REBT)

Central to rational emotive behaviour therapy (REBT) is the ABCDE model described by Dryden (1999). A diagrammatic representation of this model is shown in Figure 16.1.

This model is dependent on the notion of irrational beliefs. It is assumed that a sequence of events, as described in Figure 16.1, occurs, which leads the client to experience uncomfortable emotions and/or to engage in maladaptive behaviours. The letters ABCDE are the first letters of words which describe the sequence. The letter A represents the first stage of the sequence, which is an *activating event*. According to REBT theory,

A	Activating event
B	Beliefs – rational or irrational
C	Consequences – emotional or behavioural
D	Disputing irrational beliefs
E	Effects of disputing irrational beliefs

Figure 16.1 The ABCDE model

the activating event triggers off an irrational *belief*, represented by the B. The *consequence* (C) of this irrational belief is the person's response, involving unhelpful emotions and/or behaviours. D represents the stage where the counsellor *disputes* the irrational belief, helping the client to replace the irrational belief with a more constructive belief. Finally, E represents the *effects* of disputing, as a result of which the client will hopefully experience more helpful emotions and/or behaviours.

Once an irrational belief has been disputed and replaced by a more useful belief, it is expected that similar activating events in the future will result in more positive consequences as the client moves through the A, B, and C stages.

It can be seen that the REBT approach does not encourage the client to express emotions but instead encourages them to focus on their beliefs and behaviours.

Challenging self-destructive beliefs within an integrative counselling approach

We are all entitled to have our own attitudes, beliefs and thoughts. They are ours, and no one has the right to tell us that we should change them. Our attitudes are intrinsically ours, and we have the right to choose what we will believe and think and what we won't. Consequently, counsellors need to respect their clients' right to do this. However, an important role for counsellors is to help clients to change so that they will feel better. As discussed in Chapter 11, as integrative counsellors we believe that the most effective long-term change is achieved if emotions, thoughts, and behaviours are all addressed. In order for this to happen, exploration of the client's attitudes, beliefs, and thoughts needs to occur. Although any changes to attitudes, beliefs, and thoughts need to be made by clients as a result of their own choice, counsellors have a legitimate responsibility to help clients recognise when attitudes, beliefs, and thoughts may be self-destructive.

Counsellors may confront clients, as discussed in Chapter 13, if their attitudes, beliefs and thoughts are incongruent or may have socially un-desirable consequences (see Chapter 26 regarding ethical issues). Although as we have said, as counsellors we do not have the right to impose our values on our clients, it is most certainly a legitimate part of our role, and a responsibility, for us to raise our clients' awareness of their choices. As a consequence of our helping clients to bring into focus the choices that are available for them, they can be enabled to make new choices, if these fit for them and are appropriate, so that positive change can occur in their feelings, thoughts and behaviours.

Many clients do not seem to be aware of the possibility that they may, if they wish, change the way they are thinking, or the beliefs they have, in order to help them lead more satisfying lives. Many clients hold on to beliefs which are unhelpful for them, and indeed may be self-destructive.

As explained previously, Albert Ellis, the originator of rational emotive behaviour therapy, introduced the idea of challenging what he calls 'irrational beliefs'. Although we think his idea is excellent, we believe that there is often an advantage in using the word 'self-destructive' rather than 'irrational'. This is because some beliefs which are self-destructive are not necessarily irrational. We have found that sometimes when we use the word 'irrational' a client will correctly argue that their belief is not irrational. It is clearly not helpful for counsellors to get into arguments with clients. Also, some clients may feel offended if we suggest that their beliefs are irrational, as most people like to see themselves as rational beings. In comparison, if we gently suggest that what a client believes may be unhelpful for them and therefore self-destructive, they may be more willing to accept our suggestion.

> Most people like to see themselves as rational beings

We consider that there are two categories of self-destructive beliefs, or SDBs for short. These are:

1 'should', 'must', 'ought' and 'have to' beliefs; and
2 beliefs involving unrealistic expectations.

'Should', 'must', 'ought', and 'have to' beliefs

Clients often make statements using the words 'I should', 'I must', 'I ought', or 'I have to'. Sometimes the words are spoken with enthusiasm, firmness, and meaning, and it is clear that the client feels good about doing whatever it is that they 'should do', 'must do', 'ought to do', or think they 'have to do', and that's OK. At other times the words are spoken in an unconvincing way, as though some other person is saying to the client 'you should' or 'you must', 'you ought' or 'you have to', and the client is reluctantly, uncomfortably, and maybe resentfully accepting that message.

When this occurs, the client is likely to feel confused and emotionally disturbed. If the client conforms with the 'should' message, they may feel like a small child reluctantly and miserably doing as they are told by others. They will not feel as though they are fully in control of their life, and will not recognise their behaviour as being of their own choosing. If, on the other hand, they disregard the 'should' message, they may feel guilty, with consequent negative results. The goal of counselling in such instances is to help the person to feel more comfortable with their decisions, so that when they make a choice they do it willingly, and without feelings of either resentment or guilt. Provided underlying issues are correctly and fully addressed, this goal is usually achievable.

Where do 'should', 'must', 'ought', and 'have to' beliefs come from?

As children, we grow up in a world in which we have no experience. We do not know the difference between right and wrong, and we cannot distinguish good behaviour from bad behaviour. However, we learn, initially from our parents and close family, and then from others such as teachers, friends, and social and/or religious leaders. We learn from the people who care for us, from what they tell us verbally, and by watching and copying their behaviour. Gradually we absorb a system of values, attitudes and beliefs. It is right and proper that we do so.

As we grow through childhood and adolescence, there comes a time when we start to challenge and rebel against some of the beliefs we have absorbed from others. Interestingly though, many people, by the time they are young adults, have rejected some but hold on to most of the beliefs and values of their parents. As children, it is clearly appropriate that we learn and absorb the beliefs of our parents and significant others. There is no other way for us to learn, because as children our experience is too limited for us to make mature judgements for ourselves. As adults, we do have experience, and it is appropriate for each of us to determine for ourselves which beliefs fit and make sense for us as individuals and which beliefs do not fit. We can then keep what fits and reject that which does not. We can replace what doesn't fit by something new that does.

Beliefs that don't fit

Sometimes, when a client uses the words 'should', 'must', or 'ought', they are stating a belief that has its origins in their childhood, and which they are holding on to, but which does not fit for them now. If they really accepted the belief as their own they would be more likely to say,

'I've decided', or 'I want to', or 'I choose to', rather than 'I should', or 'I must', or 'I ought', or 'I have to'. Of course, we are describing the general case and this is not always true. What is important is to encourage the client to own their choices as being morally right and fitting for them, rather than for them to attribute their decisions to an external moral code imposed on them by others or through childhood conditioning.

> We must respect the client's right to stay with beliefs which fit for them

The problem with 'shoulds', 'musts', 'oughts', and 'have tos', is that often the words spoken are believed at a head or thinking level, but do not sit comfortably at a gut or feeling level. Where there is a mismatch between what is happening at a head level and what is being experienced at an emotional level, the person will be confused and emotionally distressed. Human beings are holistic beings, so we cannot separate our emotional feelings, our bodily sensations, our thoughts, and our spiritual experiences into discrete compartments. They all interrelate and must be in harmony with each other if we are to feel integrated and comfortable.

Challenging 'should', 'must', 'ought', and 'have to' beliefs

Sometimes a client will use an 'I should' statement and then express reluctance to do what they have said they 'should' do. In such a case, it can be useful to raise the client's awareness of what is happening internally so that they become more fully aware of their options. We like to explain to the client where many 'I should' messages come from, and to ask them where they think this particular 'I should' message has come from. We then encourage the client to check out whether the message sits comfortably with them. If it does, that is great. If it doesn't, they can, if they choose, challenge the 'I should' message and maybe replace it with something which fits more comfortably for them. Alternatively, they may decide that the message fits for them and accept it more willingly. A similar approach can be used when helping clients to challenge 'ought', 'must', and 'have to' statements.

Beliefs involving unrealistic expectations

Many self-destructive beliefs involve unrealistic expectations of self, others, or the world in general. Some of these beliefs include use of the words 'should, 'must', or 'ought', but others don't. Like the self-destructive beliefs described previously, these beliefs are often absorbed from others during childhood. A good example of a belief involving unrealistic expectations is the belief that life will be fair and just. Life experience clearly demonstrates that life is often unfair and unjust. It is therefore unhelpful to assume that it will be fair and just, as this sets a person up to have unrealistic expectations. A more helpful belief might be: 'Unfortunately, life is not always fair and just. If I can accept that, then I may be able to make sensible decisions to deal with those things which are unjust and unfair.'

Having unrealistic expectations of others

We frequently hear people saying things like, 'she should ...', 'people should ...', and 'they ought to ...'. By saying such things, the speaker is assuming that other people will have the same values as they do and is putting their own expectations onto other people. To do this is unrealistic and consequently unhelpful. Counsellors frequently encounter clients who are distressed as a result of others failing to live up to their expectations. When such clients recognise that their expectations are unrealistic, they often experience a sense of loss and need to be allowed to grieve. For example, a person might say, 'I expected my brother to care about me but he doesn't.' Having recognised this, the person experiences a loss of expectations and is likely to be saddened by the loss.

Table 16.1 gives some examples of common self-destructive beliefs and helpful alternatives. Notice how the self-destructive belief is certain to make the client feel bad, whereas the helpful alternative is likely to enable them to adjust and adapt to the reality of life so that they can feel better.

Challenging beliefs which involve unrealistic expectations

If a client verbalises a self-destructive belief, it can be useful to encourage them to question the belief by asking a question such as, 'Is it realistic to expect that life will be fair and just?' By doing this, the client is very likely to challenge their own self-destructive belief that life should be fair and just. If they do, you may invite them to suggest a more useful alternative.

You may wish to explain the difference between self-destructive and helpful beliefs to your client. You can then encourage them to write down a list of their self-destructive beliefs and replace them by more helpful

Table 16.1 Comparison between some self-destructive beliefs and helpful alternatives

Self-destructive belief	Helpful alternative
I must never make mistakes.	The only way not to make mistakes is to do nothing. I'm active, and all active people make mistakes.
Other people should not make mistakes	No-one's perfect. I can accept that other people will make mistakes.
Other people make me angry.	I make myself angry when I don't accept that other people don't live up to my expectations.
Other people should live up to my expectations.	Other people don't need to live up to my expectations.
My happiness depends on other people's behaviour and attitudes.	My happiness comes from within me and does not depend on others.
I must live up to other people's expectations.	I don't need to live up to other people's expectations to be OK.
I must win.	According to the law of averages most people only win 50 per cent of the time. I don't need to win to feel OK.
Life should be fair and just.	Life is not fair and just.
Other people are bad if they do not have the same beliefs, attitudes and values as me.	All good people do not think the same or necessarily have the same beliefs, attitudes and values.
I must get my own way.	I do not need to get my own way to feel OK, and I can sometimes get satisfaction out of letting other people have their own way.
I need other people's approval to feel OK.	It's nice to get other people's approval, but I do not need their approval to feel OK.
I must always please other people.	It's unrealistic to expect that I can always please other people.
I must never get angry.	It's OK to be angry sometimes.
I should always be happy.	There is a time to be happy and a time to be sad.
I must not cry.	It's OK to cry.
I can't be happy if people misjudge me.	People sometimes will misjudge me. That's inevitable. But I know that I'm OK and that's what matters.

alternatives. Remember that a client has the right to retain what you believe are unhelpful beliefs if they wish. It is their choice, so do not attempt to persuade them to change. However, you might suggest that they consider the consequences for them of continuing to hold on to these beliefs.

> Challenging beliefs needs to be done carefully and respectfully

As when confronting, skill and care are needed when challenging self-destructive beliefs. Ideally, the challenge will come from the client rather than the counsellor. However, it can be helpful for a counsellor to explain the nature, origin and effects of self-destructive beliefs, so that the client is able to recognise and challenge them.

In conclusion

As explained, the ideas expressed in this chapter have their origins in rational emotive behaviour therapy, although, in contrast to the approach described here, rational emotive behaviour therapists are usually direct in their efforts to challenge and persuade their clients and describe self-destructive beliefs as irrational. If such an approach appeals to you then you may wish to learn more about rational emotive behaviour therapy once you have mastered basic counselling skills (see 'Further reading').

LEARNING SUMMARY

- Self-destructive beliefs include 'shoulds', 'musts', 'oughts', 'have tos', and beliefs involving unrealistic expectations.
- Many self-destructive beliefs come from messages absorbed during childhood.
- Self-destructive beliefs need to be challenged so that they can be replaced by constructive beliefs.

Practice examples: Practice examples to help in learning to challenge self-destructive beliefs are provided in Part VI.

Further reading

Dryden, W. (1999) *Rational Emotive Behavior Therapy: A training manual.* New York: Springer.

Ellis, A. (1996) *Better, Deeper, and More Enduring Brief Therapy: The Rational Emotive Behavior Therapy Approach.* New York: Bruner/Mazel.

Chapter 17

Exploring Polarities

We are stating the obvious when we say that the human personality is incredibly complex, because it certainly is. Even though it is complex, it can be useful to describe the human personality in terms of easily understandable models in order to help us conceptualise aspects of human behaviour. Any model we use is certain to be an over-simplification, but even so a model can be useful in helping us to understand more fully what happens in ourselves and in our clients. In this chapter, we will consider two models which are of particular value with regard to our understanding of the existence of different parts of self in the human personality, and the way in which clients' awareness of opposites within themselves can be raised through counselling. These models can also be very useful if we explain them to our clients and use them in a way which enables them to change and feel more comfortable. The models are:

1   the iceberg model; and
2   the polarities model.

The iceberg model

A good metaphor to illustrate opposites in the human personality is the iceberg as illustrated in Figure 17.1. An iceberg floats so that most of it is below the waterline and cannot be seen. Human beings are a bit like that. As you get to know a person, you will see parts of their personality. You will see those parts that are, metaphorically speaking, above the waterline. There are other parts of that person's personality too, but you do not see these as they are submerged below the waterline. Even the person

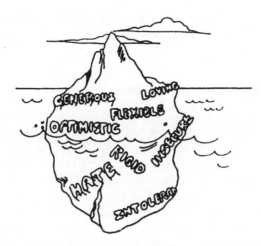

Figure 17.1   The iceberg model of human personality

concerned is unlikely to be fully aware of all those parts which are below the waterline. Icebergs have a tendency to roll over from time to time, and as they roll over some parts of the iceberg that had previously been submerged come into sight. Now and then, hidden parts of a person's personality come unexpectedly into view, rather like those parts of the iceberg that show when it rolls over. Sometimes it is other people who are surprised by what they see when this happens, and sometimes it is the person concerned who gets a surprise.

The most commonly talked about opposites in human feelings are 'love' and 'hate'. How often have you heard someone talk about a love/hate relationship? You may be aware from your own experience that a love/hate relationship can exist. If we have a strong capacity for loving, then it is likely that we also have the potential to hate. We may of course deny our capacity to hate. Just imagine the iceberg with the word 'love' sitting on the top, out in the open for everyone to see, and the word 'hate' right down below the sea, and hidden from view. The danger exists that one day the iceberg will roll over and the 'hate' side will be all that will be seen for a while. Time and time again we see a relationship where a couple fall in love, and then the relationship breaks up, and the love that was there is replaced, not by something neutral, but by hate.

Hostility and friendship are on opposites sides of the iceberg. Sometimes if we are feeling very angry with somebody, our hostility prevents us from forgiving them and being friendly towards them. Forgiveness and acceptance are on the opposite side of the iceberg to anger and hostility. If the iceberg rolls around so that anger is uppermost, then forgiveness is buried beneath the sea.

Denial of 'negative' emotions

Many of us are taught from childhood to deny what our parents, teachers, and other significant persons regard as negative emotions. Parents often put angry feelings into this category and tell their children not to be angry but to calm down. Similarly, some parents tell their children not to cry and teach them to disown feelings of pain and hurt. Stereotypically, such parental behaviour is often directed towards boys, who may be told that, 'Boys don't cry.' As a result, many children learn to think that angry feelings and feelings of pain and hurt are negative emotions and start to disown them, saying things such as, 'No, I'm not angry', when they are really very angry indeed, or, 'No it doesn't hurt', when it certainly does.

A common example of client distress caused by suppressing a part of self is the depression caused by repressed anger. We have found that many clients who are depressed are unable to express their anger. Often, when we suggest to them that maybe they feel angry with a person who has wronged them, we will be met with a denial. 'No, I'm not angry, I'm just sad', they will say. Gradually, however, as the counselling relationship builds, they will begin to express themselves more fully. After a while, as anger starts to emerge, the depression will start to lift. At first the anger will be barely expressed and will be described in very mild terms using words such as frustration, but gradually it will gain in momentum. The more this happens, the more the depression recedes.

> Repressed anger may result in depression – inappropriately expressed anger damages self and others

Similarly, repressed anger may block the ability of a person to forgive. Sometimes, a client with high moral values will be concerned because they wish to forgive someone but find themselves unable to do so. However, once they are able to get in touch with their anger towards the person they wish to forgive, and fully experience that anger, they are often able to allow the iceberg to roll over and experience forgiveness.

It is somewhat paradoxical that if we fully accept and own our anger, then we are more likely to be able to deal with it constructively rather than by expressing it destructively. By owning our anger, it will often disappear or reduce in intensity spontaneously, and in its place we are likely to experience a more comfortable emotion. It is important, however, to recognise that we have a potential to be angry, and to own that potential rather than to pretend it isn't there. Then, once it is owned, we have choice as to how we can deal with it.

Usefulness of the iceberg model in counselling

Sometimes it may be helpful for a client if a counsellor describes the iceberg model and explains that it is normal for human beings to have within them the capacity to experience a range of emotions and behaviours, some of which are opposite to others. In this way it may be possible to help the client to expand their self-awareness, and to get in touch with repressed emotions.

The polarities model

The polarities model, taken from gestalt therapy, is in some ways similar to the iceberg model but with an important difference. As in the iceberg, gestalt therapy recognises the existence of opposites in feelings, attitudes, beliefs and behaviours in each human being. This is seen as a normal human condition. In the gestalt polarities model these opposites are viewed as separated polarities that cause inner conflict and confusion to the client unless they are fully accepted and integrated. Whereas in the iceberg model it is assumed that one polarity or the other will be submerged at any one time, the gestalt model places emphasis on integrating the polarities so that both polarities are fully owned in the 'here and now' and can be accessed freely as a person chooses.

Usefulness of the polarities model

The polarities model can be useful for helping clients to feel OK about accepting and owning what they initially believe are undesirable or negative qualities or emotions. As counsellors, we can tell clients that for every so-called positive or desirable emotion, attitude, belief, behaviour, or quality, normal human beings may also have an opposite emotion, attitude, belief, or quality. This is normal and therefore OK. Such thinking frees clients to deal with all their emotions, personal qualities, traits and attributes.

Using a gestalt therapy counselling approach the process involves integrating the polarities so that any two opposite polarities are seen as ends of a continuum rather than as discrete and separate from each other. Opposite polarities can then be accepted as co-existing parts of self. This allows the client to recognise and own any two opposite polarities and to feel free to move to a more comfortable position on the continuum between these. Thus, the client is empowered by the recognition that they can if they wish choose to be at either polarity or at any intermediate point on the continuum. Through this recognition they may be enabled to strengthen those parts of themselves that they would like to strengthen, and can grow as people accordingly. For example, someone who has previously seen themselves as timid may recognise an inner ability to be assertive. Having recognised this, they then have the choice to move along the continuum – timid to assertive – to a position that suits them at any particular time and in any particular situation.

Acceptance of polarities within self

It's important for all of us to recognise and own that opposites exist within us as human beings. If we want to strengthen a particular quality, then we need to accept and deal with its opposite. To be honest with ourselves, we need to be able to say: 'I'm capable of loving and hating'; 'I'm capable of being angry and I'm capable of being forgiving'; 'I'm capable of being tolerant and capable of being intolerant'; 'I'm capable of being generous and miserly'; 'I'm capable of being optimistic and of being pessimistic'; 'of being fun-loving and of being a kill-joy'; 'of being light-hearted and of being serious'; 'of being religious and of having doubts about my religious values and beliefs'. In order to feel integrated and comfortable within ourselves, we need to accept all the parts of ourselves, and not just those parts that are socially acceptable and consistent with being 'nice' people.

> Can you accept all of you?

Clients often come to counselling because they are unable to accept parts of themselves. It seems as if parts of themselves have become submerged beneath the sea, never to be seen, and never to be owned. The submerged parts are continually wanting to surface, and there is an inner struggle to prevent the iceberg from rolling over. Naturally clients feel great discomfort when they try to keep parts of themselves submerged and try to deny parts of themselves that really want to be expressed.

Helping clients integrate polarities

There is more than one way in which to help clients to integrate polarities within themselves. We can do this by using the iceberg model with them, and helping them to recognise and own opposites within self. Alternatively, we can make use of an active experiential method which involves role-play and has its origins in gestalt therapy and psychodrama.

New counsellors are often lacking in the confidence required to enable them to use active methods where the client is encouraged to take part in role-plays. This is understandable, and it is sensible for them to stay with the skills which are comfortable for them until such time as they can use these confidently and wish to extend and enhance their repertoire of skills. Our experience is that when active methods involving client role-play are used, outcomes for clients are usually greatly enhanced. We do need to point out that in our opinion it is generally not appropriate to use active experiential methods until a sound and trusting counselling relationship has been established. Additionally, some clients are too self-conscious and unsure of themselves to be able to make use of these methods. When inviting clients to take part in an experiential exercise, we always make it clear to them that they have a choice about whether they take part in the exercise, and that they may stop the exercise at any time.

We keep a pile of coloured cushions of various shapes, sizes, colours, designs and textures in a corner of our counselling room. When exploring polarities, we invite the client to go to the pile of cushions and choose a cushion to represent each polarity. For example, let us consider a case where a client is extremely submissive, and is afraid to use the powerful part of self. In this case we might ask the client to choose a cushion to represent the submissive part of self, and to choose another cushion to represent the powerful part of self. Having done this, we invite the client to place the cushions one or two metres apart on the floor. The client is next invited to stand beside either one of the cushions. Imagine that the client chose to stand beside the cushion representing the submissive part of self. We then invite the client to say what it is like being submissive. Next we invite the client to move and stand beside the other cushion that represents the opposite part of self. Once again the client is invited to talk about what it is like to be in this position; in the example given, in the powerful position. Additionally, the client might be invited to dialogue between the two polarities, so that the submissive part of self might talk to the powerful part of self and vice versa. As the submissive part of self, when standing beside the 'submissive' cushion, the client might say to the powerful part of self represented by the other cushion, 'People won't like you if you behave like that' and, 'Nice people are like me, submissive.' When standing beside the powerful cushion, the client might say to the other cushion, 'People will walk all over you, like walking on a door mat.'

In this experiential counselling method, the counsellor needs to invite the client to move from cushion to cushion so that the dialogue continues. While the client is engaged in the dialogue, or is moving from one cushion to the other, it can be very useful for the counsellor to feedback to the client any non-verbal behaviour which is observed. For example the counsellor might notice that the client hesitates in moving, moves reluctantly, or looks much happier when going to the opposite polarity. Rather than the counsellor interpreting non-verbal behaviour, it is more appropriate and useful for the counsellor to give direct feedback of what is noticed by making a statement such as, 'You're smiling.' The counsellor might also wish to inquire, '*What are you experiencing inside right now?*' As a consequence of the dialogue and feedback from the counsellor regarding non-verbal behaviour, the client is likely to recognise times when it is useful to be in one position or the other.

Finally, the counsellor might invite the client to walk slowly backwards and forwards between the two cushions, stopping in various positions. By encouraging the client to do this, the client is likely to recognise that they can move to any position they choose at any particular time and in any particular situation. Consequently, they are empowered to use both parts of self. Additionally, they may recognise that it is possible to be in an intermediate position where they are not totally powerful or totally submissive, but are somewhere in between.

As we indicated earlier, experiential methods are extremely powerful and very helpful for the client provided that the client is comfortable with such an approach. New counsellors who would like to explore the use of such experiential approaches would be sensible to undertake some practical training in either gestalt therapy or psychodrama. Because the approaches are experiential, they are most effectively learnt through experience in a training course rather than just through reading a description in a textbook such as this.

LEARNING SUMMARY

- Human beings have polarities or opposites in their personalities.
- Generally we try to show the more acceptable polarities but sometimes the opposite polarities emerge.
- If we can accept the hidden parts of ourselves, then we will be better able to deal with them and to strengthen their opposites, if that is what we want.
- Experiential role-play methods can be useful in enabling clients to accept and integrate polarities so that they feel better.

References and further reading

Clarkson, P. (2000) *Gestalt Counselling in Action*, second edition. London: Sage.
Houston, G. (2003) *Brief Gestalt Therapy*. London: Sage.

Chapter 18

Enabling the Client to Make Use of Their Strengths

As described throughout this book, integrative counsellors like to draw on useful skills from a variety of therapeutic approaches. The skills required to enable a client to make use of their strengths mainly have their origins in Solution-Focused counselling (O'Connell, 1998) and/or Narrative Therapy (White and Epston, 1990). These approaches strongly suggest that it is more useful to focus on a client's strengths rather than to focus on their problems. Also, that it is useful to encourage the client to take an optimistic view of the future.

Clients generally come to counselling with a negative view and often see their problems as intractable. In responding to the client's description of their problem, we can use language in a way that enables the client to feel better about themselves and to take a more optimistic view about the possibility of change. This should not be taken to suggest that you are not interested in hearing about the client's difficulties or wish to minimise them. However, while listening, you can be positive in using responses which help the client recognise those inner strengths which they have already used, while also opening up the possibility that solutions to their problems will be found.

> Clients often fail to recognise their strengths

The skills involved in helping the client to make use of strengths are generally used by integrative counsellors during the stages in the counselling process where the emphasis is on thoughts. These are the stages where the counsellor is trying to help the client to clarify the problem and/or restructure their thoughts (see Figure 12.2).

There are a number of ways of helping a client to make use of their strengths. These include:

1 externalising the problem;
2 looking for exceptions;
3 identifying positive responses to negative experiences;
4 being positive about change that has occurred; and
5 being optimistic about the future.

Each of these will be discussed in turn.

Externalising the problem

The goal of externalising is to separate the problem which troubles the client from the client as a person. The easiest way to explain this is through an example. A client might come to counselling believing that they are by nature an 'anxious person'. While accepting that this is how the person sees themselves, it can be useful for the counsellor to describe the anxiety as though it has a separate and independent existence from the person. Hopefully, the result of this will be that the person will start to see themselves as someone who is troubled by anxiety, rather than as an intrinsically anxious person. If this happens, we say that the anxiety has been externalised as it is now seen as separate from the person themselves, although it troubles them. When clients are able to make such a change in their thinking, they generally become more empowered in dealing with their problem. This is because they can now start to think in terms of using strategies to control the problem rather than letting the problem control them, whereas previously they were seeing the problem and themselves as inescapably joined. In our example, if the client stops thinking about themselves as an anxious person and instead thinks about themselves as a person who is troubled by anxiety, they have a new perspective of themselves and their anxiety. With their new frame of mind they can think about how the anxiety gets the better of them and explore ways in which they can control it. When externalising, the counsellor attempts to create a different atmosphere around the problem, one in which the client sees their problem as not being intrinsic to them, but as something that is acting upon them from outside. In the example given, the client might say, 'I'm a very anxious person.' The counsellor might respond to this by saying, '*I see you as a person who is troubled by anxiety. Somehow anxiety seems to get the better of you.*' The counsellor might then follow up by asking, '*How does anxiety stop you from doing things you want to do?*' By taking this approach, the client's frame of reference changes from 'I am an *anxious person*' to '*Anxiety* causes a problem for me.' They are then in a position to be able to take responsibility for dealing with the anxiety rather than seeing the anxiety as a part of self.

> Externalising can help a person to feel better about themselves

Externalising makes it possible for the client to experience a part of themselves that is separate from the problem. By doing this, the client is able to feel that they she can control their her problem, or central issue, if they wish she wishes, because it is something external to them her which can be controlled, rather than something inherent in them her which cannot be controlled. This then opens up new possibilities for action. By externalising, the power is to some extent taken away from the problem and instead the client becomes empowered to control the problem.

It can be seen that the concept of externalising is based on the premise that the problem is the problem, as opposed to the person being seen as the problem.

A good example of the use of the skill of externalising relates to helping clients who have anger control problems. In such a case the counsellor might externalise the anger by asking questions such as: '*Does your anger have control of you, or do you have control of your anger?*' and, '*How does your anger manage to trick you into letting it control you?*' Can you see how in asking these questions the person is able to see themselves not as an angry person, but as a person who is troubled by anger, who has a responsibility to learn to control the anger rather than letting it control them? Clearly, externalising questions often lead to discussion about issues of control. The aim is to help the client gain control of unhelpful or unacceptable behaviour.

Externalising requires a particular shift in the use of language. Rather than using sentences which begin with 'I am . . .', externalising statements use sentences beginning with the name of the problem. For example, instead of saying, '*I am* anxious' the language changes to '*Anxiety* stops me from doing the things I want to do.'

Good examples of situations where it may be useful to externalise problems are when clients sees themselves as an alcoholic, a drug addict, a depressed or anxious person, or as a failure. The counsellor might ask such clients how they came to think of themselves this way and encourage them to expand on their self-perceptions. If this is done, often the client will talk about how the problem influences or interferes with their behaviour. At this point the counsellor has an opportunity to separate, or *externalise*, the problem from the client by talking about the way that 'depression', 'alcohol', 'failure', or 'anxiety' is causing trouble for them, instead of talking about *the client* being depressed, being an alcoholic, being a failure, or being anxious.

When externalising a problem, it can be helpful to find out how 'the problem' has interfered with or influenced the client's life, and then to discover how the client has attempted to overcome the problem. Here are some questions which can be used to help clients discover how a problem has interfered with or influenced their life (in these questions we will use 'depression' as the problem):

- '*When and how did depression first gain a foothold in your life?*'
- '*How has depression restricted your life?*'
- '*How does depression manage to trick you into letting it control you?*'
- '*What is the worst thing that depression has done to your life?*'
- '*When you try to get control of depression what does it do to hook you back in?*'
- '*How is depression stopping you from doing what you'd like to be doing?*'
- '*How is depression holding you back?*'
- '*What is helping depression continue to cause a problem for you now?*'
- '*What have you noticed about yourself that has made you think that you might be able to overcome depression?*'
- '*What retaliatory measures could depression use to try to put you back where it wants you?*'
- '*What would depression do as a last desperate measure if you continue to become stronger and more independent?*'

These questions help the client to recognise that they can separate the problem from themselves and that because the problem has an entity of its own they can, if they wish, use their own inner strength to control or manage it.

Looking for exceptions

A powerful technique to enable clients to get in touch with their strengths is to highlight exceptions by using exception-oriented questions. Exception-oriented questions aim to promote change by drawing attention to times or situations where an undesirable behaviour did not, or does not occur. With almost every client there will have been past and present problem-free times. However, it is quite possible that many clients will not have recognised these problem-free times. A task for the counsellor is therefore to help the client to identify those times or situations when the client's current difficulty didn't occur. Once these have been identified, the counsellor can inquire about them in detail. The counsellor can ask what, when, and with whom this exception to the difficulty occurred. For example, the client might say, 'I'm concerned because I'm drinking every night', and the counsellor might respond by looking for exceptions by saying, '*Are there any nights when you haven't had a drink?*' The client might be able to identify some times when they haven't been drinking. In this case the counsellor might explore further by saying something like, '*Tell me about those times.*' The counsellor then may use the client's views of facts, feelings and ideas associated with these times to help the client to pro-actively plan how to spend another night without drinking. It needs to be recognised that the client may be unable to identify any recent times when they have not been drinking. In this situation, the counsellor will suggest that there must have been a time when the client didn't drink every night. The counsellor will then ask questions to help the client remember the skills they used in times when the problem didn't occur. This may include exploring thoughts, behaviours, and emotional feelings which the client experienced in those times when the problem did not occur.

> People often forget the times the problem did not, or does not, occur

When looking for exceptions it can be useful to look for times when the client expected the problem to occur, but something happened differently or the client acted differently. For example a client might say, 'Last year on my birthday was the only time we didn't fight', and the counsellor might respond by saying '*What did you do differently?*' or, '*What is your guess about why you didn't fight?*' The focus is on what worked, helping the client to expand on the details of how it worked, and helping the client to retrieve how it felt to have things work.

Here are some examples of statements or questions a counsellor could use to find out about exceptions when the problem did not, or does not, occur:

- *'Tell me about the times when you don't ever get angry.'*
- *'When do you and your father get on well without arguing?'*
- *'In what situations do you have control of your impatience?'*
- *'Tell me about times when you have felt happy.'* (for a person who is troubled by depression)

Often it is helpful to explore exceptions after externalising the problem. Suitable questions might then be:

- *'Can you recall some occasions when you have prevented the problem from influencing your life?'*
- *'How did you restrict the problem's influence on these occasions?'*

Exception-oriented questions aim to help the client discover that there are times and/or situations where they behave, or have behaved, differently, and to recognise what it is that enables them to behave differently at those times or in those situations. Gaining understanding in this way enables them to get in touch with their own inner strength so that they he can take more control of their his behaviour and/or their his environment. By recognising this, they he may be able to make choices to bring about positive change.

> Highlighting exceptions can empower a person to find solutions

Once the counsellor has discovered that there were times when the problem did not occur, the counsellor can ask questions to explore in detail what was happening at those times. For example, when a problem has been externalised and exceptions have been identified the counsellor might ask questions like:

- *'What were you doing at the time when you were able to beat the problem?'*
- *'Can you describe your relationship with your partner at the time when the problem wasn't present?'*

■   *'What's your main experience when this problem is not around?'*
■   *'What strategies do you know that you have called upon in the past and that you can also use now?'*

When looking for exceptions the focus is on helping clients to recognise that at times they are confident and feel at ease, and to identify situations where they are, or have been, competent and effective, rather than focusing on times when they feel despairing, worthless, and overwhelmed by a problem. For example, a young client might say, 'The teachers at school say I'm not good at anything.' In response, the counsellor might say, *'Your mother told me that you spend a lot of time skateboarding. How did you become good at that?'* The young person might reply by saying, 'I repeat the same tricks over and over until I get expert at doing them. Each time I do a trick I notice the things that I do wrong so that I can correct them the next time.' By asking, *'How did you become good at that?'*, the counsellor will have enabled the young person to recognise the strategies they have used for learning particular skills. The counsellor might then be able to help the client to transfer these strategies and/or skills which the client has identified for use in the problem area.

Looking for positive responses to negative experiences

Clients will often talk about their past experiences as contributing to their current problems. In doing this they often fail to recognise the personal strength which they used in coping with their past experiences. Additionally, it can often be found that negative experiences in the past can be viewed as experiences that, while being negative, have brought about something positive. For example a client may blame their current situation, on the actions of an excessively punitive father. In such a situation the counsellor can express curiosity about how the client was able to cope and survive despite receiving harsh punishment. The client might then be able to recognise that they now have some useful inner resources which enable them to cope with difficult and/or unpleasant situations.

> Focusing on past success can help a person to feel more positive about themselves

When looking for positive responses to negative experiences, counsellors need to let their clients know that they have heard and understood their problems and concerns, their experiences, and their points of view. They can then make it clear that they believe that the client is in control of their own life and consequently suggest that any successful achievement must be a result of the client's efforts. For example, a client, when talking about her daughter, might say, 'She walks all over me. She'll only do things if she knows there is a reward,' and the counsellor might respond by saying, '*It seems to me that you have been able to change her behaviour by using rewards as a useful strategy.*' By saying this, the counsellor clearly attributes positive change to the efforts of the client instead of exclusively focusing on the negative part of the client's statement.

It can be useful for counsellors to explore in detail times when the client made a choice or a change which resulted in a positive outcome. They may share with their client what has worked for them in similar situations, or what has worked for other people with the same difficulty. For example, the counsellor might say, '*When I feel like that I know it's best for me to go for a long walk by myself.*' Alternatively, the counsellor might say, '*Other people have told me that when they experience what you are describing, they find it is helpful to do something active.*'

Some particular questions can be used to help a client recognise that they have coped extremely well under adverse situations. These are aimed at encouraging the client to view their behaviour in a positive light and discover unrecognised strengths. Such questions can be extremely useful for clients who are unsure about how well they are coping with life. Examples of this kind of question are:

- '*How come things aren't worse?*'
- '*What stopped total disaster from occurring?*'
- '*How did you avoid falling apart?*'

These questions can be followed up by the counsellor positively affirming the client with regard to any action they took to cope.

Being positive about change that has occurred

When things have been bad and things start to change, clients often fail to recognise that positive change has occurred. Consequently, it is important for counsellors to be vigilant in looking for the possibility that positive change has occurred as a consequence of the client's actions. There are two useful ways of helping a client to feel better as a result of past or recent achievements. One is to ask a question which presupposes positive change, and the other is to use a cheerleading question.

An example of a question which presupposes change is:

'*What has been different or better, since you saw me last?*'

This question presupposes that some change has occurred since the last meeting and may help the client identify things which have improved, so that they can feel good about the progress they have made, or their recent achievements. Quite often, positive change goes unnoticed unless a deliberate question is asked in order to identify change. For example, although they may have had fewer arguments during the week, the client might not have recognised this. By using a question which presupposes change, the counsellor can bring the change which has occurred into focus and make small changes newsworthy so that there is a recognition that improvement has begun. Once improvement has been identified, there is an incentive to make further improvement so that significant change can occur.

> Positive change is often minimised or not noticed

The use of cheerleading questions has been described by Walter and Peller (1992). Counsellors engage in cheerleading when they show enthusiastic reactions of emotional support when clients tell them that they have used behaviours which are positive and different from behaviours which previously led to undesirable outcomes. Typical cheerleading questions are:

- '*How did you do that?*'
- '*How did you manage to make that decision?*'
- '*Well done. That must have been really difficult to do; how did you do it?*'

Additionally, there are some statements which have a similar effect such as:

- '*That sounds good!*'
- '*That's amazing!*'

Cheerleading questions are useful as they help the client to recognise and be encouraged by the knowledge that they have the ability within themselves to behave differently so that positive outcomes occur.

Being optimistic about the future

Sometimes, in order to help the client to be optimistic about the future, it can be useful for a counsellor to describe the client's current situation as a stage, or to speak about the problem concerned as a stage; something that the client might grow out of, or will get over. For example, a client might say, 'My mother died six months ago and I still feel depressed.' In response, the counsellor might say, '*Losing your mother was a major loss. Before you can move on, you will need to take time to grieve. That's normal for all people when someone close to them passes away, but in time, for most people, their grief diminishes and they start to feel better.*' This statement is designed to help the client recognise that they are in a stage where it is appropriate to grieve, and that the stage is likely to pass.

When helping a client to establish goals for the future, it is important to be both realistic and optimistic. It can be useful to suggest that at some time in the future the problem will end or things will be better, whenever it seems likely that this will happen. When a client talks about their problem, it can be helpful if the counsellor re-states what the client has said in terms of goals to be achieved rather than problems to be removed. For example, the client may say, 'I'm worried because my husband and I fight all the time', and the counsellor might respond by saying, '*You would like it if your husband and yourself could get along better together. Have you thought about how this might be achieved?*' By responding in this way the counsellor has shifted the focus from the negativity of fighting and instead directed it towards a positive goal.

LEARNING SUMMARY

- externalising separates the problem from the person
- externalising invites the person to take control of the problem
- looking for exceptions draws attention to past successes, enabling the person to learn from them
- focusing on successes achieved while experiencing negative experiences puts a person in touch with their inner strength
- drawing attention to positive change is likely to promote more change
- being optimistic about the future may enable the client to look for solutions

References and further reading

O'Connell, B. (1998) *Solution Focused Therapy*. London: Sage.

Parry, A. and Doan, R. E. (1994) *Story Re-visions: Narrative Therapy in the Postmodern World*. New York: Guilford Press.

Walter, J. and Peller, J. (1992) *Becoming Solution Focused in Brief Therapy*. New York: Bruner/Mazel.

White, M. and Epston, D. (1990) *Narrative Means to Therapeutic Ends*. New York: Norton.

Chapter 19

Using the 'Here and Now' Experience

We all know people who are in the habit of continually complaining about their life situations, and who like to talk at length about the injustices of the world. They talk about things 'out there', which are apparently out of their control and are the responsibility of others. Rather than saying, 'What can I do to change this situation?', they use statements with words in them like 'They should . . .', and 'They ought to . . .', and 'It's disgraceful that they don't . . .'. Such people often go over the same ground again and again. It is almost inevitable that they will fail to move ahead, because no one can change a situation that is not within their own sphere of control.

Do you ever behave like the people we've just described? Do you ever grumble, moan, and complain about 'out there' things, things that are apparently other people's responsibility rather than yours? We both have to admit that at times, we do.

Taking personal responsibility

Notice how we started talking about other 'people who complain' in this chapter and are now looking at ourselves. My guess is that you were more comfortable when the discussion was about others than you were when owning your own ability to grumble and complain. It's usually easier for us to distance ourselves from our own dysfunctional behaviour and to blame others for our problems.

> We can't change other people but we can change ourselves

Unfortunately, if we complain about things that other people are doing or not doing, or about external events or situations, then we are likely to get stuck in a rut of complaining, and to feel frustrated because we are powerless to bring about change. Conversely, if we focus on what we ourselves are doing, and on what is happening inside us, then we can, if we choose, take action to change what we are doing, or we can change our thinking so that we are better able to accept what is happening.

Focusing on the 'here and now'

Similar logic to that just discussed applies to the present when compared with the past and future. We have no control over past events; they have already happened and we can't change them. Similarly, we have limited control over future events; they have not happened yet and we cannot be sure what the future will bring. Inappropriately focusing on the past or future is likely to lead us into unending philosophising, complaining, and worrying, whereas focusing on the present allows us to make sensible choices for our own satisfaction.

> We can't change the past but we can value the present moment

The preceding discussion is not meant to imply that it is inappropriate and of no value for a client to talk about what other people are doing, to talk about situations beyond their control, or to talk about past or future events. It does imply that there is little point in a client doing these things unless they also focus on what is happening inside them at the present time when they think about these situations or events. The focus in counselling needs to be on what is happening within the client at the moment in question, in the *here and now*, if the intervention is to be optimally therapeutic. The need to focus on the here and now is one of the central concepts of Gestalt therapy (Houston, 2003).

Imagine a situation where a client is angry about the way his father treated him when he was a young child. He could talk about this past relationship time and again and make little progress. However, if the counsellor brings the focus onto what is happening within the client at the time when he talks about the past, then progress is more likely to be made. The counsellor might then tap into anger, resentment and bitterness that is present right now. As the counsellor listens to descriptions of past experiences, it is appropriate for the counsellor to ask the client how he feels as he talks about them. The counsellor might say, 'Tell me how you feel emotionally *right now*, as you talk about those past events.' By doing this, the counsellor brings the focus into the present, and brings current emotional feelings that are associated with the past experiences of trauma into the client's awareness. The client is then able to fully experience those feelings and deal with them appropriately. It is only by experiencing these emotional feelings fully that the client will be able either to reduce them or get rid of them, or to discover ways of dealing with them constructively.

Helping the client to focus on the present

One way of bringing a client's focus into the present is to watch their non-verbal behaviour and to tell them what you notice. Alternatively, you might ask a question about what they are experiencing emotionally. For example, the client's eyes may become watery as they recount some past event. Sensitively interrupting with the words, 'I notice the tears starting to form in your eyes', or 'Tell me what you are experiencing emotionally right now', is very likely to bring the client more fully in touch with their present internal experiences.

> Feedback of non-verbal behaviour is often helpful

It can be useful to give a client permission to take time, to stay with their feelings and to experience them. In that way they are allowed to cry if hurting, are allowed to express anger if angry, and are allowed to own whatever other emotions are being experienced, so that they can move forward into a more comfortable space. If this is done, gradually the client will learn to allow themselves to experience their feelings rather than to deny them. This learning in the counselling situation will hopefully extend into the client's daily life and enable them to be more responsive to their feelings generally. Thus, they will be enabled to deal with their feelings as they arise, rather than letting them build up to an intolerable level.

'Negative' feelings

As discussed in Chapter 17, a common cause of client distress is an inability to properly and appropriately express 'negative' feelings towards others. For example, for many people the expression of anger is repressed from childhood. Whenever small children get angry, their parents tend to say, 'Don't behave in that angry way. Don't throw a tantrum.' As a result, the child learns, incorrectly, that it isn't appropriate to express anger towards others, even when an angry reaction is justified. Unfortunately, blocked anger often leads to depression, anxiety, or stress. What is worse, if we don't let other people know how we feel towards them, or how we feel about their behaviour, then we prevent ourselves from having fully functioning, open, and genuine relationships. Bringing issues out into the open, and discussing them enables emotional feelings to be expressed, rather than suppressed with the pretence that they don't exist. The immediacy of the counselling relationship can be used to demonstrate how feelings can be shared in a constructive way that enhances rather than damages a relationship.

Modelling

In the immediacy of the counselling situation there is a real-life relationship between the client and counsellor. A skilled counsellor will naturally model adaptive and constructive ways of relating, and will also help the client to explore feelings that are generated by the counselling relationship. By learning to explore these feelings and bring them into the open, the client learns appropriate ways in which to deal with the feelings generated by relationships with others, and hence is likely to improve the quality of their relationships generally.

> What is learnt in the counselling relationship will hopefully influence other relationships

Imagine that by carefully observing the non-verbal behaviour of a client, a counsellor suspects that the client is angry with them. The counsellor may have noticed, for example, an angry look flash across the client's face. However, because it is easy to misinterpret non-verbal behaviour it is important for the counsellor to check out whether in fact it was an angry look. The counsellor might say, '*I've got the impression that you looked angry then*', and as a result the client may become aware of anger and may be willing to explore it, or may get more fully in touch with whatever it was they did experience. In this way, the client's feelings are brought into the open and the counsellor can respond appropriately and genuinely so that the relationship with the client is more authentic.

Feedback

If counsellors are to be genuine in their relationships with clients, they need to stay in touch with their own feelings rather than suppress them so that they are not owned. Additionally, a counsellor's emotional feelings may provide important information about the counselling process. Consequently, by recognising, owning, and responding appropriately to their own feelings in the immediacy of the counselling relationship, counsellors may be able to respond more effectively to the counselling process to the benefit of the client. However, counsellors do need to be careful in sharing their own emotional feelings, particularly if these are not positive, as it is not appropriate for a counsellor to unload their own feelings onto the client.

> Counsellors need to deal with their own feelings in supervision

It does need to be recognised and admitted that some clients engage in annoying behaviours. Consequently, sometimes a counsellor may recognise that they are starting to be annoyed by a client as a consequence of a particular behaviour. When this happens, the counsellor firstly needs to recognise and own their feelings, and make a decision about how to deal with these. If the counsellor is not able to deal with these feelings in a way which ensures that they will not adversely affect the counselling process or intrude on the counselling relationship, then the counsellor needs to explore these feelings in supervision with an experienced counsellor. Having dealt with their own feelings, a counsellor may recognise that a client engages in a behaviour which interferes with the counselling process and may also be annoying to others. In this case, it may be useful to give the client feedback in a way which is acceptable to the client. This may enable the client to learn how the behaviour is perceived. Then the client can, if they choose, change (see Chapter 11, Figure 11.2, regarding the influence of counselling on the Johari window). Such change might significantly affect the client's life in a positive way, because it could be that the way in which the client behaves in counselling is similar to the way in which they behave when interacting with other people in the wider environment.

Unfortunately, most people are too polite to give useful feedback to friends, even when their friends exhibit quite destructive and maladaptive behaviours. However, sometimes it is possible for a counsellor to give useful and appropriate feedback in a respectful way.

How to give feedback

Imagine that a counsellor was unable to finish a sentence when making appropriate counselling responses because the client continually interrupted. Initially, the counsellor would need to allow the interruptions to occur and to observe the process. However, after a while, it might be appropriate for the counsellor to give the client some feedback. The feedback would need to be given in a gentle way that enabled the client to feel respected rather than attacked. In giving feedback, a counsellor in this situation might say to a client, *'Right now I'm starting to feel concerned because I've noticed that I'm not able to finish what I've started to say.'* Thus, the client might discover that their tendency to interrupt was interfering with the communication process, and they could, if they wished, change that behaviour. Obviously, such feedback would need to be given in such a way, and at such a time, that it was as non-threatening as possible and acceptable to the client. In any ensuing discussion, it might be helpful for the counsellor to ask the client whether they have noticed any problems occurring when they are talking with other people. By doing this, the person might start to explore the way they communicate in their work and social situations and recognise the usefulness of making changes.

> Feedback must be given sensitively

When giving feedback, it is sensible to avoid starting a feedback sentence with the word 'you' because this is almost certain to be seen as attacking and lead to a defensive response. Instead it is preferable to use an 'I' statement. Additionally it is often useful to start with the words, 'Right now' so that the statement is heard in the context of the present moment. A typical feedback statement will often have one of the following structures:

- 'Right now I feel ... because ...'
- 'I feel ... when ...'

■ 'I'm (puzzled, or interested, or concerned, or some other feeling word) because I've noticed that ...'

By starting with words which describe how they are feeling, the counsellor is open and honest in their relationship with the client. Hopefully this openness will make it easier for the client to hear and accept what is being said. After describing the way the counsellor is feeling, a feedback statement continues with a concrete statement of fact. Consider the example previously given: 'Right now I'm starting to feel concerned because I've noticed that I'm not able to finish what I've started to say.' The statement after the word 'because' is a concrete statement of fact describing exactly what the counsellor noticed. It is not an interpretation. An example of inappropriate feedback in this situation would be to say, 'I feel irritated when you interrupt me, because you don't want to listen to what I'm saying.' This statement would be likely to result in the client feeling criticised and attacked because the word 'irritated' implies blame. The statement also involves an interpretation of the client's behaviour which might be quite incorrect. As counsellors, we need to be careful not to include interpretation in feedback statements.

When giving feedback we do need to recognise that it is possible that the client may respond negatively and defensively. If this happens, the immediacy of the counselling relationship will be brought into sharp focus. This provides an opportunity for the counsellor to explore the client's perceptions of what is happening in the here and now so that the counselling relationship can be explored and enhanced.

The following are some examples of appropriate and inappropriate feedback statements. See if you can decide which are appropriate and which are not, and then check your decision by reading the comments at the end of this chapter.

Examples of appropriate and inappropriate feedback statements

Example 1

You keep coming late to appointments because you don't think it's worthwhile coming for counselling.

Example 2

I am puzzled because I've noticed that you continually come late for appointments.

Example 3

You have put a barrier between us because you dislike me.

Example 4

You are treating me like a father, and I'm not your father.

Example 5

I am concerned because it feels to me as though you are relating to me like a son relates to his father.

Example 6

Right now I have a shut-out feeling, as though there is a closed door between us.

From these examples and the comments provided at the end of the chapter you will have noticed that appropriate feedback involves the counsellor's owning their own feelings in the relationship and sharing these together with a concrete statement of fact. Inappropriate feedback accuses, blames or interprets the client's behaviour, and often starts with the word 'you'.

It is sometimes useful to teach clients how to use 'I' statements instead of 'you' statements. We teach them using the 'I feel ... when ...' structure, as this is easy to understand. We also stress the importance of making concrete factual statements and of not making interpretations.

Appropriately given feedback should have the goal of leaving a client feeling cared about, respected, and valued. Remember that a counsellor does not need to like a client's behaviour to be accepting of the client. It is not inconsistent to say, *'I'm concerned because you don't seem to be able to get to appointments on time'* while respecting, caring about and accepting the client as they are. We don't need to like everything a person does in order to care about them and/or like them.

Transference and counter-transference

The immediacy of the counselling relationship often raises questions regarding what psychoanalysts in particular, and counsellors in general, call *transference* and *counter-transference*. Transference occurs when a client behaves towards a counsellor as though the counsellor were a significant person from the client's past, usually the client's mother or father.

Naturally, it is quite possible for a counsellor to inadvertently fall into playing the role in which the client sees them. That is, if the client relates to the counsellor as though the counsellor were his father, the counsellor might start feeling and behaving like a father. Such behaviour, on the part of the counsellor, is called counter-transference.

It is inevitable that transference and counter-transference will occur at times in the counselling relationship but, provided that this is recognised, brought into the open, and discussed, it is not a problem. It would, however, be a problem if it were not brought out into the open, as it is not useful for the client to treat the counsellor as though they were someone from the past.

> It is important to recognise when transference and counter-transference are occurring

It may be that in some ways the counsellor is like the client's parent, but in other ways they are not, and it is important for the counsellor to make the distinction clear. This enables a genuine relationship between client and counsellor to be maintained, instead of the relationship being inappropriately coloured by the client's past experiences with a significant other. When a male counsellor realises that transference may be occurring, the counsellor might say, '*I have an impression that you are relating to me rather like a son relates to his father.*'

Where counter-transference is occurring, the relevant counsellor statement, for a female counsellor, might be: '*Right now I feel rather like a mother to you.*' The counsellor needs to point out caringly that she is not the client's mother or any other significant person from the client's past, and that she is herself – unique and different. As a consequence of bringing the feelings into the open they may be discussed and dealt with directly, so that an inappropriate relationship does not persist. In situations where the counsellor does not feel as though it is appropriate to bring the transference or counter-transference issue directly into the open, the issue needs to be addressed in supervision.

Sometimes a counsellor will not recognise when transference or counter-transference is occurring. It is here that supervision can play an important role in helping a counsellor to recognise what is happening and to explore appropriate ways of dealing with the issue.

Projection

Through the immediacy of the counselling relationship the client may learn something about their tendency to project characteristics of significant others from the past onto people in their current life. Thus, they may be able to recognise when inappropriate projection onto others is damaging relationships.

Usually when a counsellor notices what is happening in the relationship between themselves and their client, it is sensible to bring this into the open. If as a counsellor you sense that something unusual, different, or important is happening in the relationship, it will usually be useful to tell the client what you are observing so that it can be fully discussed and explored. By exploring such material, the client is able to learn more about themselves, to realise what they do in relationships, and to become more in touch with their emotional experiences and thoughts. As a result, they may be able to move forward and to develop more fully as a person.

Resistance

New counsellors are troubled at times by a client's apparent lack of co-operation with the therapeutic process. This is called 'resistance'. A good example of resistance is provided by clients who come late for appointments or who miss appointments repeatedly. Of course, there may be good reasons for a client doing such things. It is well to be aware, though, that often the explanations given may be more in the nature of rationalisations or excuses than the real reason why the behaviour is occurring. For example, a client may be finding counselling very threatening and worrying, and may, for subconscious reasons, be postponing attending. It is important for the client to realise what is happening so that the real issue is resolved, and the client's fear is addressed. Once again, what the counsellor needs to do is to verbalise what is noticed, rather than interpreting this.

> Resistance enables a client to avoid experiencing painful emotions

Resistance may often involve the client deflecting away from talking about important issues when these are painful. Once again, the most useful strategy is for the counsellor to give feedback of what is noticed by saying something like, '*I noticed that you change the subject whenever you start to talk about ...*'

An example of resistance

As a trainer of counsellors, David noticed that often trainee counsellors came to supervision sessions and said to him, 'Unfortunately I haven't been able to make a videotape of a counselling session as promised.' He was then given a very convincing reason why it was quite impossible for them to make the videotape: 'Oh, I couldn't find a blank cassette', or 'The machine jammed when I put the cassette in', or 'I put the cassette in and unfortunately I pushed the wrong button and it didn't record', or 'Unfortunately somebody else borrowed the video before I did, as I had forgotten to book it.' Of course, all of those 'excuses' were valid. They were all genuine. The trainee counsellor was at no time lying but was being genuine and honest. However, resistance was usually uncovered when David said something like, 'I notice that for three weeks you have been unable to make a videotape, and have had perfectly good reasons. However, I am puzzled by this because you are a very capable person. I am wondering what happens emotionally inside you when you think about making a video.' Giving feedback in this way often enabled a trainee to explore more fully what was happening, and as a result it was often recognised that it was threatening for the trainee to produce a video, and, yes, if they had made a little more effort, it would have been possible to have produced the recording. David never needed to say, 'You must produce a video next week.' Rather, just drawing attention to what he had observed was sufficient to overcome the trainee's resistance.

Dealing with resistance

In the counselling process with clients, if a client is repeatedly late, or has missed several appointments in a row, it can be useful to draw the client's attention to what has happened. It may be necessary to say, '*Yes, I have heard your reasons and I understand and believe them, but I am still left wondering whether at some other level something else is happening. I am puzzled that you should be late so often.*'

Resistance can, of course, take many forms. Sometimes resistance blocks a client from exploring a particularly painful area in their life, and as a counsellor you may feel frustrated by such avoidance. However, in our opinion, it is important to explore the resistance rather than try to burst through it. There are differences of opinion here, however, as some counsellors believe that directly breaking through the resistance is preferable. We prefer the opposite approach, probably because, while being integrative counsellors, we do have a special interest in Gestalt therapy theory and practice. We explore resistance by drawing a client's attention to what is happening. We might say to a client, '*I notice that whenever you mention* (a particular subject) *you quickly change the subject. My guess is that it is too painful to talk about* ... (the subject in question).' The client is then able to experience the avoidance fully and usually something important will emerge spontaneously. If it doesn't, then we might ask the client what they are currently experiencing emotionally. As a result, the client would probably be brought in touch with what it felt like to avoid exploring a painful area of their life and consequently might decide how to deal with their avoidance. Alternatively, they might say, 'I'm not prepared to explore that really painful area of my life. To do so would be like opening up Pandora's box. It's far too scary for me.' We need to remember that the client has a right to make that choice and to leave Pandora's box closed. If that is what they choose to do, we respect their wishes.

Uses of the 'here and now' experience

In this chapter, we have dealt with the ways in which the immediacy of the counselling relationship can be used to:

1 help the client to focus on their own behaviour, inner feelings, and thoughts, in the present, rather than focusing on past behaviours or on the behaviour of others, over which the client has no control;
2 help the client to learn to own and deal with their emotional feelings as they arise. This includes owning and dealing with so-called 'negative' feelings towards others;
3 give the client constructive feedback, in an acceptable way, with regard to inappropriate behaviours that result in negative feelings in the counsellor and may annoy others;
4 help the client to recognise and deal with the human tendency to project the characteristics of significant persons from their past onto others; and
5 help the client to deal with their own resistance.

An effective counsellor will verbalise their observations of what is occurring in the immediacy of the counselling relationship so that client growth is promoted. Hopefully, what is learnt from the counselling experience will be carried into the client's everyday life.

Comments on examples of appropriate and inappropriate feedback statements

Example 1

Inappropriate Feedback
The statement is threatening as it starts with the word 'you'. The words 'because you don't think it's worthwhile coming for counselling' are an unverified interpretation of the client's behaviour.

Example 2

Appropriate Feedback
The counsellor starts with an 'I' statement which describes how they feel: 'I am puzzled.' A concrete statement of what has been observed is then given: 'You continually come late for appointments.' The counsellor does not attempt to interpret the client's behaviour, but merely states what has been observed.

Example 3

Inappropriate Feedback
The statement is inappropriate because it consists of a 'you' statement which could make the client feel attacked. Moreover, the counsellor is interpreting the client's behaviour. The statement, 'You dislike me', is guesswork and could be wrong.

Example 4

Inappropriate Feedback
An inappropriate statement starting with 'you' which could be received by the client as a put-down.

Example 5

Appropriate Feedback
This statement starts appropriately with an 'I' statement of the counsellor's feelings: 'I am concerned.' Instead of accusing the client by using a 'you' statement, information about how the relationship feels for the counsellor is given. Compare this statement with Example 4. It is very different.

Example 6

Appropriate Feedback
Notice how in this statement the counsellor's own feelings are described, rather than blaming the client for putting up a barrier. Compare this statement with Example 3.

LEARNING SUMMARY

- Talking about the past and future, and about other people, is not constructive unless the client also focuses on the 'here and now' experience.
- Staying in the 'here and now', and focusing on current experiences, emotional feelings and thoughts is therapeutically useful.
- The immediacy of the counselling relationship can be a useful learning experience for the client.
- A counsellor can model adaptive behaviour and relationship skills and give feedback to the client.
- Appropriate feedback can start with 'I feel . . .', followed by a concrete non-interpretative statement.
- 'Transference' is when the client treats the counsellor as a parent (or significant other).
- 'Counter-transference' is when the counsellor responds to the client's transference as a parent (or significant other).
- Transference and counter-transference usually need to be brought into the open when they occur.
- 'Resistance' may involve a client's apparent lack of co-operation with the therapeutic process or direct avoidance of painful issues.
- A good way to deal with resistance is to raise the client's awareness of what is being observed.

References and further reading

Clarkson, P. (2000) *Gestalt Counselling in Action*, second edition. London: Sage.
Houston, G. (2003) *Brief Gestalt Therapy*. London: Sage.

Chapter 20

Exploring Options

When a client comes to see a counsellor, it is often because they feel hopelessly stuck in an intolerable situation in which they do not know what to do to ease their pain, and believe that there is no apparent solution to their problems. This hopeless feeling may lock a client into depression, anxiety and tension. Use of the reflective and other skills described previously enables the client to explore their issues and to clarify them. This process alone may be helpful in reducing their distress, and they may spontaneously move towards exploring options and finding solutions for their problems. Sometimes, however, the client does not move forward in this way and appears to reach an impasse, without properly exploring possible options. An appropriate way for the counsellor to deal with this situation is to reflect the feeling of being 'stuck' and then to ask the client whether they can see any options.

As an integrative counsellor, while searching for and exploring options it can be very advantageous to make use of those questions which come from solution focused counselling and reality therapy as described in Chapter 8.

Finding options

An open question such as, '*You are obviously in a very uncomfortable situation. What do you see as your options?*' can be useful as a starting-point in helping the client to identify options. By asking this question, rather than suggesting options, the counsellor encourages the client to take responsibility for solving their own problems. The client is then able to think about and hopefully suggest options for consideration. Solution-focused questions may then be used to help the client discover additional options. The identified options can then be explored, again through the use of solution-focused questions. Some of these options might be discarded immediately as being impossible or unacceptable. However, be careful to remember all the options the client suggests, because an option that the client has ruled out initially may turn out to be the one that will eventually be chosen.

> Help the client to discover their own solutions

New counsellors often feel pressured into trying to find options for their clients. Our experience is that generally it is not necessary to do this, and that it is far better if clients are able to come up with their own options. Of course there are times when for some reason a client fails to see an option that is obvious to the counsellor, and in such a case the counsellor may choose to tell the client about that option. However, when a counsellor does put forward an idea of their own, it's preferable that it should be put forward in a tentative way, so that the client sees it as nothing more than a possible suggestion and does not take it as advice which needs to be followed.

Exploring options

When helping a client to explore options, we let the client talk in a general way about the various alternatives and then summarise them clearly. We then encourage the client to explore each idea individually and to talk about the positive and negative aspects of each option. There are some advantages in dealing with the most unlikely or least preferred options first.

Thus, the client gets these out of the way, and this leaves a smaller range of options, which makes it easier for the client to move towards a decision.

It is sensible to encourage the client not only to look carefully at the consequences, both negative and positive, of each option, but also to take into account their own gut feelings about the various alternatives that are available. Quite often a person's logical thinking will be pulling in one direction whereas their gut feelings will be pulling in a different direction. It is, for example, quite common to hear a client say: 'That is what I really ought to do, that is what I should do, but I don't want to do that, it doesn't feel right for me.' Obviously the client needs to feel very comfortable with the decision they make, or they are unlikely to stay with it. Logical thinking alone does not provide sufficient grounds on which to choose an option. In fact, we believe that it's more important for the client to feel comfortable at a gut level with an option than to think that the option is the most sensible one. However, any option chosen obviously has to be the client's choice and may not be the choice the counsellor believes to be the most desirable, sensible, or appropriate.

Making a choice

Imagine that your client is in a dilemma and is unable to make a choice between two options, option A and option B. In order for the client to resolve the dilemma, we suggest that you might wish to help the client to fully explore what it would feel like to have chosen option A, and to explore what the consequences of this choice would be. After this is completed, encourage the client to do a similar exploration for option B. This enables a clear comparison between the two options to be established.

One of the problems in making a choice between two alternatives is that whenever we make a choice, almost invariably there is a loss or cost involved. Let's give you an example. We are both working on the manuscript of this book on a Saturday and don't have to work today unless we choose to. It's a warm sunny day and we are only five minutes walk from a beautiful sandy beach. We have two options. One option is to continue writing and the other option is to stop work and to go down to the beach for a swim, so we have a dilemma. In situations like this we might ask ourselves the question, 'What should we do?' However, remembering Chapter 16 on self-destructive beliefs, it would be better for us to replace the 'should' question by the question, 'What do we *want* to do?' By asking this question we can make a choice which is genuinely ours, is not excessively influenced by injunctions from the past, and fits with our current experience. We enjoy writing and quite enjoy what we are doing now, but it would also be enjoyable to go for a swim and maybe lie on the beach afterwards. Now this is not a heavy choice, but whichever choice we make will involve a loss. If we decide to keep on writing then we lose out on the exercise, the fresh air, and the relaxed feeling of being down at the beach; but if we go down to the beach we'll have a different loss. We'll lose the satisfaction of continuing to do something creative – our writing – and we may feel frustrated by not having made more progress with our writing when tomorrow comes. So, whether we continue to write or whether we go to the beach, we have to accept that there is a loss either way. If we choose one alternative, we lose the other.

The loss or cost involved in making a choice

One of the main blocks to making decisions occurs when people don't properly look at the loss or cost component involved. Frequently, we discover that accepting the loss or cost associated with a decision is more difficult than choosing between the positive aspects of the alternative choices.

> Many decisions involve the acceptance of a loss

It can be very helpful to tell clients about the loss or cost component in decision-making, and to explain this as applied to their particular dilemma. We might say to a client, 'If you choose option A, what are your losses going to be?' and, 'If you choose option B, what are your losses going to be?' We then ask them whether they would be able to accept those losses. The choice is not just a choice between two positives, but also a choice that involves choosing between two losses and deciding which loss is acceptable, if either. By focusing on the loss or cost component as well as the positive component of options, clients are more readily able to make decisions and resolve their dilemmas.

The effect of polarities

Resolution of dilemmas is difficult for most people. Part of that difficulty is due to the polarities that exist within us. Let me, Kathryn, go back to the previous example where David and I looked at the dilemma of continuing to write or going to the beach. Right now it is as though there are two parts of me. One part of me wants to go for a swim, and the other part of me wants to stay here and continue writing this book. I have found that it is very helpful for clients if I describe their dilemmas in terms of parts of themselves. Sometimes I say to a client, 'Part of you wants to make choice A and another part of you wants to make choice B. These are both valid parts of you. They both exist in you at the same time.' I ask the client to tell me about the part that wants option A and to explore that part fully, and then to tell me about the part that wants option B and to explore that fully. By doing this, I allow the client to integrate and own two opposite parts of self and not to feel confused, but rather to accept that both are valid parts of self (see Chapter 17, which dealt with parts of self). The client is then empowered to accept that choosing one of the options means letting go of the other option, and that involves a cost or the acceptance of a loss, the loss of the option that is not chosen.

The myth of the 'right' choice

Many people have been taught as children that there is always a correct choice, and that in dilemmas the choice of one option is correct and the choice of the other is wrong. Confusion often arises from the unrealistic expectation that choice involves a decision between black and white, or between right and wrong. In reality, most human decisions involve deciding between shades of grey where both options have advantages or positive qualities and both have costs or disadvantages.

> The only right decision is the one that fits for the client

Remember, if I choose option A, I lose option B, and that loss is part of the cost of choosing option A. To resolve a dilemma, and choose one option, I have to let go of the other. The letting go is the hard part. If you let your client know that, they may find it easier to reach a decision.

Finding creative solutions

At times, dilemmas can be resolved by doing some creative thinking and introducing a new option so that the extent of any loss is reduced. If we use the example regarding whether David and I should continue writing or go to the beach, there is a third option. We could decide to continue writing for a while and then stop and go to the beach. This new option might provide a win–win solution! In fact, having talked about our choice with each other, this is what we have both decided to do. We have decided to continue writing for another hour and then go to the beach. This is convenient because we both like working and relaxing together.

Giving the client permission to stay stuck

Sometimes a client will stay stuck and will be unable to resolve a dilemma even though the issues are clearly understood. As new counsellors, we often worried when a client was stuck and would sometimes prolong a counselling session unnecessarily in an effort to try to 'unstick' the client and lead the client to a satisfying solution. We now realise that such counsellor behaviour is not very helpful. It is much more helpful to reflect back to the client their 'stuckness', and to say, '*Look, it seems as though we've come to an impasse. There doesn't seem to be an easy solution, and today you seem to be stuck and don't know which way to go. Let's leave it there. Come back another time and we will talk together again.*' By saying this, the counsellor gives the client permission to remain stuck, reduces the pressure to make a quick decision, and lets the client know that they are welcome to come back again to continue working on the issue. Sometimes the client will come back the next time saying, 'I've made a decision', because they were given permission to stay stuck and effectively given time to think through what was discussed in the previous session without pressure. At other times, a client will remain stuck. Then the counsellor's goal is to assist the client to come to terms with the consequences of being stuck in what may be a painful or uncomfortable situation. The counsellor does this by assisting the client to verbalise emotional feelings about being stuck, and then encouraging them to talk about how they will cope with being stuck.

> Sometimes it's OK to be stuck and not feel pressured to make a decision

In the next chapter we will try to develop a deeper understanding of the process required to help clients deal with blocks to decision-making. However, remember that it is OK to allow a client to remain 'stuck'. Often experiencing being stuck for a while is necessary before progress can be made.

LEARNING SUMMARY

- It is preferable for counsellors to ask their clients to suggest their own options before suggesting additional ones.
- New options may be tentatively suggested if important alternatives have been missed (for example, are there any 'win–win' options?).
- All the options need to be summarised clearly before discussing each in turn.
- Dealing with the least desirable options first may be helpful as it may exclude them.
- It can be useful for the client to examine the positive and negative aspects of each option, carefully considering likely consequences.
- There is a loss or cost involved in making any choice and often accepting the inevitable loss is the hardest part of making a decision.
- Many, if not most, decisions are not choices between black and white, but rather choices between shades of grey.

Chapter 21

Facilitating Action

By using the counselling skills described in the previous chapters, a client can be helped to move out of their troubled state and into a more comfortable emotional space. If that is achieved, then they have clearly been helped by the counselling process in the short term, and for some clients that is sufficient. However, for other clients, their emotional distress is a consequence of either unhelpful behaviours or entrenched life situations. For them, unless action is taken to help them make choices and to take action to change their unhelpful behaviours and/or life situations, then emotional distress may well recur.

As we explained in the previous chapter, clients will often feel stuck and unable to make a decision or to move forward into taking action. It is as though they are blocked by their thoughts and emotions and cannot move forward. When this happens there is a temptation, particularly for new counsellors, to try to encourage, persuade, or in some other way push the client into making a decision and into putting that into action.

Have you ever experienced resistance from a person when you have tried to persuade them to do something which is different from what they have been doing? We human beings are rather like the proverbial donkey. The more someone pushes or pulls us, the more we tend to resist! If we are to enable clients to make choices and to follow through by taking action to change then we must resist the temptation to try to push them into making decisions and taking action and instead use a different strategy.

> The harder you push the more resistance you will feel!

As integrative counsellors, we believe that we can learn from one particular aspect of Gestalt therapy theory when we are trying to help people to overcome blocks which are preventing them from changing their behaviours or situation. The relevant theory regarding how to deal with such blocks or resistance was admirably described by Zinker (1978) and more recently by Houston (2003). Zinker illustrated the change that occurs in counselling through the use of an awareness circle.

The Gestalt awareness circle

Before discussing the awareness circle, we would like to remind readers that as integrative counsellors we believe that the processes of change in counselling generally occur as described in Chapter 12 and illustrated in Figure 12.1. In this process we tend to firstly emphasise emotions, then thoughts and then behaviours. Gestalt therapists work differently as they address somatic experiences, emotional feelings, and thoughts simultaneously, because they place a strong emphasis on the interconnectedness of these. They work by raising awareness of the client's bodily experiences, feelings, and thoughts as they connect with each other. As integrative therapists we also raise awareness of feelings and thoughts. We do this through the use of the various counselling skills described earlier in this book. However, as explained, unlike gestalt therapists we tend to address emotions prior to focusing on strategies which might influence changes in thinking. Even so, the concept of awareness is a useful one. As integrative counsellors, we need to recognise that during the counselling process an important goal is to raise the client's awareness of what is occurring internally for them; in other words to help them express their emotions and thoughts.

Now that we have identified the differences between the way a gestalt therapist and an integrative counsellor works, let's have a look at the Gestalt Awareness Circle. This circle describes the way that raising a client's awareness can enable them to clarify their problems, explore options, and make decisions about the future. A modified version of Zinker's Gestalt Awareness Circle is shown in Figure 21.1.

As shown in Figure 21.1, clients generally come for counselling when they are emotionally distressed. That is when they are at the *arousal* point on the awareness circle, with their emotions unpleasantly aroused. The counsellor's task is to enable the client to move around the circle towards *satisfaction* or *rest*. This is achieved by raising the client's *awareness* of their whole situation as it is. As integrative counsellors what we do is to

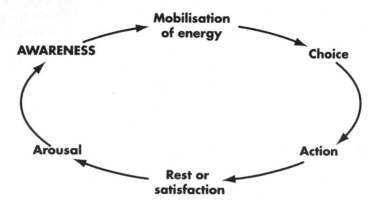

Figure 21.1   Gestalt Awareness Circle

actively listen while the client tells their story, enable them to get in touch with their emotions and then to clarify their thoughts. By doing this we raise the client's awareness of their internal experience and perceptions of their situation and problem.

We will now discuss the awareness circle in some detail starting at the point of *arousal*.

The arousal stage

In the *arousal* phase, the emotionally disturbed client is unable to focus clearly, and sees a confused picture of their world. It is as though they are looking at an overgrown forest, choked by too many trees and too much undergrowth. They are unable to clearly see any one tree, but instead are overwhelmed by a blurred and confusing picture. In this state, the client's energy is depleted. They will be unable to see their options, and will therefore have little hope of taking any action to change their situation.

Raising awareness to mobilise energy

If the client is to feel better, they need to *mobilise their energy* so that they can work constructively to resolve their issues. The counsellor can facilitate this mobilisation of energy by raising the client's awareness of their inner experiences. As a trainee counsellor, if you have mastered the skills described in the previous chapters, then you have the tools required to do this. By using these counselling skills, you will inevitably raise the client's awareness of their emotional feelings and thoughts regarding their situation as it is, and consequently they will become more energised in seeking change.

Moving round the awareness circle

Sometimes, once awareness is raised, the client will move with ease around the awareness circle. To use the previous analogy, the overgrown forest of trees will become a background against which the clear outline of one tree will emerge. The client's confusion will disappear and they will move naturally around the circle into making a *choice*, taking *action*, and coming into a state of *satisfaction* or *rest*.

In life, we do not stay in a state of rest, and if we did we would probably achieve nothing. What we do is to move around the awareness circle again and again.

Blocks to progress around the circle

Unfortunately, most people don't move naturally and easily around the awareness circle but instead get stuck as discussed previously. This occurs because they are blocked in the process of moving forward by internal emotional and psychological constraints. Such blocks often occur, as shown on the circle in Figure 21.2, before *choice* or *action*. If a client is blocked in either of these places, then it is tempting for the counsellor to focus on encouraging the client to make a choice or to take action. Such

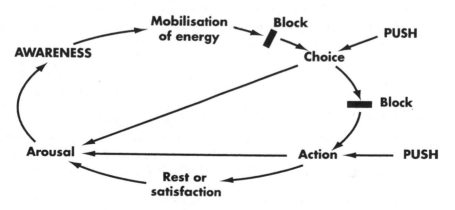

Figure 21.2 The effect of pushing for choice or action

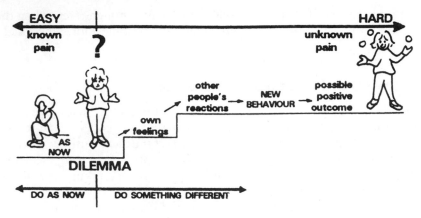

Figure 21.3 Dilemma model

counsellor behaviour is usually very unhelpful as it is likely to be pressuring, creating greater difficulties for the client. Instead of achieving the counsellor's goal of helping the client to make a choice or to take action, pushing for choice or action usually returns the client to an even higher state of emotional arousal (see the arrows in Figure 21.2).

If you want to help your client to make a choice or to take action, then a prerequisite is to enable the client to fully explore, understand, and deal with any block which might be impeding progress around the circle. Some common blocks which inhibit choice and action are identified in the simple dilemma model in Figure 21.3.

A client who makes decisions and takes action to change their life has to cope firstly with their own feelings, and then with other people's reactions. This is often difficult, particularly if the decisions or actions displease others. Also, if a client does something new, then they take a risk: there may be unknown consequences, and these could be painful. It may be easier to go on living as now, with no changes and with known pain, rather than to take a risk and do something new and different with its unknown pain. Thus, it is easy to understand how client choices and actions are often blocked by internal fears and anxieties, including the following:

- inability to deal with own feelings;
- inability to cope with the reactions of others;
- fear of consequences;
- fear of a repetition of past bad experiences;
- the intrusion of inappropriate 'shoulds', 'musts' and 'oughts';

- fear that something comfortable or rewarding will be lost; and
- lack of skills to carry out the desired action.

Dealing with blocks

Whenever a client is blocked and unable to make a choice or take action, resist the temptation to push the client into doing so, and instead return to the awareness point on the circle. In particular, raise the client's awareness of their block and encourage them to explore how it feels to be blocked and unable to move forward. Encourage them to become aware of what they are experiencing internally when they experience their inability to decide or act. Ask them how it feels to be blocked and allow them to express the relevant emotions. Then explore their thoughts which contribute to the block.

The goal is to enable the client to explore and to deal with what is blocking them from making a decision and taking action; are they afraid of their own feelings (for example, they might feel guilty if they did what they wanted), or are they afraid of offending others? There may be other reasons. Also it is possible that by focusing on what is blocking the decision, the client may discover that they have another more important issue which needs confronting.

Remember, the more you push a client to make a choice or to take action, the more blocked they are likely to become. If you want to help a client to move on then you need to raise their awareness of, and focus on, whatever is blocking their decision making so that they can fully explore this block and deal with it.

> Focusing on a block is more helpful than trying to push through it

Suitable questions to help clients explore blocks are as follows:

- *'Tell me what you are experiencing emotionally as you think about making this decision (or taking this action)?'*
- *'What are you aware of happening inside you when you think about making this choice (or taking this action)?'*
- *'As you experience that emotion, what thoughts do you have?'*

For many clients, if you, the counsellor, use the counselling skills you have learnt to raise awareness of and to work through blocks, then the client is likely to move spontaneously around the awareness circle, to make *choices* and to take the necessary *action* to achieve goals. However, for some clients this approach alone is not sufficient. Some clients will stay stuck and unable to make a decision, in which case let them know that it is OK to be stuck, as explained in the previous chapter. For others, help is required to enable them to follow through by taking action.

Clients who need additional help to take action

Some clients repeatedly use the counselling process to enable them to continue to exist in unsatisfactory life situations without change. Sometimes in the counselling process it appears as though they are replaying the same tape over and over again. When they do this, they may well sink further into despair and hopelessness. Such clients need specific help in facilitating action, if they are to bring about meaningful changes to their lives. Also, there are some clients who, after deciding what they want to do, find themselves unable to move forward into action, not because of psychological blocks, but rather because they do not have the necessary skills or confidence to carry out the action they wish to take. These clients need additional help. The rest of this chapter deals with ways of helping clients who do not have the necessary confidence or personal resources to make and implement action plans on their own.

Clearly, it is not helpful for a counsellor to do the client's work. By doing that, the counsellor would reinforce the client's sense of helplessness, and lead the client to believe that they needed assistance each time new goals were to be targeted. What is helpful is for the client to learn how to organise, plan and execute decisions so that in the future they are able to do these things for themselves. A good way of helping a client to learn is to walk alongside them, and to work with them as they struggle with the issues involved in achieving one important goal. You can then, if you wish, explore with them the processes used in achieving their goal. Thus they may identify those processes which were most useful to them so that they can use them in achieving future goals.

Although every situation is different, there are some basic steps that are useful in enabling clients to take action to achieve goals. These steps are listed in the action plan below:

Action plan

1 Make psychological preparation.
2 Identify the goal.

3   Identify the first step towards goal achievement.
4   Concretise the first step towards goal achievement.
5   Decide how to carry out the first step.
6   Acquire the skills to carry out the first step.
7   Decide when to carry out the first step.
8   Carry out the first step.
9   Reward self for carrying out the first step.
10 Reassess the overall goal.

We will now look in detail at these steps in the order presented above. In order to make the exercise more meaningful, we are going to consider the specific example of a father who has a dysfunctional relationship with his teenage son.

Psychological preparation

This has been dealt with earlier in this chapter. The counsellor raises client awareness, to enable the client to work through blocks and to come to a decision.

Identifying the goal

Imagine that the father in our example had come to the decision that he wanted to work on improving his relationship with his son. For many clients, identifying such a goal would be sufficient to facilitate action, and the counsellor's work would be over. For other clients, further help would be needed.

Identifying the first step towards goal achievement

For some clients, the goal of trying to improve a relationship with a son would be too broad and non-specific. It might not be clear how the goal could be achieved and consequently positive action would be unlikely to occur. Such a client may need to identify the first step towards achieving the goal. This first step needs to be realistically achievable, so that the client is likely to be rewarded by success rather than discouraged by failure.

> The first step needs to be realistically achievable

The counsellor might ask, '*How are you going to set about improving your relationship with your son?*' Maybe the father would respond, 'Well, I'd like to start by having a talk with him, but that's scary, because we haven't said anything pleasant to each other for some months.'

Clearly at this point the counsellor would move the focus away from the contemplated action and return to raising awareness of the client's fear of talking with his son. If this were not done then the client might be blocked from action.

Concretising the first step in goal achievement

Once the first step in goal achievement has been identified, it needs to be concretised, so that it is clear and specific rather than vague. For example, the statement 'I'd like to have a talk with my son' is very general. The value of such a talk is likely to depend on what the purpose of the talk is, and on what the content of the conversation is likely to be. Questions by the counsellor, such as, '*What do you want to say to your son?*' and '*What do you hope to achieve as a result of this talk?*', might yield more specific information such as, 'I want to tell him why I am so angry with him, so that I can get that rubbish out of the way and can start relating to him in a positive way.'

Deciding how to carry out the first step

This decision needs to take into account the likely consequences of the proposed action. For example, the statement in the paragraph above, 'I want to tell him why I am so angry with him . . .' suggests that the client intends to confront his son in a way likely to lead to further alienation rather than reconciliation. At this point the counsellor could usefully carry out some role-plays to allow the client to experience what it would be like to be the recipient of the intended message.

Acquiring the skills to carry out the first step

The client may need to acquire new skills to be able to competently carry out the first step. In our current example, the counsellor might coach the client in the use of 'I' statements, and carry out further role-plays to determine the likely impact of client statements.

Deciding when to carry out the first step

Sometimes when people have to carry out unpleasant tasks, they will delay doing what they have decided to do by using the excuse that the time is not right. Do you do that? We think that most people do, and delayed action often results in no action. We find that for us it is usually easier to carry out what we plan if we have made a clear decision about the proposed timing. We think that it's the same for many clients, and it's therefore useful to explore the issue of timing with them. This may result in more awareness raising – back to the awareness circle again!

Carrying out the first step

Whether or not the client carries out the first step is unimportant. If they do, then they can feel good about that, and if they don't then there will be some learning from the process. The client can once again get in touch with their inner experiences to discover what stopped them from carrying out the first step, and from that awareness a new decision can be made.

Rewarding self for carrying out the first step

Do you ever minimise your achievements? We sometimes do, but we are getting better at taking pride in what we do well. Many clients fail to give themselves positive messages when they succeed in performing difficult tasks. As a counsellor, help your clients to feel good about themselves by maximising their achievements. A client who is properly rewarded for carrying out the first step is more likely to continue making positive decisions and carrying them out.

Reassessing the overall goal

Often when the client has gone some way in one direction, they will realise that the goal originally targeted is one which is no longer desired. That is clearly OK, but the client will consequently need to reassess their overall goal.

In conclusion

In this chapter we have discussed the skills involved in facilitating action. Generally, if you use the previously learnt counselling skills and remember what you have discovered here about the awareness circle, you will be successful in helping clients to take appropriate action to bring about meaningful changes in their lives. Additionally, the action plan described above can be used when it is clear that the client is unable to move forward without more specific help.

LEARNING SUMMARY

- Pushing directly for choice or action is likely to fail and increase emotional distress.
- To maximise the possibility of choice or action, raise awareness of blocks.
- A major client dilemma concerns the choice 'to do as now' or 'to do something different'.
- Doing as now involves known pain.
- Doing something different involves unknown pain and outcomes. It's risky!
- Action plans are helpful for some clients.
- Action plans involve preparation for action, setting a specific goal, and having a reward for taking the first step.

References and further reading

Clarkson, P. (2000), *Gestalt Counselling in Action*, second edition. London: Sage.
Houston, G. (2003) *Brief Gestalt Therapy*. London: Sage.
Zinker, J. (1978)) *Creative Process in Gestalt Therapy*. New York: Vintage.

Part V

Practical, Professional, and Ethical Issues

Chapter 22

The Counselling Environment

In earlier chapters, we have discussed the way in which counselling involves the creation of a safe, trusting relationship between the client and the counsellor. In order to assist in the promotion of such a relationship it can be helpful, when counselling a client in a face-to-face situation, if the counselling environment is one which will enable the client to feel comfortable and at ease.

Unfortunately, it is not always possible for counsellors to have the use of a specially designed counselling room. In some situations, counsellors are visitors to a home, agency, school, or government department and have to make the best use of spaces that are intended for other purposes. Where this is the case, it is desirable for the counsellor to do whatever is possible to protect the privacy of the client. Many adults and children don't like others to know that they are seeing a counsellor. In offices and schools the confidentiality of the counselling process may be compromised at some level by lack of privacy. Clearly, counsellors need to do their best to seek the most private facilities and arrangements as possible.

The counselling room

Whenever we walk into a room, that room has an effect on us. Is it the same for you? Have you noticed that sometimes when you have entered a room you have felt comfortable and at ease, almost as though the room welcomed you? At other times, you may have entered a room that felt clinical, cold and unwelcoming. A well designed counselling room will have a warm, friendly feel about it. In addition to being warm, pleasant, welcoming, and comfortable, it is an advantage if the room can be set up so that it is especially suitable for counselling.

Where a counsellor has their own personal room, that room can reflect something of their individual personality. Our counselling rooms are decorated with plants and pictures. Pictures on the walls are peaceful, showing natural scenes of trees and landscapes. The colours are muted and not harsh, and these combine with comfortable furnishings to provide a welcoming, relaxed atmosphere.

Your room will be different from ours because we are all different and have different tastes. We suggest that you try to make your room an extension of yourself so that you feel at ease in it, and then in all probability your clients will feel comfortable in it too.

> The counselling room needs to be inviting

Preferably the furnishings in your counselling room should include comfortable chairs for yourself and your client, together with other

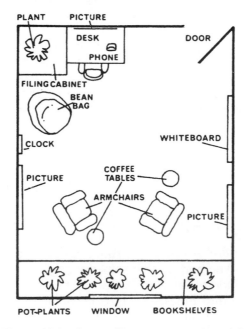

Figure 22.1 Counselling room arrangement

furnishings appropriate for a professional office. You may need to write reports, draft letters, keep records and carry out some administrative duties. Hence a desk, telephone and filing cabinet will be useful, together with bookshelves for a professional library.

Layout of the room

The sketch in Figure 22.1 shows a suitable layout for a counselling room for the personal counselling of individual clients. Notice that the desk and filing cabinet are unobtrusively in a corner facing the wall, where their importance for clients is diminished. When a client is in the room we prefer to sit in a comfortable chair similar to the client's, facing the client and at their level. We avoid sitting at a desk, as to do so brings inequality into the relationship. Additionally, we prefer to have open space rather than a table separating us from the client. Using this set-up enables clients to join with us as equal partners as they explore their issues, and ensures that we are not perceived as powerful experts separated by a desk. If we do need to sit at the desk to do some written work in a client's presence, we make sure that the desk doesn't separate us from the client.

> Formality doesn't enhance the relationship

We don't have a client chair and a counsellor chair, but rather two chairs that are similar. When a client enters the room they are invited to sit in whichever chair they choose. Only if they hesitate will we direct them to a chair. This is a small point, but an important one. Remember that clients are usually anxious when they enter a counselling room, because it is not their space and they may be worrying about the counselling process. They may be more at ease if you make it clear what is expected of them, rather than leaving them to decide what is appropriate.

We try to arrange the chairs so that they do not face directly into light coming from a window. Looking towards a window can be unpleasant, as after a while the glare may cause eyestrain. During a counselling session, the client and counsellor will be looking at each other most of the time, so the background against which each is framed is important for comfort. Preferably, the client's and counsellor's chairs will face each other, but at a slight angle with enough space between them so that the client does not feel that their personal space is being invaded.

Equipment needed

We prefer to have a whiteboard in every counselling room. Clients who predominantly operate in a visual mode are likely to focus more clearly and gain in awareness if important statements are written on the board, and if their options are listed there. Sometimes a client's dilemma can be expressed through a sketch that metaphorically describes their situation. A whiteboard is particularly useful for helping clients to challenge irrational beliefs or to construct assertive statements. It may also be used as an aid when carrying out educational and administrative tasks which counsellors inevitably undertake as part of their duties.

We always have a box of tissues in a handy place in our counselling rooms. It is inevitable that some clients will cry and having tissues at hand reduces embarrassment.

The need for privacy

As will be discussed in Chapter 26, confidentiality is essential when counselling. A client will not feel comfortable about disclosing intimate personal details unless they are confident that they will not be overheard. If a client can hear voices from outside the counselling room, then they may be justified in fearing that they can be heard by others. It is therefore preferable if counselling rooms are suitably soundproofed, although this ideal is often not achievable.

> Privacy is essential

If at all possible, the counselling process should be uninterrupted by the intrusion of people knocking on the door, entering the room, or phoning in unnecessarily. For this reason, many counsellors have a rule that when a counselling room door is closed, no attempt should be made by others to enter the room except in unusual circumstances. In many counselling agencies, when a counselling room door is shut, the procedure for contacting the counsellor when unusual circumstances make this necessary is for the receptionist to use the phone. Except in serious emergencies, the receptionist allows the phone to ring a few times only and if it is not answered then the counsellor is left undisturbed. This minimises the possibility that the client might be interrupted at an important stage in the counselling process. It enables the client to feel that confidentiality is assured, and allows them to express their emotions in privacy without the risk and embarrassment of being observed by others.

Safety issues

It is important for counsellors to take whatever measures are required and appropriate for their own protection. It is inevitable that at some time a counsellor will be confronted with a client who has violent or sexually aggressive tendencies. This is a problem for all counsellors, but it needs to be recognised that female counsellors are especially vulnerable.

> The safety of counsellors needs to be ensured

We believe that it is essential for all agencies and government facilities which provide counselling services to have alarm buttons in their counselling rooms. Then, if a counsellor is in danger the alarm can be pressed to alert other workers so that they can respond appropriately. Clearly, there needs to be a suitable protocol in place so that when an alarm does sound the action taken is appropriate. Because of the safety issue, some counsellors prefer to arrange the seating so that they are seated nearest to the door, enabling them to leave the room without being obstructed by the client.

Setting up your own room

Setting up a counselling room gives a counsellor an opportunity to be creative, and to use their own personal ideas to generate a suitable environment in which clients may feel comfortable and do useful work. We have found that it can be an enjoyable task when we experiment with the layout and decoration of our counselling rooms so that they reflect our personal tastes and are welcoming to others.

LEARNING SUMMARY

- Counselling rooms need to be client-friendly.
- Client and counsellor chairs that are similar and have no barriers between them help in the creation of an empathic relationship.

LEARNING SUMMARY (cont'd)

- Looking towards a window is unpleasant.
- If chairs are too close, personal space may be invaded.
- Counselling rooms should ideally be soundproofed, and have whiteboards and a supply of tissues.
- Procedures to ensure that counselling sessions are not interrupted are useful.

Chapter 23

Keeping Records of Counselling Sessions

Many counsellors, including ourselves, find the administrative and clerical duties associated with counselling a chore. However, we believe that it is generally in clients' best interests to keep detailed and up-to-date records on each counselling session. The British Association for Counselling and Psychotherapy's *Ethical Framework for Good Practice* (BACP, 2002) states that 'practitioners are encouraged to keep appropriate records of their work with clients unless there are adequate reasons for not keeping any records. All records should be accurate, respectful of clients and colleagues and protected from unauthorised disclosure. Practitioners should take into account their responsibilities and the rights under data protection legislation and any other legal requirements.'

Ideally, report writing should be done immediately after the counselling session, while all the relevant information is fresh in the counsellor's mind, and before other inputs have had time to intrude.

In today's society we can either type or dictate records using speech recognition software directly into a computer. Alternatively we can keep handwritten records on printed forms or cards. Where records are computerised adequate security measures are required to protect client confidentiality. Similarly, handwritten records need to be kept in secure locations (see Chapter 26).

Identifying the client

Client records need to be clearly identified so that there can be no confusion regarding identity, because in large agencies it is not unusual to find two clients with the same name. Identifiers might include:

1 client's family name (surname);
2 other names;
3 date of birth (if known);
4 address; and
5 contact phone numbers.

Where handwritten records are kept, it can be an advantage to label each page of the client record with the client's full name so that the possibility of pages being inadvertently placed in the wrong file is minimised.

Additional demographic information about the client

Commonly, when the information is available, records may include any of the following:

1 marital status;
2 name of partner or spouse;
3 names and ages of children; and
4 referral source.

Notes about each counselling session

The notes for each counselling session may include:

1 date of the session;
2 factual information given by the client;
3 details of the client's problems, issues, or dilemmas;
4 notes on the process that occurred during the session;
5 notes on the outcome of the counselling session;
6 notes on interventions used by the counsellor;
7 notes on any goals identified;
8 notes on any contract between client and counsellor;
9 notes on matters to be considered at subsequent sessions;
10 notes on the counsellor's own feelings relating to the client and the counselling process; and
11 the counsellor's initials or signature.

We will now describe the content of the notes in more detail under the headings listed above. However, although these headings are discussed individually, in practice notes often flow together as the headings overlap.

Handwritten notes should preferably be legible so that if a client transfers to another counsellor for some reason notes can easily be read, with the client's permission.

Date of the session

This heading is self-explanatory. When reviewing a client's progress over time, it's very useful to know the dates of counselling sessions.

Factual information given by the client

During a counselling session, the client is likely to divulge factual information which may be useful in subsequent sessions. Sometimes small facts which may appear to be insignificant provide the key to unlock a closed door in the client's mind or could, if remembered, provide the counsellor with a clearer picture of the client's background. An example of information that might be included in a counsellor's notes could be:

'The client has been married for 13 years and during that time left her husband twice, once two years ago for a period of two weeks, and secondly six months ago for a longer unspecified period. She has considerable financial resources, lacks a social support system, had an affair some years ago and has kept this a secret from her husband.'

Details of the client's problems, issues, or dilemmas

Keep the record brief, so that it can be read quickly when required. An example of this part of the record would be:

'Mary suspects that her husband may be sexually involved with another woman, is afraid to ask her husband whether this is so, and is confused about her attitudes to him. She can't decide whether to pluck up courage and confront him, to leave him now, or to continue in what she experiences as an unsatisfactory relationship with him. She is not willing to consider relationship counselling with her husband.'

Notes on the process that occurred during the session

The process is independent of the facts presented and of the client's issues, and is concerned with what occurred during the counselling session, particularly in the client/counsellor interaction. For example:

'The client initially had difficulty talking freely, but as the counselling relationship developed he was able to explore his confusion and to look at his options. Although he was unable to decide which option to pursue, he seemed pleased by his ability to see his situation more clearly.'

Notes on the outcome of the counselling session

The outcome could be that a decision was made, or that the client remained stuck, or that a dilemma was identified. Alternatively, the outcome might be described in terms of the client's feelings at the end of the session. Examples of notes under this heading are:

- *'She decided to confront her husband.'*
- *'She left feeling sad and determined.'*
- *'She said that she could now see things clearly.'*

Notes on interventions used by the counsellor

Notes under this section are intended to remind the counsellor of particular interventions used. For example, the notes might say:

- *'Taught relaxation.'*
- *'Coached client in the use of assertive statements.'*
- *'Discussed the anger control chart.'*

Notes on any goals identified

These may be goals for the client to achieve in the world outside, or in counselling, for example:

- *'The client wants to learn to be more assertive.'*
- *'She wants to use the counselling process to sort out her confusion and make a decision regarding her marriage.'*
- *'She wants to experiment by taking risks.'*

Notes on any contract between client and counsellor

It is important to remember any agreements that are made with clients. These may be with regard to future counselling sessions, for example:

- *'The client contracted to come for counselling at fortnightly intervals for three sessions and then review progress.'*

■ *'It was agreed that counselling sessions would be used to explore the client's relationships with people of the opposite sex.'*
■ *'I have contracted to teach the client relaxation during the next session.'*

Notes on matters to be considered at subsequent sessions

Often during the last few minutes of a counselling session a client will bring up an important matter that is causing pain and is difficult to talk about. If this is noted in the record, then the counsellor can remind the client at the start of the next session, thus enabling the client to deal with the issue in question, if they wish. Sometimes, as a counsellor, you will realise at the end of a session that aspects of the client's situation need further exploration. It can be useful to make a note as a reminder.

Notes on the counsellor's own feelings relating to the client and the counselling process

These are required to help the counsellor to avoid letting their own feelings inappropriately interfere with the counselling process in future sessions. Such notes can be invaluable in the counsellor's own supervision and may be useful in helping them to improve their understanding of the counselling process. An example is:

'I felt angry when the client continually blamed others and failed to accept responsibility for his own actions.'

The counsellor's initials or signature

By initialling or signing case notes, a counsellor takes responsibility for what is written in them. In many agencies, counsellors work together with other counselling team members. In such agencies, over a period of time more than one counsellor may see a particular client. Also, a client may come back to an agency for further counselling after a particular counsellor has left. In such situations it can be helpful to the client if the client's counselling history is available, subject to the normal constraints of confidentiality.

As stated previously, writing records of counselling sessions can be a chore. However, a counsellor who does this diligently will quickly become aware of the advantages. The effectiveness of future counselling sessions is likely to be improved if the counsellor reads the client's record before meeting with them each time. By doing this the counsellor is able to 'tune in' to the client right from the start of the interview and will not waste time on unnecessary repetition.

Clearly, records need to be detailed, accurate, and legible if they are to be maximally useful. However, when writing records, be aware of the confidentiality issue (see Chapter 26) and of the possibility that the legal system may demand that such records be made available to a court. Also, bear in mind when writing records that clients may later ask to read them. Clearly, clients have the right to read their own records if they wish to do so.

LEARNING SUMMARY

- Ideally, report writing should be done immediately after a counselling session.
- Records need to include:
  - the date;
  - factual information and details of the client's problems;
  - notes on the process and outcome of the session;
  - notes regarding interventions used, goals set, contracts made, and matters to be considered in the future; and
  - notes regarding the counsellor's own feelings.

References and further reading

British Association for Counselling and Psychotherapy (2002) *Ethical Framework for Good Practice in Counselling and Psychotherapy*. Rugby: BACP.

Chapter 24

Cultural Issues

Some contentious issues arise when considering counselling in the context of ethnic and racial diversity. A major area of contention centres on the extent to which counsellors should have specific knowledge of, and sensitivity to, race relations in order to counsel effectively. Important questions emerge; for example, should clients be counselled by counsellors of the same race or ethnic background? Additionally, given that relationships between black and white majority and minority groups over several centuries have been typified by oppression, exploitation, and discrimination, can satisfactory and effective relationships within counselling be created by counsellors working with clients who come from different cultural and ethnic groups from their own? These are questions which you, the reader, will need to evaluate yourself after considering the many complex issues which we will discuss in this chapter.

Awareness of assumptions, attitudes, beliefs, values, prejudices and biases

Some counsellors believe that counselling experience and expertise are all that is required for effective counselling with any client. Others suggest that it is essential to understand the relationships between various cultures and to have knowledge of the historical backgrounds of differing racial groups in order to be capable of counselling people from these groups. They believe that an understanding of how contemporary society functions with regard to race is required. Additionally, they suggest that counsellors must have personal awareness of their own position with regard to racial issues such as the exercise of power, the effects of discrimination and stereotyping, and the way ideologies can influence policies.

> We need to understand our own cultural heritage

We believe that, as counsellors, each of us needs to be aware of our own racial and cultural heritage and to understand how that heritage has affected our attitudes, beliefs, values, prejudices and biases. By being aware of these, it is easier for us to recognise whether the problems we encounter while counselling stem from our own cultural background, or come from some other source. When we recognise that our own issues are interfering with the counselling process, we need to explore and resolve these in supervision.

Stereotyping

When counselling clients from other cultures, we need to put aside stereotypic descriptions and cultural myths. We need to strive to understand the cultural influences which contribute to the client's sense of personal and community identity. We must value the client as someone who is influenced by their cultural background and try to understand their beliefs, values, attitudes, and behaviours.

It is dangerous to assume that a person from a particular community necessarily belongs to a homogenous group where all group members share an identical common culture and heritage. Often, although there are likely to be similarities between people from a particular ethnic group, there may also be considerable diversity with regard to culture, language, religion, history, and many other attributes.

> There are both similarities and differences within each culture

Instead of stereotyping, it is more useful to remember that cultural attitudes develop and change with time. It is inevitable that members of minority ethnic groups who have settled in a new country, while maintaining some of their original cultural beliefs and attitudes, will have adopted into their own value systems, to varying degrees, some of the values and cultural patterns of the majority population.

Difficulties facing clients from other cultures

In our modern world, many people have to cope with living in a society where the cultural beliefs, values, and behaviours prevailing in their country of residence are different from, and in some ways incompatible with, the cultural beliefs of their family, close friends, and their ethnic group. This inconsistency often creates psychological and emotional problems with the consequence that counselling help may be sought.

Living within a different culture

A major problem for many clients who live in a society where the cultural environment is different from that of their families is stress arising from internal conflicts. These conflicts occur when the culturally determined social and moral values of their families conflict with those of the wider society. Consequently, while recognising that the client is an individual who is experiencing difficulties which might be faced by any other person, counsellors also need to be aware of the possibility that the difficulties being experienced may be related to, or compounded by, issues of race, ethnicity, gender, or socio-economic status.

> Each client is a unique individual

There are many different client groups for whom cultural considerations are important. A broad client group is that of migrants or descendants of migrants and their children who are at varying levels of assimilation into the mainstream culture. Another group is that of temporary visitors to a country, such as overseas students and expatriate workers. The issues clients bring to counselling with regard to their adjustment to living in a country and culture which is different from their own are diverse, but often relate to issues such as:

- cultural and racial discrimination;
- cross-cultural relationships where partners come from different cultures;
- intergenerational conflict;
- gender role and gender equality issues;

- coming to terms with living in a new culture at a time of opportunity where matters such as language, housing, education, and employment are pressuring;
- coping with stress, which many migrant refugees develop following past traumatisation, witnessing violence, torture, and other disturbing experiences;
- support when first arriving to settle in a new country;
- in the case of temporary visitors, support with regard to returning to their home country; and
- adjustment to different approaches to teaching, learning, and assessment, attitudes to time-keeping, communication between workers, and communication within workplace hierarchies.

Personal search for identity within a different culture

Many people who live in cultures that are different from their own encounter personal identity problems. Waterman (1984) has suggested that there are generally a number of stages during which such people engage in a search for personal identity. Similarly Dupont-Joshua (2002) outlines the stages of a process which she sees happening in minority groups. In the first stage, she claims people of minority groups identify more strongly with the dominant culture's values and tend to lack awareness about their personal ethnicity. She calls this the conformity stage. Following this stage, as awareness of issues involving racism, sexism, oppression, and so on, begin to develop, minority group members begin to search for their own group's role models. A rejection and distrust of the dominant culture develops, with much greater identification with their own culture. This is followed by a questioning of, or the outright rejection of, the dominant group's values, which may have been causing conflicting feelings about loyalty to their own group. This stage involves resolution of previous conflicts and a sense of fulfilment in the search for a personal cultural identity. In the final stage, an appreciation of the dominant group's values is achieved, but with the desire to get rid of all forms of oppression.

When a client is experiencing the emotional problems involved in an ethnic identity search, the counsellor needs to try to help the client to achieve a satisfactory outcome with regard to this search, so that the person concerned can develop a deeper sense of belonging to a group.

How culturally different clients view the world

Some counsellors have suggested that many emotional and psychological problems that clients bring to counselling are culture-specific, while others suggest that most problems are universal. We agree with Laungani (2002) who states that it is reasonable to suggest that just as there are culture-specific problems, emotional and psychological problems are a universal experience.

> Emotional and psychological problems are universal

Before considering specific strategies which are useful for counsellors when counselling clients from cultural groups which are not their own, we need to consider a number of dimensions which influence the way individuals perceive their world.

Laungani (2002) believes that the dimensions of individualism, materialism, free will and cognition are more likely to influence the way individuals and groups in British and Western cultures view their world. On the other hand, the dimensions of communalism, spiritualism, determination, and emotionality are more likely to influence the way individuals and groups in Eastern cultures view their world. The influence of these dimensions will affect a person's emotional responses, thoughts, beliefs, attitudes, biases, relationships, and behaviours. It can be helpful for counsellors to understand the influence of these dimensions when working with clients from cultures different to their own. We will explore how these dimensions influence thoughts, feelings, and behaviours, under the following headings:

- Individual and relationship issues
- The way decisions are made
- Who is perceived to be a natural helper?
- Attitudes of the extended family
- Gender and gender roles
- Perceptions of time
- Use of language
- Spirituality
- Physical and/or emotional issues

Individual and relationship issues

In Western society we place considerable emphasis on individuality and uniqueness, and a high value on a person's individual rights. In particular, it is generally believed that people have the right to make their own decisions and to follow a lifestyle of their individual choice. Many other cultures place a much greater emphasis on community and see an individual person in terms of the community rather than as a separate entity. In these cultures there is a sense of corporate responsibility and collective destiny. There is often a focus on harmonious blending and co-operation, accompanied by a high respect for the role of the elderly. These views are common, in various degrees, in many families from countries such as India, Pakistan, West Indies, Africa, Southern Italy, China, and Japan.

> Some cultures emphasise the individual and others the community

The way decisions are made

While personal choice is central to individuals within an individualistic society, in community-oriented cultures personal choice may be virtually non-existent. Pressures and threats of ostracism ensure that individuals stay within the confines of the community and behave in accordance with the community's norms. For example, in some cultural settings individuals have little or no input into the choice of a marriage partner; in the traditional Indian culture marriages are arranged by parents.

Individualism allows an individual to choose to do almost whatever they want. If an individual's choices lead to success, they can take credit for their success. If the outcome is unsuccessful, the individual has only themselves to blame. Hence there is a high value put on individual responsibility in Western culture. In some other cultures, individuals are not seen as being responsible for life's successes and failures in the same way. In Hindu and Buddhist thinking the law of Karma shapes the individual's view of life. According to the law of Karma individuals do benefit from the results of their own actions but things are believed to happen because they are destined to happen. Thus, the person does not have the same level of personal responsibility for the outcome. This belief system has the advantage that it may help a person to be more accepting of failure without becoming as anxious or depressed. A disadvantage is that the belief may lead to a state of resignation and inactivity and the person may avoid dealing with a disturbing or troubling issue.

Decision-making is also influenced by the way in which families function. In many Western families, decisions are made through democratic discussion and negotiation. However, this is not the case in other cultures. For example, in Chinese families communication patterns flow down from those of higher status. Consequently, in many traditional Chinese families the father, who is considered to have the highest status, makes major decisions with little input from other family members.

> People make decisions within a cultural context

Clearly, inner conflict may well arise for people coming from community-oriented and/or hierarchical cultures who are living in a country where the majority culture is individualistic and many families rely on a democratic decision-making process.

Who is perceived to be a natural helper?

Knowledge about the helping options available to clients who come from Eastern cultural groups can enable counsellors to provide their clients with sensitive alternatives. In India, there is some reliance on indigenous therapeutic interventions. Yoga appears to be one of the most popular forms of treatment used, but is not seen as suitable for treating all types of emotional and psychological difficulties. Where psychological problems are seen as a result of negative spiritual influences, it is accepted practice to take a person to a spiritual helper who is attributed with healing powers. The helper may encourage the person to recite prayers, meditate or perform religious rites. Fasting and other personal practices are often undertaken by extended family members to ensure that the person's emotional well-being is restored.

Some African and other cultures have spiritual beliefs which include a belief in evil spirits. A person from these cultures may be helped by consulting with a person who is believed to be specially qualified to help in dealing with evil spirits. In times of serious and sudden illnesses within families, such experts may be summoned by family members to undertake religious ceremonies to counteract negative influences in order to help the afflicted person (Kakar, 1990).

> We must respect the client's spiritual beliefs

It is difficult for people from some cultures to seek counselling help from a person who is not a member of their community. For example, many Nigerians believe that personal matters can only be discussed with family and friends present (Idowu, 1985). This means that counsellors may need to spend time developing a trusting relationship with family members before they can be of help.

Some Asian cultures put a high value on age and respect for elders, and will consult with the elders when they need advice or counselling help. Because of this, people from these cultures prefer to seek help from older counsellors, and may find it difficult or impossible to work with younger ones. In this regard, it is sometimes useful for counsellors to seek the assistance of someone who is aware of the relevant cultural norms. This person can then assist by acting as a consultant to provide guidance and information with regard to possible ways of helping a particular client.

Attitudes of the extended family

When helping people from Eastern cultures, counsellors often need to take account of the influence and/or needs of the extended family. For example, in traditional Indian family life a person's individuality is absorbed into the collective family community. Consequently, when an emotional problem affects a particular family member, it is likely to be perceived as a communal problem which affects the entire family.

In traditional Chinese families, there is a close-knit bond between the individual and the family. It is expected that for an individual to stay part of the family the individual will submit to community norms and will not deviate (Yang, 1997). For such individuals living in Britain where the majority view is different, the pressure to conform may cause acute stress and anxiety. However, for those family members who are comfortable with conformity the extended family network may provide inbuilt safety against mental disturbance. Clearly, there are individual differences. These are illustrated by Johnson, and Nadirshaw (2002), who suggest that South Asian communities have been stereotyped in terms of the claim that they look after their own within the extended family. While the extended family may offer care and support to its members, it may also be a source of tension and conflict. For example, Beliappa (1991) claims that the most severe concerns for women in South-East Asian communities are related to marital relationships, yet many of these women feel that the extended family is not an appropriate source of help for their difficulties. Mental distress remains hidden or bottled up, as it is not appropriate to talk about one's situation outside of the family.

> The family culture may encourage or inhibit personal disclosure

Whenever possible, counsellors need to gain an understanding of the social systems in their clients' families. They need to familiarise themselves with family customs and rules, particularly with regard to verbal exchanges between people. For example, many Africans often see disclosing personal problems to a counsellor not only as a sign of weakness, but also as divulging family secrets (Idowu, 1985).

It can also be useful for counsellors to learn about the child-rearing practices of their clients if these are relevant to counselling, as these practices vary markedly across cultures. For example, in some cultures there may be emphasis on the nuclear family, whereas in others the emphasis is on the extended family. In many Eastern cultures (for example, Indian, Pakistani, and Chinese), child-rearing practices are focused on emphasising the importance of family ties and obligations. Praise is given for actions that are seen as benefiting the family and guilt-inducing techniques are used to maintain discipline. Children are expected to retain emotional ties with their mother and a respectful attitude towards their father, even when they have become adults. Consequently, it is not unusual for counsellors to find that some clients will find it difficult to make the choices they would prefer to make because of concern that they may upset their parents. From a Western perspective, this concern could be incorrectly perceived as the client being overly dependent. However, Western counsellors need to take care when working with such clients, because assisting the client to become more independent may lead to even greater conflict (Lee & Richardson, 1991). Clearly, a client's cultural background needs to be respected so that they are empowered to make decisions which fit for them.

Gender and gender roles

The norms regarding relationships between members of the same sex and members of the opposite sex vary markedly across cultures. In order to join effectively with clients when trying to help them with relationship issues, it is advantageous if counsellors are able to gain some understanding of cultural norms with regard to relationships. Additionally, gender-based norms regarding behaviour, roles and expectations vary.

In traditional Chinese families, the mother is usually responsible for socialising the children. If they become rebellious, it is seen as reflecting poor parenting on her part. She also has to mediate between the dictates of her husband and the demands of the children. The greatest responsibility is placed on the eldest son as he is expected to help raise his younger siblings and be a role model for them. Daughters are expected to help in the household. Generally, fewer demands are placed upon them because they become members of their husband's family when they marry (Lee & Richardson, 1991).

Clients from male-dominated societies may find difficulties adjusting to a society where male and female roles are largely regarded as interchangeable. Misunderstandings could arise in daily interactions, particularly if these are social or romantic.

Perceptions of time

Time does not have the same meaning in relationship centred societies as it does in Western societies. At a subjective level, time in these cultures is more flexible and relaxed. Time is often conceptualised in terms where time has no beginning or end. As a result, clients from these societies do not exhibit the same sense of urgency that is often experienced in Western society. There are exceptions to this flexibility, and differences may occur in situations where an event is considered to be important. For example, undertaking an important journey or fixing a time for weddings, funerals and other family functions is seldom left to chance.

Use of language

The way language is used will have a significant influence on the effectiveness of communication between a client and a counsellor. Figures of speech, complex communication, proverbs and quotations may either be familiar or confusing depending on the client's culture. Additionally, it is important to recognise that there may be significant or subtle differences in the vocabulary and meanings of words in different cultural environments. Consequently, the fact that a client is communicating in English with an English-speaking counsellor may be misleading if the counsellor does not realise that there are subtle differences in the use of particular words.

> It is easy for words to be misunderstood

Spirituality

For many people throughout the world, spiritual beliefs hold a very high level of importance. If these beliefs are challenged or questioned, the person concerned may be alienated. When counselling people from other cultures, or people who have different beliefs from ours, we need to put our own beliefs to one side. In order to join with and help any client we need to try to understand their spiritual beliefs and to see their world in the context of those beliefs. This may be particularly important with respect to a client's beliefs regarding the role and function of traditional healers, or with regard to spiritual and religious influences. For example, the belief in a materialistic world is not consistent with most Eastern cultural thinking. For some, the external world is not composed of matter and is seen as being illusory. Reality is not seen to be external to the individual, but the perception of reality lies within the individual. Consequently many clients from Eastern cultures are more inward-looking than most Westerners. The Eastern way of looking at life may therefore lead clients to formulations where material and spiritual, physical and metaphysical, natural and supernatural explanations of phenomena coexist with one another. Eastern beliefs and values revolve around the notion of spiritualism and obtaining a heightened state of spiritual awareness. Any activity which is likely to promote such a state is to be encouraged. In keeping with ideas about spiritualism, emotional and psychological disturbance may also be explained in terms of sorcery, bewitchment, and by the posession of one's soul by evil and malevolent spirits (Kakar, 1990).

Physical and/or emotional issues

Particular cultural groups who have a common history of past experiences that unite them and help them to define who they are may also experience emotions which are common to the group. It is useful to understand the common history and the emotions which are associated with that history. For example, counsellors who see clients of any ethnic group with a history of oppression need to understand, appreciate, and respect the anger that this generates; understand their own response to that anger, whatever that may be; and deal with that response appropriately so that the counselling relationship is enhanced. As counsellors, if we are to be helpful to our clients so that we maximise their opportunity to change in ways which are appropriate for them, then we must fully respect and work within frameworks which make sense to them and which result from their cultural heritage.

> A person's cultural background may affect their ability to express feelings

In traditional Chinese culture, emotional expression is restrained and displays of emotional reactions do not typically occur outside the family. Feelings are usually not openly expressed except by young children. Often, if counsellors attempt to encourage clients to express emotions directly they may be met with resistance and this is likely to be counterproductive. Additionally, such clients may lack the experience to identify, acknowledge, and communicate emotional states. The emphasis in counselling should therefore be on the indirect expression of positive and respectful feelings. For example, interest may be shown in the ways in which members of a family show how they care for each other. This focus on behaviour is respectful and indirect.

Issues for counsellors when counselling clients from other cultures

As counsellors, we need to develop culturally relevant ways of helping each client. Ideally, we should have knowledge about the client's particular group and culture. However, it is obvious that this will not always be the case. There are many occasions when a counsellor will not have much information about the client's cultural background. In such cases, it may be useful to encourage the client to extend their story to include relevant information relating to their culture. If a counsellor can do this successfully, they may be able to further their knowledge about the client's family, values, attitudes, beliefs, and behaviours. Additionally, they may discover information about the characteristics of the client's community and the resources in that community and in the family, enabling them to understand, join with, and be more helpful to the client. While exploring cultural issues with clients, it is important for counsellors to recognise their own cultural beliefs so that these do not intrude on the client–counsellor relationship. In any exploration of cultural issues, the aim is to produce a better relationship with the client and to understand the client's problems more fully. During a counselling session it is not justifiable for a counsellor to explore cultural issues just out of curiosity, or to satisfy the counsellor's own personal needs.

Expectations

Sue and Sue (1990) identified the way that typical counsellor expectations may be unhelpful for clients from some ethnic groups.

Many counsellors expect that their clients will be comfortable with a collaborative process which enables the client to find solutions to their problems. However, this expectation is not realistic for some cultural groups. For example, Nigerian students expect to be given a 'cure' by the counsellor (Idowu, 1985). Similarly, Pedersen (1991) discovered that African and Iranian students had high expectations that the counsellor would be direct, expert, and concrete. Although most counsellors hopefully have expertise, many tend to be facilitative rather than direct and concrete. Pederson also found that foreign students on the whole had high expectations of counsellor nurturance, whereas many counsellors try to encourage self-reliance. Additionally, counsellors usually expect that clients will disclose their feelings, but this may not fit for many Asians, as they generally associate maturity and wisdom with the ability to control, rather than express, emotions and feelings.

> The client's and counsellor's expectations may differ

Clearly, it is important for both the counsellor and client to discuss the counselling process and their individual expectations in order to avoid misunderstandings.

Ethical considerations

There is an important and contentious issue regarding the counsellor's role in either accepting or challenging cultural beliefs. Stuart (2004) suggests that counsellors who are able to see the world from the client's perspective do not need to necessarily accept everything in the client's view as healthy. His opinion is that at times it may be appropriate for counsellors to attempt to change beliefs. For example, if a husband believes that his culture gives him permission to beat his wife when she does not submit to his will, counsellors have an obligation to attempt to change this belief, even if the man's wife accepts the doctrine. The counsellor has a professional obligation to prevent harm, and this takes precedence over respecting cultural diversity. However, great care needs to be exercised when challenging cultural beliefs with the goal of ensuring the client's safety. Farrant (2003) argues that some ways of attempting to prevent harm may, in some circumstances, put clients at further risk. She points out that screening to identify abused women in Asian contexts challenges other equally powerful beliefs within those cultural communities. Cultural factors such as forced marriage, restrictions on lifestyle, and the belief-based concept of honour and shame play a fundamental role in how some Asian women react to domestic abuse. In some communities, it may not just be the spouse who is the perpetrator; the extended family and wider community may be involved in, or collude with, the violence. Some women are expected to uphold the honour of their family and/or husband at all costs. Failure to do so results in shame and that can have severe consequences for their personal safety. Counsellors therefore need to be extremely careful in trying to understand the client's complete picture with the goal of doing all they can in an attempt to ensure the client's ongoing safety.

> The safety of the client is paramount

Meeting the needs of a client from a different ethnic group

Although we recognise that ideally, to be most helpful, it is an advantage if the counsellor comes from the same ethnic background as the client, we believe that it is usually possible for counsellors to be of help to clients from different backgrounds. In order to be of help, there are a number of guidelines which can usefully be followed.

Deliberately inquire about the person's cultural identity

As counsellors we need to remember that each individual is unique. Stereotyping is almost certain to prevent us from joining empathically with the client. If we stereotype we will inevitably fail to recognise the complexities of the client's individual cultural outlook. What we need to do is to concentrate on listening and joining with the client as we would with a client from our own ethnic group. While doing this, if we pay attention, we will be likely to recognise verbal and non-verbal clues that might suggest that we are not fully understanding. Alternatively, we may realise that we are uncertain about the client's values regarding a particular issue. In these situations we need to deliberately seek information so that we can better understand the client's cultural identity and associated beliefs and attitudes.

Deal with our personal prejudices and biases

In our view, it is inevitable that all of us will have personal prejudices and biases. Stuart (2004) suggests that some of our prejudiced beliefs may be derived from what we read and some from our own personal experience. He points out that when our biases go unchecked, our perceptions of the client say more about us than the client! This is clearly not useful. We are left with the question, how do we deal with our prejudices and biases? Perhaps the most useful way is to recognise and own them and talk openly about them with a supervisor. In that way, we can explore our own personal issues that drive our prejudice. If we resolve these issues, we will be more able to let go of unhelpful thoughts, attitudes, and beliefs, so that we can join with the client with an accepting openness, and thus get more fully in touch with the unique person we are trying to help.

Remind ourselves of the many influences on personal ethnic identity

If we are to try to fully understand an individual client, we need to be careful to take into account the many personal attributes which will influence their beliefs and attitudes. These attributes include age, developmental stage, gender, sexual orientation, occupation, health, disability, position in the family, and religious orientation. There is often a complex interaction between attributes such as these and a person's ethnic background. A person's sense of cultural identity is clearly going to depend on this interaction. As counsellors, we need to try to get a picture of the whole person because it is only by doing this that we will be able to effectively join with them.

Be flexible in the way we work

At the present time in the United Kingdom, counsellors are generally trained in one or more counselling approaches. However, these approaches all have their origins in Western society and this may be unsatisfactory for some clients. A more open and accepting approach to other models of counselling and helping may be more useful.

Counsellors who consistently work with clients from particular ethnic groups may find it useful to gain insights into non-Western therapeutic approaches. Additionally, as a counsellor, when contracting with a client you may find it useful to fully discuss the client's expectations and to be clear in letting them know the extent to which you believe that you can meet those expectations. If you are able to work in a way which suits your client, then you are more likely to be helpful. For example, some clients prefer a more direct approach than others. An example of this is that studies involving Asian college students have suggested that the use of a directive counselling style is perceived more positively by them than a non-directive style (Atkinson and Matsushita, 1991).

Establishing rapport

When counselling clients from some cultural groups, joining may involve a lengthy process in order for trust to be established before useful work can begin on the client's problems. Be clear about what help it is that you are offering and allow more time for the counselling session than you normally would. Remember that many concepts like truth, honesty, politeness, and self-disclosure are culturally bound. This may affect what the client feels they can or cannot say and to what degree they can expose their feelings in relation to the issues they are bringing.

The counsellor needs to take responsibility for helping clients to understand the counselling process and issues relating to goals, expectations, legal rights, and the counsellor's orientation. Negotiation and contracting is required in order to provide a counselling service that is acceptable and useful for the client.

Attending behaviours

Attending behaviours vary from culture to culture and also from individual to individual. In fact, individual differences among clients may be as important as cultural patterns.

What is considered to be appropriate eye contact varies with culture. For example in some cultures, when listening to a person, direct eye contact is appropriate, but when talking, eye contact should be less frequent. However, this pattern is not the same in all cultures. Perhaps the best advice is to try to match the client's level of eye contact.

Most counsellors pay a lot of attention to their client's body language. However, as counsellors, we need to be very careful about interpreting body language. The only person who can accurately and consistently interpret a person's body language is the person themselves. Even so, as counsellors, it is important for us to learn what we can from the body language cues which clients give us. When a counsellor works with a client from the same cultural background, the meaning of body language is often fairly clear, and this can easily be confirmed by checking with the client. When working with clients from a different culture, it is far more difficult to make interpretations regarding body language because there is considerable variation in cultural norms.

In most cultures, when two people are holding a conversation they prefer the distance between them to be at least an arm's length. However, this norm is not universal. In Arab and Middle Eastern cultures, a conversational distance of 300 mm or even less is generally the accepted practice. Such close proximity would be uncomfortable for many Western people.

Shaking hands is generally seen as a sign of welcome in Western culture. However it is dangerous to assume that this is the case in other cultures. Indeed, in some cultures, if a male gives a female a handshake, this may be seen as giving a sexual invitation.

Language and translation issues

As counsellors working with different ethnic groups, we need to be aware of our use of language. Words and phrases which are familiar to us may have quite a different meaning for someone from a different culture. We may inadvertently use expressions which have racist overtones. To minimise misunderstanding we need to try to be aware of the effect of our language on the client and to check with them if we suspect that what we have said has been interpreted in a different way to that intended. Some colloquial expressions may be confusing for a client. For example, if you were to say, 'I'm afraid I haven't been able to help you', some clients might focus on the word 'afraid' and believe that you were fearful. Thus the intention of the message would be misunderstood.

It is obvious that generally clients are able to express themselves more meaningfully in their own language (Ivey, Ivey and Simek-Morgan, 1996). It may therefore sometimes be sensible and appropriate for a counsellor to make use of an interpreter in a counselling session. We have done this on a number of occasions with success, but recognise that there are some problems in doing this. Firstly, unless the client feels comfortable with and trusts the interpreter, they may not feel able to disclose important and relevant personal information. Secondly, it is quite likely, if not inevitable, that the interpreter's own personal issues might to some extent intrude on the counselling process. Additionally, where highly emotional personal issues are raised, it may be necessary for the counsellor to help the interpreter to debrief. If this is not done, the interpreter may be left with uncomfortable and disturbing feelings.

When working with an interpreter the counsellor's understanding of the client's and the interpreter's use of language is important. Sometimes, in the transfer of information from the counsellor to the interpreter to the client, and from the client to the interpreter to the counsellor, subtle and important changes in meaning may occur.

Use of micro-skills

Counsellors need to be familiar with the use of all of the micro-skills described earlier. However, early in the process of relationship building it may be useful to focus more heavily on active listening than on using other skills. In particular, it needs to be remembered that a question-and-answer style of gathering information is alien to clients from many cultures, so until you are confident of the client's cultural norms in this regard, it is wise to minimise the use of questions as much as possible and to use a less intrusive and more indirect style of relating.

> Use of questions can be unhelpful for some clients

When working with a client from a different cultural background, it is essential to create a trusting relationship. This may mean making progress more slowly than usual. In particular, it may be unwise to attempt to encourage the client to talk through sensitive personal issues too early in the process. It is also important to be congruent, and this requires the counsellor to be honest and open about their limitations particularly with regard to their understanding of the client's cultural background.

Once rapport has been developed, it may be sensible and possible for a counsellor to invite the client to give feedback if they feel uncomfortable at any time with the counselling process.

Using an integrative approach to counselling the culturally different client

It can be argued that using an integrative approach has advantages when working with culturally different clients. An integrated approach offers the client a process which is broadly based and flexible whereas a 'purist' approach carries the danger of exposing the client to the hidden

Eurocentric assumptions that are invariably present in conventional therapies (Lago and Moodley, 2002). The flexibility of an integrative approach allows the influence of these to be minimised.

> There are advantages in using an integrative approach

An integrative model of counselling motivates the counsellor to select effective methods of helping the client to achieve desired goals. Thus the approach that the counsellor uses at any specific point in time during the counselling process will depend on the counsellor's understanding of the attitudes and beliefs of the client and the nature of the problem.

When using integrative counselling the client and counsellor in partnership engage in a mutual exploration of problems; together, they establish desirable goals and outcomes and agree on strategies for reaching them. The counsellor keeps an open mind and is able to recognise the usefulness of particular approaches for dealing with specific problems.

LEARNING SUMMARY

- The most important factor in producing successful outcomes when counselling clients from other cultures is the counsellor's ability to join with the client so that a good trusting working relationship is established.
- Counsellors need to be aware of their own racial and cultural heritage and to understand how that heritage has affected their attitudes, beliefs, values, prejudices, and biases.
- The client's emotional responses, thoughts, beliefs, attitudes, biases, relationships, and behaviours will be affected by a number of factors including: individual and relationship issues, the way decisions are made, who is perceived to be a natural helper, attitudes of the extended family, gender and general roles, perceptions of time, use of language, spirituality, physical and/or emotional issues, and experience of trauma.

References and further reading

Atkinson, D. R. and Matsushita, Y. J. (1991) Japanese–American acculturation, counselling style, counsellor ethnicity, and perceived counsellor credibility. *Journal of Counselling Psychology*, 38, 473–78.

Beliappa, J. (1991) *Illness or distress?: Alternative models of mental health*. London: Confederation of Indian organisations.

Dupont-Joshua, A. (2002) Working with issues of race in counselling. In S. Palmer (ed.), *Multicultural Counselling: A reader*. London: Sage.

Farrant, A. (2003) Fighting back. *Nursing Standard*, 17(51), 20–21.

Idowu, A. (1985) Counselling Nigerian students in United States colleges and Universities. *Journal of Counselling and Development*, 63, 506–509.

Ivey, A., Ivey, B. and Simek-Morgan, L. (1996) *Psychotherapy: A Multicultural Perspective*. Boston: Allyn and Bacon.

Kakar, S. (1990). *Shamans, mystics and doctors*. Chicago: University of Chicago.

Lago, C. and Moodley, R. (2002) Multicultural issues in eclectic and integrated counselling and psychotherapy. In S. Palmer (ed.) *Multicultural counselling: A reader* (pp. 40–56). London: Sage.

Laungani, P. (2002) Understanding mental illness across cultures. In S. Palmer (ed.), *Multicultural Counselling: A reader*. London: Sage.

Lee, C. C. and Richardson, B. L. (1991) *Multicultural Issues in Counselling: New Approaches to Diversity*. Alexandria, VA: American Association for Counselling And Development.

Pedersen, P. (1991) Counseling international students. *The counselling psychologist*. 19, 10–58.

Stuart, R. B. (2004). Twelve practical suggestions for achieving multicultural competence. *Professional psychology: Research and Practice*, 35(1), 3–9.

Sue, D. W. and Sue, D. (1990) *Counseling the culturally different – theory and practice*. New York: Wiley.

Waterman, A. (1984) *The Psychology of Individualism*. New York: Praeger.

Webb Johnson, A. and Nadirshaw, Z. (2002) Good practice in transcultural counselling: An Asian perspective. In S. Palmer (ed.), *Multicultural Counselling: A reader*. London: Sage.

Yang, K. S. (1997) Theories and research in Chinese personality: An indigenous approach. In H. S. R. Kao and D. Sinah (eds), *Asian perspective on psychology* (pp. 236–64). New Delhi: Sage.

Chapter 25

Influence of the Counsellor's Values and Beliefs

In Chapter 2, we discussed the need for counsellors to try to be non-judgemental. Can you imagine what it would be like if you were a client talking to a counsellor and as you were talking you formed the impression that the counsellor was disapproving of you, or of what you were saying? We suspect that in such a situation you would feel inhibited and might decide that it was not wise to talk openly to this counsellor. Alternatively, can you imagine what it would be like for you if the counsellor seemed to be troubled by what you were saying and was questioning whether your values and beliefs were acceptable? Once again, we suspect that you might feel uncertain about continuing to disclose information. Clearly, there is a risk that the counselling process will be compromised if the counsellor appears to be judgemental.

Sometimes it is very hard not to be judgemental. We have found that it is especially hard when we are confused or not clear about our own values or beliefs. When we are not clear about these, we find that it is harder not to be disapproving, or we get distracted by spending time thinking about our own values and beliefs instead of attending to the client. It is therefore important for counsellors to know where they stand with regard to their own personal values and beliefs.

Sometimes a counsellor's values and beliefs will match those of the client, but often they will not. If we are to be able to help clients with different values from ours, then we need to understand the client's world in

251

the context of their value system and not ours. If we are not able to do this, then we will not be able to join empathically and what we say to the client will be likely to jar, confuse, or create a barrier between us. At worst, we might get into an argument about values instead of helping the client to sort out their confusion!

We have no right to try to impose our values onto clients. However, we believe that there are times when it is appropriate for us, as counsellors, to be open with a client about our values in order to be congruent.

> counsellors need to be congruent to ensure that the relationship is authentic

If we have a clear understanding of our own values, we will have additional inner strength. We will not need to be defensive in trying to justify our values; they are ours and they will stand in their own right without the need for justification.

If we don't understand and know our own values, we may well be trapped into trying to discover what they are during a counselling session. Instead of being able to concentrate on seeing the world through the client's eyes, we may be distracted by trying to sort out our own confusion. Questions such as, 'Is this morally right or wrong?', may trouble us and prevent us from joining the client in their own struggle to work out what is right for them.

People change as they understand themselves better

The more we work as counsellors, the more strongly we believe that most people are naturally well intentioned, caring of others, socially responsible, and capable of giving and receiving love. When we meet someone who seems to be nasty, we almost always, as we get to know them better, recognise the damage that has been done to them by past life experiences. As counselling proceeds, we usually notice changes occurring as that person comes to terms with past experiences. It is as though a plant that looked like a thistle is changing into something more attractive. With this belief, we do not need to try to convince others to accept our values; we just need to understand them better and to help them to understand themselves better.

We have a friend who trained as a Christian priest, who told us that while at university an agnostic lecturer told him that arguments from strongly evangelical Christian students never threatened, or made him question, his agnostic beliefs. However, this lecturer found that our friend made him think about his agnosticism. Rather than confront him with a different point of view, my friend respected him enough to accept him as he was and tried to see the world through his eyes when he talked with him. Our friend knew clearly what he himself believed and openly owned his beliefs, but did not push them onto his lecturer or attack his lecturer's position. As a consequence, he was able to join with this lecturer in a way which allowed the lecturer to explore different ways of thinking in safety and without feeling pressured. Although the lecturer did not change his beliefs, he had the opportunity to expand his thinking so that his relationship with our friend was enhanced as they gained a better understanding of each other.

Being non-judgemental isn't easy

As children, our values and beliefs are initially those of our parents and significant others such as teachers. It is appropriate that as young people we accept without question the values and beliefs of those adults who are important in our lives. To use a gestalt therapy concept, these values and beliefs are swallowed whole. In gestalt therapy, they are said to have been introjected and are called *introjects*. As we grow up, our values and beliefs will change as we accept some of our earlier values and beliefs but modify others in the light of our own experiences. Clearly, though, our values and beliefs are likely to be influenced by both the cultural background in which we grew up as children and by the contemporary culture of the societal group within which we live. As counsellors we are therefore certain, at times, to work with clients who may have quite different values from our own.

Being non-judgemental is not so easy at times. Counsellors are sometimes faced with situations where a client's values strongly conflict with their own. When this happens, it is easy for a counsellor to become emotionally aroused by the fear of threat to their own value system.

> We need to be able to accept the client's values if we are to be helpful

The first step in dealing with a values conflict between yourself and a client is to recognise it. You will probably be able to do this fairly easily if you remember that the warning sign of a values conflict is likely to be emotional arousal in yourself. If you feel your body tensing, or other bodily symptoms of emotional arousal, then stop and think. Ask yourself, 'What is happening?' Check out whether your values are being challenged. Similarly, if you find that you are starting to disagree with a client and to argue with them, stop and think, to check out whether or not you are involved in a values conflict.

Owning your own value system

It is not going to be helpful to a client for a counsellor to deliberately try to change their point of view. As has been emphasised, effective counsellors join with their clients and try to see the world as their clients see it. When you sense that you are encountering a values conflict, then you need to make a choice by asking yourself, 'Can I put my own values to one side in order to join with this client or not?' If the answer is 'Yes', then counselling can proceed. If it is 'No', then to be fair to the client you will need to tell them that while you respect them and their right to have a different point of view, you have different values with regard to the issue in question. If you feel able to do so, it will be useful for you to explain to the client that you are not saying that your values are better or worse than their values; they are just different because you are two different people. You can then offer the client the option of continuing to talk with you if they wish, or talking to someone else. If the client wants to talk with someone else, then it is best to refer them to someone who may be able to meet with them on their own value-ground.

Sometimes you may recognise an important values difference between your client and yourself, but will feel able to put your own values to one side while counselling and suspend judgement. When this happens, you may need to continually remind yourself to imagine you are the client, with their world view. When your own values start intruding on the counselling process, recognise this, and once again focus on the client's perspective. If you are able to stay fully tuned in to the client's thoughts and feelings, your counselling will be more likely to be effective. Moreover, you will be more likely to be successful in putting your own values to one side so that they remain intact as part of you.

The need for supervision

Whenever a values conflict interferes with your work with a client, it is important for you to talk with your supervisor about the issues involved.

By doing this you will minimise the possibility of future situations where the effectiveness of your counselling might be adversely affected by the particular value in question. Hopefully, if you fully explore the relevant issues, you will be able to work with clients with very different points of view from yourself without your own values influencing the appropriateness of your counselling responses.

> Talk to your supervisor about values conflicts

As discussed, it is very important for counsellors to know, as clearly as possible, what their values are.

Knowing your values

How can you, as a new counsellor, know what your values are? There are so many areas in life where values are important that it is impossible in training to cover all value-laden situations. Inevitably, some of these will emerge during counselling sessions. Counsellors have to continually address new issues. Even so, it is possible in training to examine some commonly encountered situations or beliefs where values are of importance.

A values clarification exercise

As an aid to counsellor training we suggest the following exercise in values clarification. This exercise is best done in a group where discussion of differing values can occur. A good way to carry out the exercise is to label one end of the training room 'agree' and the other end 'disagree'. Trainees, as a group, can then be asked to respond to each statement below by individually positioning themselves in the room somewhere on the agree–disagree continuum along the length of the room. Once trainees have positioned themselves in response to a statement, the facilitator can invite comment and promote discussion with regard to their positions in the room.

If you are not part of a group, then you may wish to think about and try to work out where you stand with regard to each of the statements below. Do you agree or disagree with the statement, or stand somewhere between the agree and disagree position?

Please notice that many of the statements below are statements of belief rather than value statements. However, our values are determined by our beliefs, so in determining our values, it's important to also consider beliefs.

Statements for values clarification exercise

Warning!

Some of these statements are intentionally provocative and may offend.

- Unemployment benefits should be terminated after three months.
- People from other ethnic groups should be treated with suspicion.
- Termination of pregnancy is a woman's right.
- Men are always to blame for domestic violence.
- Women and men are equal.
- Guns don't kill; the people who fire them do.
- Gun laws are for the benefit of the community as a whole.
- With modern contraceptive methods, sexual fidelity is no longer necessary.
- Censorship is socially desirable.
- Homosexuality is a normal condition.
- Delinquency is due to parents being too permissive with their children.
- Counsellors wouldn't be needed if people would turn to God.
- Usually one partner is mostly to blame when a marriage breaks up.
- Marijuana should be legalised.
- Welfare benefits are too high.
- Couples should stay together for the sake of their children.
- Children in two-parent families are happier than children in single-parent families.
- If a person has an affair, their spouse should leave them.
- Contraception is wrong.
- People who have had psychiatric treatment are not suitable for leadership positions.
- Lying is sometimes justifiable.
- Charities deserve regular donations.
- Good people should not associate with immoral people.
- Anyone can get a job if they try hard enough.
- Life is to be enjoyed.
- Striving for wealth is wrong.
- Handouts do not help people.
- People can be too honest.
- Sex is overrated.
- Smoking in public places should be banned.
- Love and forgiveness are more important than punishment.
- Alcohol more frequently gives pleasure than it creates problems.

- Alternative medicine is more useful than conventional medicine.
- I don't want to change other people so that they have the same values as I do.
- It's OK for a father to bath his young daughter.
- Chemicals are harmful.
- It's a good idea to build large concrete dams.
- Masturbating is enjoyable and acceptable.
- People should not be allowed to trek through national parks.
- Sex offenders are nasty people.
- Too much closeness in a family is a bad thing.
- Adult needs should take precedence over children's needs.
- Killing people is wrong.
- Swearing is offensive.
- The developed countries should feed the developing countries.
- I believe in heaven.
- Oral sex is enjoyable and acceptable.
- Divorce is wrong.
- De facto relationships are morally acceptable.
- Children who receive sex education are more likely to be promiscuous than those who don't.
- The Koran tells us what is right and what is wrong.
- Single parents shouldn't have sexual relationships with special friends.
- Single parents who have sexual relationships with special friends should be open about what they are doing and should tell their children.
- Hospital births are better for babies than home births.
- Things are either right or wrong; there are no in-betweens.
- Smacking children is unnecessary.
- Only married people should have sexual intercourse.
- It's OK for a 15-year-old to have sexual intercourse.
- You can tell what a person is really like from their appearance.
- It is good to strive for material possessions.
- Money doesn't bring happiness.
- Children should be breastfed until they want to stop.
- Families should have clear rules.
- Children should be allowed to make their own decisions.
- Children are better off in child care than with their mothers.
- We need fewer laws and more freedom.
- Most people are intrinsically good.

When considering your position with regard to the above statements, please remember that we are all unique individuals and different from each other. Consequently, in some ways, your values will probably be similar to ours, and in some ways they will be different. We are comfortable with that. Are you?

LEARNING SUMMARY

- Counsellors need to know their own beliefs and values so that:
  - they can respect their clients' values
  - they are not distracted during counselling by trying to sort out their own values
- Counsellors have no right to try to impose their own beliefs or values on clients.
- Whenever a values conflict interferes with your work, consult your supervisor.

Further reading

Ridley, C. R. (1995) *Overcoming Unintentional Racism in Counseling and Therapy: A Practitioner's Guide to Intentional Intervention.* Thousand Oaks: Sage.
Worthington, E. (ed.) (1993) *Psychotherapy and Religious Values.* Grand Rapids: Baker.

Chapter 26

Confidentiality and Other Ethical Issues

The first part of this chapter will be devoted exclusively to confidentiality, because it is one of the most important ethical issues for a counsellor. Other aspects of professional ethics will be considered in the second part of the chapter.

Confidentiality

Respecting client confidentiality is a fundamental requirement for keeping trust (BACP, 2002). For counselling to be maximally effective, the client must feel secure in the knowledge that what they tell the counsellor is to be treated with a high degree of confidentiality. In an ideal world, a client would be offered total confidentiality so that they would feel free to openly explore with the counsellor the darkest recesses of their mind, and to discuss the most intimate details of their thoughts. As new counsellors, we naively believed that we could at all times give our clients an assurance that what was said in a counselling session was between them and us and would not be discussed with others. We very soon learnt that this was an idealistic belief and found that in practice it is generally not possible, advisable, or ethical to offer total confidentiality.

As a counsellor, you may at times be troubled by some personal difficulties regarding confidentiality and may need to talk with your supervisor about these. Counsellors are faced with a dilemma with regard to confidentiality. Unless we give our clients an assurance that what they tell us will be in confidence, they are unlikely to be open with us. However, there are limits to the level of confidentiality which we can offer and we need to be clear with clients about these limits. Most importantly, as a counsellor you need to be aware of the limits to the confidentiality which you are offering.

> Absolute confidentiality is often not possible and may be unethical

Many experienced counsellors would agree with Woolfe and Dryden, who, in the *Handbook of Counselling Psychology* (2003) go so far as to say that promising total confidentiality is unethical. It is certainly true that confidentiality is compromised by the following:

- the need to keep records;
- the requirements of the counsellor's own supervision;
- the need to protect others;
- working in conjunction with other professionals;
- participation in educational training programmes, conferences, workshops and seminars; and
- cases where the law requires disclosure of information.

The above list will now be discussed in detail.

The need to keep records

As explained in Chapter 23, there are compelling reasons for keeping good records. Counsellors who work in agencies frequently use computerised systems or centralised filing systems for such records. This may make it possible for other counsellors and non-counselling staff such as receptionists and filing clerks to have access to confidential records. Some counsellors omit to note certain categories of sensitive material on their record cards as a way of protecting clients. However, there are obvious consequences if this policy is adopted, as important information may be overlooked or forgotten during subsequent counselling sessions. Clearly, for the protection of clients, computerised records need to be protected by adequate security systems. Similarly, hard-copy records should not be left lying around in places where they can be read by unauthorised people, and should be stored in lockable filing cabinets or in a secure filing room.

The requirements of the counsellor's own supervision

The requirements of professional supervision, as described in Chapter 27, demand that counsellors be free to fully disclose client material to their supervisors. This is essential if clients are to receive the best possible service, and is also necessary for the wellbeing of counsellors themselves. Some counsellors openly talk with their clients about the requirements of professional supervision, and sometimes it can be reassuring for a client to know that their counsellor is receiving supervision.

> Counsellor supervision is essential and in the client's best interests

The need to protect others

Experienced counsellors sometimes work with suicidal clients, with dangerous clients, and with clients who have committed serious offences against other people and may possibly repeat such behaviour. Counsellors have responsibilities to their clients and also to the community. Consequently, there may be instances where a counsellor needs to divulge information to protect a client from self-harm, to protect a third party. For example, if a counsellor knows that their client possesses a gun and intends to kill someone, then it would be unethical and irresponsible if the person at risk, the police and/or the psychiatric authorities were not informed. As stated by the British Association for Counselling and Psychotherapy (2002), 'situations in which clients pose a risk of causing serious harm to themselves or others are particularly challenging for the practitioner. Consultation with a supervisor or experienced practitioner is strongly recommended, whenever this would not cause undue delay. In all cases, the aim should be to ensure for the client a good quality of care that is as respectful of the client's capacity for self-determination and their trust as circumstances permit.'

Working in conjunction with other professionals

Professionals such as psychiatrists, medical practitioners, psychologists, social workers, clergy, and welfare workers frequently phone counsellors to talk with them about mutual clients. It is sometimes in the interests of such clients for other professionals to be appropriately informed about their situations. It is also desirable for counsellors to maintain good working relationships with other helping professionals. Sensible judgements need to be made about what information can be, and is, disclosed, and what is withheld. It is important to try to avoid compromising the client's trust in you as a counsellor and to respect their rights as a person.

> Working in collaboration with other
> professionals may be advantageous for the client

If you believe that it is desirable that sensitive material be disclosed, then you need to obtain the client's permission first, unless there are unusual and compelling reasons for not doing so. Obtaining the client's permission involves informing the client about what you wish to do and why. Thus the client is able to give *informed consent*. This informed consent should be verified in writing so there can be no misunderstanding. Many agencies have a standard consent form which can be used when information is to be shared. This form is discussed with the client and then signed by both the client and the counsellor.

Where two or more members of a family require counselling help, family therapy may be useful. However, if family therapy is not available, or is considered inappropriate, then any helping professionals involved with members of the family are likely to achieve more for their clients if they consult with each other, have case conferences and work together as a team. However, if this is to occur the process needs to be made transparent to all family members involved, and their consent for the sharing of information needs to be obtained.

Sometimes, you may discover that a client of yours is also consulting another counselling professional. There is rarely justification for two counsellors working with the same client, and so after discussion with the client it is sensible to contact the other counsellor to decide who will take over the case. However, as with most situations, there can be exceptions. In a small number of cases, if good contact is maintained between two counsellors, it may be possible for them both to remain involved provided that they maintain contact with each other and each set clear boundaries and goals for their work.

Participation in educational training programmes, conferences, workshops and seminars

Another problem area regarding confidentiality concerns ongoing training, upgrading of skills, and sharing of new techniques. Counsellors need to grow and develop as people and as counsellors. This can partly be done through personal supervision and partly through large group sharing at conferences, seminars, workshops, and case conferences. Client material that is presented at such events can sometimes be disguised by changing names and other details, but often this is not possible, particularly when video-recordings of counselling sessions are used. Client material should never be used in this way without the prior written consent of the client. Moreover, there could be legal as well as ethical problems if consent is not obtained.

Cases where the law requires disclosure of information

Remember that client confidentiality may be limited by legal intervention. Sometimes, counsellors are subpoenaed to give evidence in court, and in such cases withholding information may be in contempt of court. Additionally, mandatory reporting is required by counsellors from certain professions in some countries and/or states with regard to issues such as child abuse.

Respecting the client's right to privacy

Clearly, from the preceding discussion, there are many reasons why confidentiality in the counselling situation is limited. However, it is the counsellor's task to ensure that client confidentiality is preserved as far as is sensibly, legally, and ethically possible. Assure your clients that you will do this to the best of your ability, because they need to feel that whatever they share with you is protected information which will not be carelessly or unnecessarily divulged to others. It is quite unethical to talk about clients or client material to any person whatsoever, except in the circumstances previously described in this chapter. What a client shares with you is personal property and must not be shared around, so if you do have a need to talk about a client or their issues then talk with your supervisor.

> We all like to have our privacy respected

You will need to make your own decisions, in consultation with your supervisor, about how best to deal with the confidentiality issue. Our policy is to be upfront with clients and to explain the limits of confidentiality as they apply. For example, when we worked for an agency, that agency had a policy regarding confidentiality. Consequently we needed to inform clients of that policy. As private practitioners, if we believe that it would be useful or sensible to divulge information for an ethically acceptable and professional reason, then we obtain the client's informed consent, as we would if we were working for an agency.

Professional ethics

The issue of confidentiality has been discussed in some detail. However, there are many other ethical issues for counsellors, and a new counsellor needs to be informed of these. Many counsellors belong to professional associations with codes of ethical conduct. These codes are readily available on request, and it is sensible for a new counsellor to read through the relevant code for the relevant profession. Counsellors working in the United Kingdom should be fully conversant with the BACP ethical framework for good practice in counselling and psychotherapy (2002).

Some important ethical issues are included in the list below, and these will be discussed in subsequent paragraphs:

■ Respect for the client
■ Limits of the client–counsellor relationship
■ Responsibility of the counsellor
■ Counsellor competence
■ Referral
■ Termination of counselling
■ Legal obligations
■ Self-promotion.

Respect for the client

Regardless of who the client is, and regardless of their behaviour, the client has come to you for help and deserves to be treated as a human being of worth. If you treasure your client then, through feeling valued, they will be given the optimum conditions in which to maximise their potential as an individual. Most helping professionals agree that within each of us is the potential for good, and for that potential to be realised we need to feel OK about ourselves. Counsellors therefore have a responsibility to help their clients to feel OK about themselves, and to increase their feelings of self-worth.

> Give the client the respect you would like yourself

If we try to impose our own moral values on clients, then we are likely to make them feel judged and to damage their self-worth. Moreover, they are likely to reject us as counsellors and to reject our values too. Paradoxically, if we are able to accept our clients, with whatever values they have, we are likely to find that as time passes they will move closer to us in their beliefs. This is inevitable because, as counsellors, we are, whether we like it or not, models for our clients. We have a responsibility to be good models. In this regard, it can be useful to create opportunities for clients to give feedback about their experience of the counselling process. This will demonstrate respect for their views and their right to have some influence in the counselling relationship.

We need to remember that the client's interests must take precedence over those of the counsellor during the counselling process. It is not ethical to use counselling sessions with clients to work through our own issues. The correct time for working through our issues is in supervision sessions.

Limits of the client–counsellor relationship

In all our relationships we set limits. Each of us has a boundary around us to preserve our identity as an individual. The strength of that boundary, and its nature, depends on who the relationship is with, and on the context of the relationship. The client–counsellor relationship is a special type of relationship, established by the client for a particular purpose. The client enters into the relationship entrusting the counsellor with their wellbeing and expecting that the counsellor will, throughout the relationship, provide them with a safe environment in which they can work on their problems.

As discussed previously, the client–counsellor relationship is not an equal relationship and inevitably, whether the counsellor wishes it or not, the counsellor is in a position of power and influence. They are often working with clients who are in highly emotional states and are consequently very vulnerable. The way in which a counsellor relates to a client is uncharacteristic human behaviour. A counsellor devotes most of their energy to listening to and understanding the client, and so the client sees only a part of the counsellor's character. In these circumstances, a client may perceive a counsellor as unrealistically caring and giving. The counsellor's power and the client's biased perception combine to make the client very vulnerable to offers of friendship or closeness.

The counsellor is also vulnerable. In the counselling relationship, the client often shares innermost secrets, and so inevitably there may develop a real closeness between the client and counsellor. Counsellors learn to be empathic, and so they develop special relationships with their clients. If they are not careful they too become vulnerable to offers of closer relationships than are appropriate. Counsellors therefore need to be careful not to discount signposts that the counselling relationship is being compromised.

> Counsellors are vulnerable too!

Unfortunately, it is almost always unhelpful and damaging to the client when the client–counsellor relationship is allowed to extend beyond the limits of the counselling situation. If such an extension occurs, the counsellor's ability to attend to the client's needs is seriously diminished, and there may well be serious psychological consequences for the client.

As a counsellor, it may at times be hard to refuse invitations to get closer to your clients than the counselling situation allows. Remember that if you do not set appropriate boundaries you will merely be satisfying your own needs at the expense of the client. You will have abused your special position of trust as a professional, and you will have to live with that knowledge, and with any more serious consequences. When counsellors breach appropriate boundaries they may damage or diminish the usefulness of the counselling process and reduce the possibility that the client will seek further counselling help. Be aware of the danger signals when your relationship with a client is becoming too close, and bring the issue into the open by discussing it with your supervisor and with the client, if that is appropriate.

Counsellors need to exercise care if they touch a client in any way. Unwelcome touching is not only unethical, but may also be construed as sexual harassment.

Responsibility of the counsellor

Counsellors frequently experience a sense of conflict between their responsibilities to the client, to the agency which employs them, and to the community. You will at times need to make your own decisions about which of these responsibilities needs to take precedence, and in our view the decision is unlikely to always be the same. If you are in doubt about any particular decision, consult your supervisor.

Clearly, the counsellor has a responsibility to the client and needs to directly address the client's request for counselling help. When a client comes to you for confidential help, you have an implied contract with them to give them that, unless you tell them something to the contrary. You cannot ethically fulfil the client's needs if doing so would:

- involve working in opposition to the policies of the organisation that employs you;
- involve a breach of the law;
- put other members of the community at risk; or
- be impossible for you personally.

However, in these situations you need to be clear with your client about your own position, so that they understand the conditions under which they are talking to you.

Counsellors who are employed by an organisation or institution have a responsibility to that employing body. All the work they do within that organisation or institution needs to fulfil the requirements of the employing body, and to fit in with the philosophical expectations of the employing body. For example, when we both worked for the Child and Youth Mental Health Service in Queensland, it was our responsibility to comply with the policies of the Queensland Department of Health. If we had not been able to do that, then we would have had an ethical responsibility to discuss the issue with our employers, or to resign.

> We have a responsibility to the client, our employer, the community, and ourselves

Counsellors have to be aware at all times of their responsibilities to the community at large. As discussed earlier, this raises problems with regard to confidentiality. Whenever a member of the community is at risk, or property is likely to be damaged, or other illegal actions are likely to occur, or have occurred, then a counsellor needs to make a decision regarding what action is needed. Often, such decisions do not involve choosing between black and white, but rather between shades of grey, and sometimes counsellors find it difficult to decide what is most appropriate in order to serve the needs of the client and the community in the long term. At these times, the sensible approach is for a counsellor to talk through the ethical issues with their supervisor.

Counsellor competence

A counsellor has a responsibility to ensure that they give the highest possible standard of service. This cannot be done without adequate training and supervision. All counsellors need to attend to their own professional development and to have supervision from another counsellor on a regular basis. Failure to do this is certain to result in the counsellor's own issues intruding into the counselling process, and this will be to the detriment of the client (see Chapter 27).

A counsellor also needs to be aware of the limits of their competence. We all have limits professionally and personally, and it is essential that as counsellors we are able to recognise our limits and to be open with our clients about those limits. The client has a right to know whether they are seeing someone who has, or does not have, the necessary abilities to give them the help they require.

Referral

When a client's needs cannot be adequately met by a counsellor, then that counsellor has a responsibility to make an appropriate referral, in consultation with the client, to another suitable professional. However, it is not appropriate for a counsellor to avoid all difficult and unenjoyable work by excessively referring clients to others. There is a responsibility on all counsellors to carry a fair load, and to be sensible about referral decisions. Such decisions are best made in consultation with a supervisor.

It may sometimes be appropriate for a counsellor to continue seeing a client while under intensive supervision, instead of referring. If this happens, then the counsellor has a responsibility to inform the client.

Often, referral is useful where people have special needs. For example, people with particular disabilities, people from other cultures and people who speak another language may benefit from referral to an agency (or professional) which (or who) can provide for their specific needs. When referring clients to others, it may be useful to contact the professional to whom the referral is being made, with the client's permission, to ensure that the referral is acceptable and appropriate.

Termination of counselling

Termination of counselling needs to be carried out sensitively and with appropriate timing (see Chapter 10). It is not ethical to terminate counselling at a point where the client still needs further help. If for some unavoidable reason (such as leaving the district) you need to do this, then it is incumbent upon you to make a suitable referral to another counsellor who can continue to give the necessary support.

Legal obligations

Counsellors, like all other professionals and every other member of the community, need to operate within the law. Therefore, as a counsellor, you need to familiarise yourself with the relevant legal requirements for your profession. It is particularly important to know whether mandatory reporting of specific behaviours such as suspected child abuse is required.

Self-promotion

Most professional associations for counsellors have specific rules about advertising. There is clearly an ethical issue with regard to the way in which counsellors describe themselves and their services. It is unethical for a counsellor to make claims about themselves or their services which are inaccurate or cannot be substantiated. Counsellors who do this not only put their clients at risk, but may also face the possibility of prosecution.

LEARNING SUMMARY

- For counselling to be most effective a high degree of confidentiality is required.
- Confidentiality is limited by the need to keep records, professional supervision, the law, the protection of others, participation in training conferences, and co-operation with other professionals.
- Professional ethics relate to issues such as respect for the client; limits to the relationship with the client; responsibility to the client, the employing agency and the community; competence; referral to others; termination of counselling; legal obligations; and self-promotion.

References and further reading

British Association for Counselling and Psychotherapy (2002) *Ethical Framework for Good Practice in Counselling and Psychotherapy*. Rugby: BACP.
Corey, G., Corey, M. S. and Callanan, P. (2002) *Issues and Ethics in the Helping Professions*, sixth edition. California: Brooks/Cole.

Shillito-Clarke, C. (1996) Ethical Issues in Counselling Psychology. In R. Woolfe and W. Dryden (eds) *Handbook of Counselling Psychology* (pp. 555–580). London: Sage.

Woolfe, R. and Dryden, D. (1996) *Handbook of Counselling Psychology*. London: Sage.

Chapter 27

The Need for Supervision

As counsellors, we must value our clients and offer them the best help we can. It is therefore not ethical for a client to be seen by a new counsellor unless that counsellor is being adequately supervised. Additionally, our belief is that all counsellors, new and experienced, should have ongoing supervision. This belief is supported by the ethical framework of the British Association for Counselling and Psychotherapy (2002) which states that all counsellors are required to have regular and ongoing formal supervision or consultative support for their work. There are several important and quite different reasons for this including the following:

- to enable the counsellor to work through their own personal issues;
- to enable counsellors to upgrade their skills;
- to provide an external review of the counselling process for particular clients; and
- to address issues concerning dependency and professional boundaries.

We will now consider each of the above.

To enable the counsellor to work through their own personal issues

You may be surprised at the suggestion that supervision is required to enable a counsellor to work through their own personal issues. You may ask, 'If counselling is for the benefit of the client and not the counsellor, why should the counsellor use counselling supervision in order to deal with their own issues?' The answer is simple: unless a counsellor owns and deals with their own issues, these issues are quite likely to interfere with the counselling process to the detriment of the client. Frequently, a counsellor will feel emotional pain when their client discusses issues similar to the counsellor's own unresolved emotional issues. Consequently, when issues are discussed which are painful for the counsellor as a result of unresolved issues, the counsellor may consciously or unconsciously avoid their own pain in a number of ways, for example:

- the counsellor might deflect away from the painful issue by encouraging the client to talk about something else;
- the counsellor might try to comfort the client rather than to help the client to deal with the issue;
- the counsellor might attempt to encourage the client to pursue a course of action that in some way satisfies the counsellor's own needs. The counsellor may wish, for example, that they had taken a particular course of action in their own life and may encourage the client to take a similar course; or
- the counsellor may avoid facing both their own issue and the client's by failing to recognise the issues and subconsciously suppressing them.

A perceptive supervisor will spot counsellor behaviour that demonstrates avoidance of painful issues and will ask the supervisee to explore whatever was happening emotionally within them when the avoidance occurred. This means that counsellors need to be prepared to own and explore their own issues on an ongoing basis. Otherwise, these issues are likely to diminish the effectiveness of counselling.

> Effective counsellors own and explore their personal issues

Most people don't look closely at their own emotional problems unless they are causing them considerable distress. It is a natural human defence to suppress uncomfortable feelings and not to delve into them without good reason. However, a counsellor must delve into uncomfortable feelings, because if they have a problem that they can't face, then it will be quite impossible for them to help a client with a similar problem. As counsellors, therefore, we need to explore and deal with all of our own painful issues as they come into our awareness. The spin-off for us is that our personal growth is enhanced when we do this.

To enable counsellors to upgrade their skills

Even experienced counsellors find it useful and valuable to learn from other counsellors. We all have a different range of skills and use differing styles when counselling. During our counselling careers, we have both discovered that our own counselling styles have continued to change. This has enabled us to integrate new skills into our work and to continue to take a fresh approach to counselling rather than sink into a rut and become stale.

We find that it is sometimes useful for us to receive input from counsellors who use different frameworks from ours. By doing this, we usually find that we learn some new ideas for enhancing our work.

> The best counsellors never stop learning

Although didactic learning can be useful for counsellors, it seems to us that the experience of personal supervision is more powerful in promoting professional development. Learning through supervision can integrate skill training with personal growth. Additionally, the counsellor is reminded in supervision of how it is to be a client. This can be helpful in enabling a counsellor to continually meet with the client as a person of equal value.

To provide an external review of the counselling process for particular clients

Often a client will not see what seems obvious to the counsellor. This is because the client is personally and deeply involved in their situation. In comparison, the counsellor, after joining with the client and trying to see the world in the way the client does, can stand back to take a more objective view and thus see more clearly. A parallel process happens when a counsellor is being supervised. The supervisor is able to view the counselling process and the case details in a different way from the counsellor. The supervisor may recognise processes which are occurring for the client or the counsellor which have been unrecognised. Thus a supervisor is able to provide useful input on ways of working with particular clients. Additionally, good supervisors have the benefit of experience which can be a source of useful information for the supervisee.

To address issues concerning dependency and professional boundaries

As discussed in the previous paragraph, a supervisor may recognise processes that have not been recognised by the counsellor. Of specific importance are issues of dependency and respect for professional boundaries.

It can sometimes be hard for new counsellors to recognise when the time for terminating a series of counselling sessions has been reached. This may be partly due to issues of dependence that inevitably will develop in some counselling relationships (see Chapter 10). Sometimes, it is hard for a counsellor to recognise whether the client really does have a need for further counselling or whether dependency is occurring either on the part of the client or the counsellor themselves.

> Both clients and counsellors experience dependency issues

Dependent clients sometimes produce new material for discussion when the counselling process is moving towards closure. This may be as a consequence of a subconscious or conscious desire to prolong the counselling relationship. By discussing cases in supervision, a supervisor may be able to recognise when dependency is interfering with appropriate termination processes. Additionally a supervisor may be able to help a counsellor devise suitable strategies for managing dependency issues.

Some counsellors have difficulty in recognising when their own personal feelings towards a client could result in behaviours which would inappropriately transgress professional boundaries and consequently interfere with the counselling process. Additionally, new counsellors sometimes have difficulty in knowing how to respond to direct and/or indirect client invitations for friendship and closeness. Once again, supervision can help a counsellor to recognise inappropriate processes that are occurring and to develop appropriate strategies to deal with these processes.

What does supervision involve?

There are a number of ways in which supervision can occur:

1 by direct observation with the supervisor in the counselling room;
2 by direct observation through a one-way mirror;
3 by observation using a closed-circuit TV;

4 by use of audio- or video-recording and analysis;
5 by direct observation together with audio- or video-recording and analysis; or
6 by use of a verbatim report.

These methods will be discussed in turn.

Direct observation with the supervisor in the counselling room

Trainee counsellors are usually apprehensive about seeing their first few clients. A good way to help them adjust to the counselling environment is for trainees to sit in on counselling sessions conducted by their supervisors. Naturally, the permission of the client is required. Student counsellors who are allowed to do this need to understand what their supervisor expects of them. We prefer our students to take a low profile and to sit quietly out of the line of vision of the client. This reduces the necessity for the client to feel the need to interact with one of us and the student simultaneously, leaves us free to conduct the session in the way that we choose, and enables the trainee to observe without feeling pressured to participate. As the trainee's level of comfort increases, some participation by them can occur. Adopting this approach allows them to directly observe the counselling process, and to feel at ease while being in the same room as the client in a counselling situation. The method allows the trainee gradually to make the transition from being a passive observer to being an active counsellor under supervision.

The process just described is excellent for beginners who have had no previous counselling experience, but there are problems connected with having both the trainee and supervisor in the room together. Obviously, some of the intimacy of the counselling relationship is lost, and as a consequence the client may find it difficult to deal openly with sensitive issues.

Direct observation through a one-way mirror

The one-way mirror system as shown in Figure 27.1 provides an alternative to direct observation. Many counselling centres have a pair of adjacent rooms set up like this for training purposes and for family therapy. The one-way mirror allows a person in the observation room to watch what is happening in the counselling room without being seen. A microphone, amplifier, and speaker system provide sound for the observer, so that they are able to see and hear what is happening. Ethically, it is imperative that a client who is being observed from behind a one-way mirror is informed in

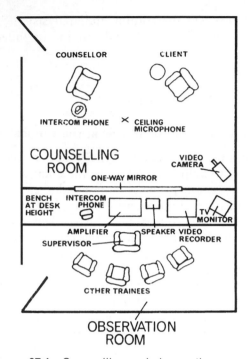

Figure 27.1 Counselling and observations rooms

advance about the presence of the observer or observers, and that consent is obtained for the session to proceed in this way.

The one-way mirror system can initially be used to enable a trainee or trainees to watch an experienced counsellor at work. Later, the trainee can work as a counsellor while being observed by their supervisor, and possibly by other trainees also. The system has the advantage that the supervisor is not present in the counselling room and therefore does not intrude on the counselling process. However, they are available to take over from the trainee if that becomes necessary, and they can give objective feedback after the session is completed.

Observation using a closed-circuit TV

A similar method to the one-way mirror system is to have a video camera in the counselling room connected to a TV monitor in another room. However, this method doesn't provide as much visual detail as is obtained with the one-way mirror system. It is often difficult to see facial expressions if the camera has a wide-angle lens to enable most of the room to be in the picture.

One of the best methods of supervision is by use of video-recordings. Audio-recordings can also be used, although their usefulness is more limited because non-verbal behaviour cannot be observed. Video-recordings of counselling sessions are a rich source of information. Not only may selected segments of a session be viewed repeatedly, but it is also possible to freeze the picture so that non-verbals may be studied.

Whenever an audio- or video-recording is made it is essential to obtain the prior written consent of the client, and to tell them who will have access to the recording and when it is to be erased. Many agencies have standard consent forms for clients to sign. It is sensible to have such forms checked for their legal validity.

Use of audio- or video-recording and analysis

Sometimes counsellors audio- or video-tape sessions without their supervisor observing at the time. Such tapes provide an excellent opportunity for supervision. The supervisor and counsellor can then review and analyse parts of the tape. Often it can be useful for the counsellor to review additional tapes on their own in order to recognise unsatisfactory processes and to improve their counselling techniques.

> Video-tapes are an excellent learning tool

Direct observation together with audio- or video-recording and analysis

A combination of a one-way mirror system together with audio- or video-recording is a very powerful arrangement for counsellor training. Trainees can be directly observed during practice sessions, and may later process their work in detail with their supervisors by analysing and reviewing the audio- or video-recordings.

Use of a verbatim report

Another method of supervision is by use of the verbatim report. A verbatim report is a written report which records, word for word, the client's statements and the counsellor's responses. It may be produced from memory, or as a transcript of an audio recording. Here is an example of a verbatim report. Note that this example is invented and does not relate to a real client or counsellor.

Example of a verbatim report

Name of counsellor: Fiona Smith
Name of client: Simon Anonymous
Date of counselling session: 19.1.05
Background information about the client: Simon is 36 years old, has been married twice, and has two children. These are a girl, 12, and a boy, 10. Both children are in the custody of Simon's second wife. He lives alone.

This was Simon's second visit to see me. He came a week ago feeling tense and depressed. He told me that he was worried about his inability to build relationships with women, and he couldn't understand why.

My feelings and attitudes prior to the session: I was feeling good and was looking forward to working with this client again. I believed that I had built a good relationship with him during the previous session and that this would enable him to talk freely with me.

What occurred prior to the responses given below: When Simon arrived for this session he looked pale and was very subdued. During the first 15 minutes of our time together, his body looked tense and he seemed reluctant to talk. After a few minutes of silence, I felt as though he had put a barrier between us and I spoke.

F1 Seems like there's a barrier between us. (Said quietly.)
S1 *Ah what ... what da ya mean? (I thought he sounded defensive.)*
F2 Like we're separated by a barrier. (I used my hands to suggest a barrier.)
S2 *Separated? (Said with non-verbals that suggested disbelief and questioning. I felt very shut out from Simon now.)*
F3 Yes, I feel shut out by an invisible barrier. Sometimes you open it up a ... (Simon interrupted heatedly.)
S3 *No, no, it's a double brick wall with a door in it. The door is usually closed and that's because it keeps me safe.*
F4 That brick wall's important to you!
S4 *It sure is!*

F5   It protects you. (Simon started to talk freely and easily after this.)

S5   *Yes, it does ... (He went on to explain how vulnerable he would feel without the wall, and then started to cry. I waited.) ... You see, I've been hurt too much in the past, and I'm scared that if I'm me, if I'm really me, and open up, then I'll be rejected again.*

F6   The barrier protects you from the pain of rejection. (Long pause.)

S6   *It also prevents me from getting into a relationship and I'm not sure that I like that. (Said carefully, slowly, and firmly.)*

F7   You don't sound sure about whether you want the barrier or not.

S7   *Well, it would be hard to tear it down. I'm so used to it now. You know I realise that the barrier's been there for a long time now. Goodness knows what might happen if I didn't have it there.*

F8   It would be risky to tear it down.

S8   *It would. (He paused to think for what seemed a long time. I had difficulty staying silent because I wanted to tell him what he was discovering for himself.) ... You know, I would get hurt for sure, and what's worse, I'd have to take responsibility for the ways I hurt the women I get close to. (He laughed.) That's worse. That's worse! I can't bear it when I hurt someone I love.*

F9   Getting close involves lots of hurt. (He interrupted, fortunately, before I was able to take him off track by suggesting getting close could also involve pleasure. I was bursting to tell him!)

S9   *Yes, it seems like that to me ... (He then told me in detail about his pain at losing his wife. He couldn't understand how he hurt so much when he had left her) ... It's not over yet. How can I still be hurting after so long?*

F10 I get the impression that you're still grieving.

S10 *I should be over her by now! (Said despairingly.)*

F11 It takes time to grieve. Can you give
     yourself time?

From here on the process flowed naturally as he dealt with his grief. I got the strong feeling that his barrier would gradually disintegrate as he worked through his grief.

My feelings after the session: I felt good because Simon had moved forwards to a fuller awareness of himself and his behaviour. Additionally, I realised that I had been infected by some of his sadness.

What I have learnt from the session (or things I would do differently another time): I learnt that it was helpful for the client when I shared with him my own feelings (of separation, see F1, F2 and F3). Because he interrupted (F9 and S9), I discovered that it was better to follow his path. If I had brought the focus on to the pleasure associated with closeness then I would have made it more difficult for him to address the underlying issue of his grief. I learnt that my desire 'to make the client feel good' could have been counterproductive. I'm pleased he interrupted and prevented me from doing this.

Structure of the verbatim report

As you will see from the example of a verbatim report, the report begins with background information about the client, their problems, and their emotional state. The first part of the report may also summarise the process and outcome of previous counselling sessions.

The next section of the report concerns the counsellor's own feelings and attitudes prior to the counselling session. This information is required because a counsellor's behaviour and performance are often influenced by their mood, feelings generally, and feelings towards the client, and their preconceived ideas and attitudes concerning the client and the client's behaviour.

A central component of the verbatim report is the section containing client statements and counsellor responses. This section usually contains only about 10 to 20 responses from each person. It would be very laborious to write out a transcript of a substantial part of a counselling interaction and this is unnecessary. Preferably the trainee counsellor will select a portion of the session that demonstrates some important learning or highlights some difficulties. Often a new counsellor will find that a part of the interaction seems to 'go wrong' inexplicably. Such a segment provides ideal material for a verbatim report and subsequent discussion in supervision. Notice that responses are numbered and identified by the initial letter of the person's name. For example, statement F7 is Fiona's seventh in the report. After each statement other significant information is recorded, in parentheses, including non-verbal behaviour, silences, and the feelings and thoughts of the counsellor.

Immediately before the verbatim client and counsellor statements is a description of what occurred in the session prior to them, and immediately after them is a brief description of what occurred in the remaining part of the session. These descriptions are required so that the statements that are recorded verbatim are seen in the context of the whole session.

The verbatim report concludes with sections that describe the counsellor's feelings after the session and what they have learnt for the future. It is then signed.

The value of verbatim reports

Verbatim reports enable a supervisor to tap into trainee issues that might have blocked them from satisfactorily helping the client to work through their issues. Such reports also enable the supervisor to identify unsatisfactory processes and inappropriate counsellor responses and to help the trainee discover better ones.

Confidentiality

Audio-recordings, video recordings, and verbatim reports require the same level of protection as client records in order to ensure that confidentiality is preserved (see Chapter 26). It is essential that tapes and reports are not left in places where they might fall into the hands of unauthorised persons.

In conclusion

By using any of the methods described in this chapter, a supervisor can help a new counsellor to improve their skills and to understand the process that occurred during a particular counselling session. This chapter has discussed ways in which you may be supervised as a new counsellor. Your initial training is just the beginning, and there is no end to the ongoing need for further training. A good counsellor never stops learning from their own experiences and from what others can teach them. In order to improve, it is essential to continue in supervision even as an experienced counsellor.

> Ongoing supervision is the key to good counselling

The counselling strategies described in this book are the basic ones. Once you have mastered them, you may wish to continue to learn from experienced counsellors who have advanced skills or who are skilled in specialised counselling techniques. We believe that ongoing training can best be carried out through experiential training in workshops and seminars, together with hands-on experience under the supervision of a qualified and experienced practitioner.

LEARNING SUMMARY

- It is not ethical for a new counsellor to see clients without adequate supervision.
- A counsellor's own unresolved issues will adversely affect the counselling process.
- Common supervision methods involve direct observation, observation using a closed-circuit; TV, audio- or video-recording and analysis, and use of verbatim reports.

Further reading

British Association for Counselling and Psychotherapy (2002) *Ethical Framework for Good Practice in Counselling and Psychotherapy*. Rugby: BACP.

Feltham, C. and Dryden, W. (1994) *Developing Counsellor Supervision*. London: Sage.

Holloway, E. L. (1995) *Clinical Supervision: A Systems Approach*. Thousand Oaks: Sage.

Chapter 28

Looking After Yourself

A counsellor's own wellbeing is of paramount importance, for the following reasons. Firstly, counsellors are human beings with their own needs so it is appropriate for them to be sensible in caring for themselves. Additionally, from a professional point of view, it is essential for counsellors to look after themselves because counsellors who are not feeling good are unlikely to be fully effective in helping their clients. Counselling can be draining, so counsellors need support; otherwise they are likely to find themselves emotionally depleted. If they are to feel good they must resolve their own personal issues satisfactorily while receiving the support they need. This can be done as described previously, through regular supervision from an experienced counsellor (see Chapter 27).

> All counsellors are susceptible to burnout

In recent years, it has become clear that all counsellors at times experience what is known as 'burnout'. Burnout is disabling, but if it is recognised in its early stages, then it is comparatively easy to take remedial action. Even experienced counsellors fail at times to recognise the onset of burnout and try to convince themselves that the symptoms they are experiencing are due to some other cause. It is difficult for many counsellors to admit to themselves, let alone to others, that they are burning out, even though there is now general acceptance that burnout is a common problem. The first step in dealing with burnout is to be aware of the symptoms.

283

Burnout symptoms

There are many symptoms that come under the general heading of burnout. These symptoms give an indication that a counsellor is becoming drained emotionally by the counselling work and is wanting to draw back. Counsellors may experience a feeling of being totally overworked and of having no control over their workload. They may perceive themselves as swimming against the tide and unable to keep their heads above water. This leads to feelings of hopelessness and helplessness.

Physical and emotional symptoms

Counsellors experiencing burnout are usually tired physically, emotionally and mentally. They start to feel that they can't face meeting another client. Typically, a counsellor may say to themselves during a counselling session: 'I really can't bear to be here. I wish this person would just go away.' The counsellor may also experience being physically debilitated and find it hard to drag themselves to work. Their enthusiasm has evaporated, and they may have physical symptoms such as headaches, stomach-aches, skin disorders, high blood pressure or back and neck pains. Their susceptibility to viruses and other infections is increased.

Negative attitudes

Burnt out counsellors may develop strong negative attitudes towards clients. They may develop a cynical attitude to their clients and blame them for creating their own problems. They may even start to treat their clients in an impersonal way, as though they were objects and not human beings. Consequently, the counselling relationship will suffer and counselling will become a chore, rather than an interesting, challenging, and creative activity. Such counsellors no longer find satisfaction in their work. Negative attitudes may also be experienced towards fellow workers, supervisors, other staff, and the employing organisation.

Disillusionment

Disillusionment with the counselling process is a major burnout symptom. Counsellors start to question the value of their work and begin to wonder if what they are doing is worthwhile. Burnt out counsellors will often be unable to see any evidence of success in their work. They feel frustrated by their inability to bring about change in their clients and are dissatisfied with their job, believing that it involves giving and getting nothing in return. This leads to feelings of failure and low self-esteem. The demands of clients become too great and the counsellor may just want to withdraw from the helping situation. In the advanced stages of burnout, counsellors start taking days off sick, and may start frantically looking for a new job so that they can resign.

Personal consequences

One of the sad consequences of burnout is that it is likely to affect the counsellor's personal life. As a counsellor's self-esteem diminishes, their personal relationships may be put in jeopardy and other people may become targets for feelings of anger, frustration, helplessness, and hopelessness.

A major cause of burnout

What is the primary cause of burnout? Well, we can't be certain, and all counsellors are different, but it seems likely that a major cause of burnout is the stress of the interpersonal counselling relationship. This is an unbalanced relationship, with the counsellor doing most of the giving and the client doing most of the receiving.

In the early chapters of this book, heavy emphasis was put on establishing an empathic relationship, and on the need to join with the client. It is essential that, as a counsellor, you learn to do this effectively, because *empathy* is one of the essential ingredients of successful counselling. However, *being empathic can be hazardous to a counsellor's health!* That is, unless proper precautions are taken.

> Emotions are infectious

Clients are often in a highly emotional state, and if a counsellor listens with empathy and joins with an emotional client, then the counsellor is likely to be infected by the client's emotional state. Emotions, like viruses, are catching, which is probably why people who aren't counsellors try to calm their friends down when they are emotional. After all, who wants to be emotionally distressed? In contrast to most friends, many counsellors encourage people to experience and express their emotions fully. Empathic counsellors are certain to experience, at some level, emotions similar to those of their clients. Clearly, no counsellor can afford to be emotionally distressed for a significant part of the working day, because to allow this to happen would be certain to result in burnout. Counsellors who are working mainly with emotionally disturbed clients are therefore very much at risk and need to take special precautions to avoid burnout.

Protecting yourself

With experience, you will learn how to walk beside a client with empathy and also how to protect yourself from the excesses of emotional pain by at times moving back for a while, grounding yourself, and then joining more fully with the client again. Certainly, if you are to protect yourself from burnout, you will need to learn how to do this. David will describe the technique he uses for himself, and then you will need to experiment for yourself, to find out what works best for you. 'In a counselling session, when I notice that I am starting to experience a client's emotional pain excessively, I immediately set about grounding myself. This grounding process takes only a second or two to happen, but will take longer to describe ...'

Using an imaginary space-bubble

'I imagine myself to be encapsulated by a plastic space-bubble which separates me from outside emotions, but enables me to observe them, and allows me to respond to them appropriately. I then slow down my breathing and relax my body, so that my troubled emotional state is replaced by tranquillity. In my imagination, I float, in the space-bubble, upwards and backwards to a position several metres behind and above my body. It is as though the part of me in the bubble is able to observe both the client and the physical me, which is still sitting in my counselling chair. I am still able to concentrate fully, but am more detached and less involved. In this position, I can make sensible decisions with regard to the counselling process. However, I can in a split second travel back in my imagination to my counselling chair, to give empathic attention and empathic responses to the client.'

'Clearly, I have a powerful imagination, and have trained myself to relax quickly, when necessary. You will need to experiment for yourself, to devise an effective way in which you can protect yourself from emotional damage due to excessive exposure to client pain.'

> If you are becoming overwhelmed move back to a more objective position

'Despite the above discussion, there will inevitably be times when, as a counsellor, you *are* affected by the emotional traumas of your clients, as at times I am. Personally, I don't think that it is helpful to let a client know that I have been emotionally affected by what they have told me. Most clients are caring people who do not like to upset others. Consequently, if a client thinks that I have been emotionally disturbed by what I have heard, then they may be less likely to tell me about other disturbing information. Counsellors therefore need to control the expression of their own emotions appropriately, so that clients feel able to talk freely.'

Recharging

If you are left in an emotionally disturbed state after a counselling session, talk to your supervisor about your feelings as soon as possible. If your supervisor isn't available, you may need to talk with another counsellor. If another counsellor isn't available, another alternative is to debrief by writing down your feelings and thoughts and allowing yourself to express your emotions in an appropriate way. Remember: the counselling relationship is substantially a one-way relationship, in which the counsellor is the giver and the client is the taker. Such a relationship will inevitably drain the counsellor of emotional energy. Clearly, unless a counsellor recharges, they will experience the symptoms of burnout as they become drained.

Other factors which lead to burnout

The dangers of over-involvement

It is important to be aware of the dangers of over-involvement with clients and their issues. We all have different personalities and differing capabilities for coping with emotionally stressful situations. Some counsellors get over-involved with their clients and take their client's problems home with them, whereas other people are more philosophical and are less affected by their counselling work. A while ago, while working at a crisis counselling agency, David trained himself so that when he left his place of work, he allowed himself to think about client material only until he reached a particular set of traffic lights. Once he had passed these lights, he gave himself the option of going back to work to think about clients, or of forgetting them and continuing his journey home. He invariably continued his journey.

Suicidal clients

Experienced counsellors who deal with suicidal or violent clients have an extremely stressful time and are particularly prone to burnout. A counsellor who has a high caseload of suicidal clients has little option but to accept that, even with the use of properly accountable practices, eventually a client may succeed in killing themselves. This knowledge creates anxiety in the counsellor and increases the likelihood of burnout. Remember that it is not appropriate to blame yourself for what you are unable to prevent. Protect yourself, as a new counsellor, by ensuring that such clients are referred for appropriate professional help.

Isolation

Being isolated and working alone puts a counsellor at increased risk of burnout, because of a lack of peer support during the working day. After all, if we are being drained of our energy, we need to be able to get some back by interacting with others who can meet with us in more equal two-way relationships.

Personal stress

A stressful personal life is almost certain to make a counsellor more susceptible to burnout because of diminished emotional resources.

Combating burnout

As stated before, many counsellors are afraid to admit to themselves, let alone to other people, that they are starting to experience burnout symptoms, because they feel that it would be an admission of failure. This is understandable for many reasons. Firstly, most of us have learnt from childhood to appear to be strong enough to cope with our load, whatever that may be. That learning is based on a myth that human beings are inexhaustible, which is obviously not true. Secondly, new counsellors invariably start counselling with very high ideals and unrealistically high expectations of what they will be able to achieve.

Having realistic expectations

Our own experiences as counsellors lead us to believe that usually the outcomes of counselling interventions are helpful for the client. However, there are times when a client does not seem to be helped by the counselling process and when this does happen, it would be easy for us to become disillusioned. At times like this we remind ourselves of the need to look at the overall picture.

Outcomes with clients are often different from what the counsellor would prefer, and it is therefore necessary to have realistic expectations in order to avoid disillusionment. The idealism of the new counsellor can easily be eroded and lead to later dissatisfaction if unrealistic expectations are not fulfilled.

Giving with no expectation of return, caring for people unconditionally, and being dedicated to counselling work are all attitudes that are implicitly absorbed as part of many counsellor training programmes. These attitudes conflict strongly with feelings that may be experienced during burnout. It is therefore not surprising that counsellors find it difficult to own burnout feelings.

Accepting that burnout is normal

It is strongly recommended that counsellor training programmes always include education for trainee counsellors about the inevitability of burnout occurring at times, even in the most dedicated counsellor. If counsellors realise that burnout feelings do occur in normal, competent, capable and caring counsellors, then they will be able to start accepting their own burnout feelings and to share those feelings with their peers and other professionals.

> If we accept that burnout is inevitable we can deal with it appropriately

Burnout comes in cycles and it is helpful to expect these cycles to occur. It is healthy to say, 'Ah-ha, I'm starting to recognise some of the symptoms of burnout.' By making that simple statement, a counsellor is able to admit truthfully what is happening and is then empowered to take the necessary action to deal with the problem.

Most counsellors start their job with some feelings of nervousness, but very soon this is followed by enthusiasm and excitement. However, it doesn't take long for other feelings to set in. These may be feelings of stagnation and apathy, or even of frustration and annoyance. In other words, the counsellor's initial enthusiasm and excitement will, from time to time, be replaced by feelings associated with burnout. In the same way, by using sensible burnout management techniques, the initial enthusiasm about counselling can be re-experienced.

Actively dealing with burnout

Quite often people look for a new job or resign as a result of burnout. That is one way of dealing with it, but it is not necessary to do that if you recognise the symptoms early enough and do something positive to deal with them. Experiencing burnout is not a disaster if it is recognised and dealt with effectively. For a counsellor, dealing with burnout can be compared to a car owner servicing a car. The car needs to be serviced regularly or the car will not function well. Similarly, as a counsellor take steps to continually look after your own needs. If you become aware of burnout feelings, take the appropriate action to recharge yourself, to regain your enthusiasm and the excitement you experienced at the beginning of your counselling career. This can be done time and again, so you can work as a counsellor for a lifetime if you choose by recharging yourself and starting afresh from time to time.

Here are some suggestions for dealing with burnout:

1 Recognise and own the symptoms.
2 Talk with someone about your feelings.
3 Re-schedule your work.
4 Cut down on your workload.
5 Take a holiday.
6 Use relaxation or meditation.
7 Use positive self-talk.
8 ower your expectations of yourself, your clients, your colleagues, and your employer.
9 Allow yourself to enjoy life and have a sense of humour.
10 Use thought-stopping to stop worrying about clients when not at work.
11 Use your religious or other belief system for support.
12 Care for yourself as a person by doing some nice things for yourself.

Consider some of these ideas. Firstly, it is interesting to note that simply admitting that you are experiencing burnout will affect your behaviour and enable you to cope better. Talking with your supervisor or someone else may also be helpful, as by doing this you may be able to clarify your options more easily with regard to suitable methods of intervention.

It can be helpful to re-schedule your work so that you have a feeling of being in control. You may need to be assertive if your boss doesn't understand your need for a reduced workload. Reducing your workload may not be sufficient initially, and you may need to take a few days off, to have a holiday or to take some days off sick. Help yourself to feel more relaxed, more in control and fitter. Build into your lifestyle proper times for rest, recreation, exercise, light-hearted relief and relaxation. Doing relaxation exercises or meditating can be helpful. Use positive self-talk to replace negative self-statements and challenge the negative self-statements you make about others. This involves changing your expectations of yourself, your clients, and your peers.

> Take action to lead a balanced life

A useful way to deal with burnout is to take a less serious view of life, to allow yourself to have a sense of humour and to be less intense in your work. Be carefree and have fun. Most importantly, do not take client problems home. If you do catch yourself doing this, practise thought-stopping. The first step in thought-stopping is to recognise that you are thinking about client problems when you should be relaxing. Then recognise your choice, to continue thinking about these problems or to focus your attention on something in your present environment. This may involve doing something physical or it may involve concentrating on something specific such as listening to music. Focus all your energy and attention on the 'here and now' to block out the intruding thoughts. Sometimes you may find that the intruding thoughts recur and you may catch yourself saying, 'If I don't think about this client problem now, then I will never deal with it and that will be bad for the client.' If such a thought comes into your mind, then write a note in your diary to deal with that issue at a particular time when you are at your place of work, and say to yourself, 'OK, at 10 o'clock tomorrow morning, at work, I will devote half an hour to thinking about that problem, but right now I will get on with doing and thinking about things that are pleasant for me.'

Many counsellors find strength in their religious beliefs and gain through prayer and meditation. They find that by doing this they receive an inner strength that enables them to be more effective in their work. Similarly, people with other philosophical belief systems can use their philosophy of life as an aid in combating burnout.

If you care for yourself, and take appropriate action to attend to your own needs by leading a less pressured and more balanced life, then your burnout symptoms are likely to fade and you will be able to regain your energy and enthusiasm. However, if you are like most counsellors, you will have an ongoing struggle with burnout which will come and go. There will always be times when you will give too much of yourself, and then need to redress the balance so that your own needs for recharging are adequately met.

Gaining satisfaction from counselling

If you are pro-active in caring for yourself, then you will be more able to care for others. You will be likely to get satisfaction from counselling and to enjoy being a counsellor. We hope that you, the reader, will gain as much personal fulfilment from counselling as we have. We wish you all the best for your work.

LEARNING SUMMARY

- Counselling can be emotionally draining for the counsellor.
- Regular supervision is a good way to avoid burnout, as it provides an opportunity for resolution of the counsellor's own issues.

LEARNING SUMMARY (cont'd)

■ Burnout includes the following symptoms: feelings of disillusionment, being emotionally and physically drained; somatic symptoms, and negative attitudes to clients.

■ Burnout comes in cycles, but with self-awareness and adequate supervision recharging can occur.

■ Methods for dealing with burnout include:
  – recognising the symptoms and talking with someone about them;
  – changing your workload or schedule;
  – taking a break;
  – using relaxation, meditation or positive self-talk;
  – lowering your expectations;
  – taking life less seriously and having a sense of humour;
  – using thought-stopping; and
  – using your religious or other belief system for support.

Further reading

Carter, R. and Gollant, S. K. (1994) *Helping Yourself Help Others: A Book for Caregivers*. New York: Times Books.

Grosh, W. N. and Olsen, D. C. (1995) Prevention: avoiding burnout. In: M. B. Sussman (ed.) *A Perilous Calling: The Hazards of Psychotherapy Practice*. New York: Wiley.

Part VI

Practice Examples
for Students

Chapter 29

Practice Examples for Students

The examples provided in this section enable students to gain practice in the use of the counselling skills which are described in Parts II and IV of this book.

Chapter 5
Client statements for use when learning to paraphrase

1 'My brother has had a serious motorbike accident and it looks as though he may be permanently crippled. He's a builder by trade and now he may never be able to walk again. I don't know how he'll be able to work.'

2 'The cancer is malignant and now I only have six months to live at the most. There is so much that I want to do and I can't decide what to do first. I am certainly going to have to do things in a hurry.'

3 'The law is very unjust. He discovered where I live, followed me, deliberately aimed the gun, and fired several shots directly at me to try to kill me. He even asked the police if I was dead, and then he's given a light sentence on so-called psychiatric grounds. It's not fair.'

4 'I've never stayed in one place for more than a couple of years. In the last few months I've lived in five different houses. It's hardly worth unpacking when I move now because I know I'll move on again. I just can't settle.'

5 'The pain starts in my head and moves down into my back. Sometimes my whole body aches. The pain never stops and is overwhelming.'

6   'I think my father is a hypocrite. He's a preacher who preaches love and forgiveness and is charming to everybody except his own family. In the family he's a tyrant who bullies everyone and is unforgiving. I'm rapidly losing my respect for him.'

Chapter 6
Client statements for use when learning to use reflection of feelings

1   'I don't know how I'm going to do it all. I have to go to work, pay the bills, look after the children, do the washing, and clean the house, all before Wednesday. I just can't do it!'
2   'I know he's got a gun and he could come round to the house at any time. The police say they can't do anything because he hasn't done anything yet. It'll be too late when they do come to help. I'll be dead.'
3   'He's a good boy and I love him but he does get into trouble. I never know what he's going to get up to next. Every day I wonder who is going to come knocking at the door to tell me something terrible.'
4   'We won. We won the big prize, the new car!'
5   'My brother died last week. I miss him dreadfully. I wish I hadn't criticised him so much recently because he was really a very good person.'
6   'My mother treats me like dirt. She never praises me for anything. Colleen gets all the praise. All I get is black looks.'

Chapter 7
Client statements for use when learning to reflect content and feelings

1   'My children are able to use computers without worrying. They learnt to use them at school. Unfortunately, I haven't been able to keep up with the times and, as a result, I don't think that my children respect me. I feel quite stupid.'
2   'Every time my father comes to visit me I dread the time when he'll leave to go home because he lives such a long way away and he's so old now. He's going back this weekend and I can't stop thinking that maybe I'll never see him again.'
3   'My son is driving me crazy. He never stops doing silly things. I have to watch him all the time. Yesterday he climbed onto the roof and then fell out of a tree. I'm starting to lose patience with him.'

4 'I can't make sense of what Freda wants. Firstly, she asks me to go to visit her on Friday and then she tells me that if I do she'll feel overwhelmed. I just don't know what to do.'
5 'Some very strange things are happening. A disreputable looking person keeps hanging around my house and I'm not sure but I think that some things have disappeared. I think I'll have to be careful to check that the house is kept locked.'
6 'My partner has left and I can't track him down. I wish I could find him and tell him that I still love him and want him back. I know that I've hurt him badly by having the affair. Now it's me that's suffering.'

Chapter 8
Examples of closed questions which can be converted to open questions

1 'Do you intend to arrive at 2 p.m.?'
2 'Are you disappointed?'
3 'Do you have two children?'
4 'Is your household always tense?'
5 'Will you achieve your goals by writing to him?'
6 'Did that happen on Thursday?'

Chapter 9
Transcript for use when learning how to summarise

Students can be asked to identify the types of counsellor responses used and to add a summary to complete the transcript.

Client: *My anxiety rises when I think about going to work. I almost start to panic ... I wonder how I am going to cope with another day at that place.*

Counsellor: You're really worried. (Counselling skill used: _____)

Client: *Worried? I feel as though I'm going crazy. I despair. The new boss is putting in place policies which infuriate me. They disadvantage our customers and are frankly disrespectful. She doesn't seem to understand the basics of modern commercial practice and if I comply with her wishes I will compromise my own standards. I just don't know what to do.*

Counsellor: You are faced with a dilemma. (Counselling skill used: _____)

Client: *Yes, I am. If I continue to work there I either have to compromise my ideals or I will be in continual conflict with my boss. I'd like to leave,* *but the pay is excellent, and in the present economic climate good jobs in my line are difficult to find.*

Counsellor: You're stuck in a frustrating situation because finding a new job wouldn't be easy. (Counselling skill used: _____)

Client: *It wouldn't. There aren't many jobs being advertised right now. But I'll keep looking because I do want to leave and eventually a new opportunity is sure to turn up. I suppose in the meantime I'll have to make the best of the present situation. That's where my difficulty lies.*

Counsellor: What ideas do you have about ways of responding to your current work situation? (Counselling skill used: _____)

Client: *Well, I suppose that I could avoid conflict by following the new policy but interpreting it fairly loosely whenever I can. Also, I could be clear with customers that I don't have any alternative but to follow company policy. That way, I would be making it clear that I wasn't being personally uncooperative. I'd need to be careful how I did that though, because I do have some loyalty towards the firm.*

Counsellor: I am getting the impression that you believe that you could accept some compromise without too much difficulty. (Counselling skill used: _____)

Client: *Yes, there are ways to alter the way I work without feeling personally compromised, particularly if I remember that I intend to leave as soon as I can … mm … Yes, I know what to do.*

Counsellor: [SUMMARY: ....]

Chapter 13
Examples for use when learning to use appropriate confrontation

Write suitable counsellor statements of confrontation for the following examples.

1 The client tells the counsellor that he is very keen to receive counselling help, but repeatedly arrives for appointments up to three-quarters of an hour late.

2 The client has made it clear on several occasions that she is coming to counselling to address the post-traumatic effects of abuse during her childhood. However, each time she arrives for counselling she deflects away from talking about the abuse by introducing a range of other unrelated issues.

3 The client admits to pushing and slapping his wife, but minimises this behaviour and blames her for his behaviour, saying that she is provocative. He doesn't see that he needs to take responsibility for what he does.
4 When the counsellor reflects back what she sees as angry non-verbal behaviour, the client denies being angry but continues to look and sound angry and to make statements which suggest that she is angry.
5 Although the client does not appear to be under any threat, he is responding to others from a disempowered, victim, 'poor me', position instead of being assertive in letting others know about his needs.

Chapter 14
Examples for use when learning the skill of normalising

For each of the case descriptions below devise suitable counsellor normalising statements and explain how you would use that statement to help the client.

1 An elderly lady who had a successful career has recently retired. She is now bored with life, has no interests, and sees herself as a failure.
2 A man in his twenties who has previously enjoyed a single life has recently moved into a close live-in relationship with a friend. He is confused because he says that he loves his friend and wants to continue the relationship. However, he feels claustrophobic and unable to do the things which he would like to do for himself.
3 The father of a young child says that he and his partner (the child's mother) are having difficulty managing the child's behaviour and are arguing with each other about how to parent the child. It has emerged in the counselling process that the father's own family of origin was very easy-going and that physical punishment was never used. However, his partner's family of origin believed in the use of strict rules, with physical punishment for disobedience.
4 A middle-aged woman is unable to work or sleep and cannot understand 'what is the matter with her'. In counselling, it transpires that there have been three deaths of near relatives in recent weeks. She herself worries about whether she has bowel cancer, but is avoiding seeking medical advice.
5 In a time of very high unemployment a 50-year-old, who was retrenched as a senior executive nine months ago, says that he has been unable to find employment. He feels deeply depressed, has lost his motivation, and feels like a failure.

Chapter 15
Examples of client statements for use when learning reframing

Reframe the following statements:

1   'My teenage daughter is a great disappointment to me. I thought that when she reached this age she and I would be good friends and would spend lots of time together. All she wants now is to do her own thing. I'm just irrelevant as far as she's concerned.'
2   'My husband interferes in everything I do. I just need to start doing something and he's there, taking over. I'm starting to think that I must be an incompetent idiot who isn't capable of doing anything for herself.'
3   ' "Don't sniff, stand up straight, don't be late, be polite", that's all I hear from Mum. She says she loves me but I don't think that she even likes me any more.'
4   'I don't know why the manager picks on me all the time. Whenever there is a difficult job to do or a difficult customer to deal with she always gives the work to me. She's obviously trying to make my life as difficult as possible.'
5   'I'm totally exhausted and realise I've been very stupid. In just a few months, I've completely redecorated my house, written several journal articles for publication while working full time in a very demanding job, driven 200 kilometres and back to see my dying brother most weekends, and organised a group project for the local community. I seem to be unable to stop working compulsively. I feel really depressed by my inability to relax and enjoy life.'
6   'My friends tells me that I'm completely stupid because I keep going out with my girlfriend who treats me in a very offhand way. Maybe they're right!'

Chapter 16
Examples for use when learning to challenge self-destructive beliefs

Replace the self-destructive beliefs below by more helpful beliefs.

1   'Other people should always agree with me.'
2   'I should be able to expect that people will be reliable and trust-worthy.'

3 'Other people should always respect me.'
4 'I should never be seen to make mistakes.'
5 'I need to be in control all the time or I will feel threatened.'
6 'Other people should care about my needs.'
7 'I need other people's approval to feel OK.'
8 'As a result of past trauma, I can't enjoy life like other people.'
9 'I should do what other people want me to do.'
10 'People should never be impatient.'
11 'I will feel bad if other people reject me.'
12 'I must work hard all the time.'
13 'Things will sort themselves out if I just wait.'
14 'I must always help other people when they ask me to.'
15 'I must never refuse invitations.'
16 'Other people should appreciate what I do.'

References

Agnew-Davies, R. (1999) Learning from research into the counselling relationship. In C. Feltham (ed.) *Understanding the Counselling Relationship* (pp. 200–36). London: Sage.

Alford, B. A. (1995) Introduction to the special issue: Psychotherapy integration and cognitive psychotherapy. *Journal of Cognitive Psychotherapy*, 9, 147–51.

Atkinson, D. R. and Matsushita, Y. J. (1991) Japanese–American acculturation, counselling style, counsellor ethnicity, and perceived counsellor credibility. *Journal of Counselling Psychology*. 38, 473–8.

Bandler, R., Grinder, J. and Andreas, C. (1989) *Reframing: Neurolinguistic Programming and the Transformation of Meaning*. Moab: Real People Press.

Beitman, B. D. (1994) Stop exploring! Start defining the principles of psychotherapy integration: Call for a consensus conference. *Journal of Psychotherapy Integrations*, 4(3), 203–28.

Beliappa, J. (1991) *Illness or distress?: Alternative models of mental health*. London: Confederation of Indian Organisations.

Bor, R. and Palmer, S. (2001) *A Beginner's Guide to Training in Counselling and Psychotherapy*. London: Sage.

Bor, R. and Watts, M. H. (eds) (1999) *The Trainee Handbook: A Guide for Counselling and Psychotherapy*. London: Sage.

Boscolo, L., Cecchin, G., Hoffman, L. and Penn, P. (1987) *Milan Systemic Family Therapy: Conversations in Theory and Practice*. New York: Basic Books.

British Association for Counselling and Psychotherapy (2002) *Ethical Framework for Good Practice in Counselling and Psychotherapy*. Rugby: BACP.

Carroll, M. (1996) *Counselling Supervision: Theory, Skills and Practice*. London: Cassell.

Carter, R. and Gollant, S. K. (1994) *Helping Yourself Help Others: A Book for Caregivers*. New York: Times Books.

Clarkson, P. (2000) *Gestalt Counselling in Action*, second edition. London: Sage.

Corey, G., Corey, M. S. and Callanan, P. (1998) *Issues and Ethics in the Helping Professions*. Pacific Grove, CA: Brooks/Cole.

Davison, G. C. (1995) Special Issue: What can we learn from failures in psychotherapy. *Journal of Psychotherapy Integration*, 5, 107–12.

De Jong, P. and Berg, I. (1998) *Interviewing for solutions*. Pacific Grove, CA: Brooks/ Cole.

De Shazer, S. (1988) *Clues: Investigating Solutions in Brief Therapy*. New York: Norton.

Dryden, W. (1995) *Brief Rational Emotive Behaviour Therapy*. London: Sage.

Dryden, W. (1999) *Rational Emotive Behavior Therapy: A training manual*. New York: Springer.

Dryden, W. (ed.) (2002) *Handbook of Individual Therapy*, fourth edition. London: Sage.

Dryden, W., Horton, I. and Mearns, D. (1995) *Issues in Professional Counsellor Training*. London: Cassell.

Dupont-Joshua, A. (2002) Working with issues of race in counselling. In S. Palmer (ed.), *Multicultural Counselling: A reader*. London: Sage.

Egan, G., (1994) *The Skilled Helper: A Problem-management Approach to Helping*, fifth edition. Belmont, CA: Brooks/Cole.

Ellis, A. (1996) *Better, Deeper, and More Enduring Brief Therapy: The Rational Emotive Behavior Therapy Approach*. New York: Bruner/Mazel.

Farrant, A. (2003). Fighting back. *Nursing Standard*, 17(51), 20–1.

Feltham, C. (ed) (1999) *Understanding the Counselling Relationship*. London: Sage.

Feltham, C. and Dryden, W. (1994) *Developing Counsellor Supervision*. London: Sage.

Feltham, C. and Horton, I. (eds) (2000) *Handbook of Counselling and Psychotherapy*. London: Sage.

Frank, J. D. and Frank, J. B. (1991) *Persuasion and Healing*, third edition. Baltimore: Johns Hopkins University Press.

Geldard, K. and Geldard, D. (2001) *Working with Children in Groups: A Handbook for Counsellors, Educators, and Community Workers*. Palgrave, London.

Geldard, K. and Geldard, D. (2002) *Counselling Children: A Practical Introduction*, second edition. London: Sage.

Geldard, K. and Geldard, D. (2003) *Counselling Skills in Everyday Life*. Basingstoke: Palgrave Macmillan.

Geldard, K. and Geldard, D. (2004) *Counselling Adolescents: The Pro-active Approach*, second edition. London: Sage.

Glasser, W. and Wubbolding, R. (2000) Reality therapy. In R. Corsini and D. Wedding (eds) *Current Psychotherapies*, sixth edition (pp. 293–321). Itasca, IL: Peacock.

Goldfried, M. R. and Castonguay, L. G. (1992) The future of psychotherapy integration. Special Issue: The future of psychotherapy. *Psychotherapy*, 29, 4–10.

Greenberg, L. S. (2002) Integrating an emotion-focused approach to treatment in psychotherapy integration. *Journal of psychotherapy integration*. 12(2), 154–89.

Grosh, W. N. and Olsen, D. C. (1995) Prevention: Avoiding burnout. In M. B. Sussman (ed.) *A Perilous Calling: The Hazards of Psychotherapy Practice*. New York: Wiley.

Hillman, J. and Stricker, G. (2002) A call for psychotherapy integration in work with older adult patients. *Journal of psychotherapy integration*, 12(4), 395–405.

Holloway, E. L. (1995) *Clinical Supervision: A Systems Approach*. Thousand Oaks: Sage.

Horvath, A. O. and Symonds, B. D. (1991) Relationship between working alliance and outcome in psychotherapy: A meta-analysis. *Journal of Counseling Psychology*, 38, 139–49.

Houston, G. (2003) *Brief Gestalt Therapy*. London: Sage.

Howe, D. (1999) The main change agent in psychotherapy is the relationship between therapist and client. In C. Feltham (ed) *Controversies in psychotherapy and counselling* (pp. 95–103). London: Sage.

Idowu, A. (1985) Counselling Nigerian students in United States Colleges and Universities. *Journal of Counselling and Development*, 63, 506–509.

Ivey, A., Ivey, B. and Simek-Morgan, L. (1996) *Psychotherapy: A Multicultural Perspective*. Boston: Allyn and Bacon.

Jacobson, N. S. (1994) Behaviour therapy and psychotherapy integration. Society for the Exploration Psychotherapy Integration. *Journal of Psychotherapy Integration*, 4, 105–19.

Johnson, W. A. and Nadirshaw, Z. (2002) Good practice in transcultural counselling: An Asian perspective. In S. Palmer (ed.) *Multicultural Counselling: A reader*. London: Sage.

Jones, E. (1993) *Family Systems Therapy: Developments in Milan-Systemic Therapies*. Chichester: Wiley.

Kakar, S. (1990). *Shamans,mystics and doctors*. Chicago: University of Chicago.

Lago, C. and Moodley, R. (2002) Multicultural issues in eclectic and integrated counselling and psychotherapy. In S. Palmer. (ed.), *Multicultural counselling: A reader* (pp. 40–56). London: Sage.

Laungani, P. (2002) Understanding mental illness across cultures. In S. Palmer (ed.), *Multicultural Counselling: A reader*. London: Sage.

Lee, C. C. and Richardson, B. L. (1991) *Multicultural Issues in Counselling: New Approaches to Diversity*. Alexandria, VA: American Association for Counselling and Development.

Luborsky, L. (1994) Therapeutic alliances as predictors of psychotherapeutic outcomes: Factors explaining the predictive success. In A. O. Horvath and L. S. Greenberg (eds) *The Working Alliance: Theory, Research and Practice* (pp. 38–50). New York: John Wiley.

Luft, J. (1969) *Of Human Interaction*. California: Mayfield.

Mearns, D. (1994) *Developing Person-Centred Counselling*. London: Sage.

Nuttall, J. (2002) Imperatives and perspectives of psychotherapy integration. *International Journal of Psychotherapy*, 7(3), 249–265.

O'Brien, M. and Houston, G. (2000) *Integrative Therapy: A Practitioner's Guide*. London: Sage.

O'Connell, B. (1998) *Solution Focused Therapy*. London: Sage.

Palazzoli, S. N., Boscolo, L., Cecchin, F. G. and Prata, G. (1980) Hypothesising circularity and neutrality: Three guidelines for the conductor of the session. *Family Process*, 19, 3–12.

Parry, A. and Doan, R. E. (1994) *Story Re-visions: Narrative Therapy in the Postmodern World*. New York: Guilford Press.

Pedersen, P. (1991) Counseling international students. *The counselling psychologist*, 19, 10–58.

Pierce, R. A., Nichols, M. P. and Du Brin, M. A. (1983) *Emotional Expression in Psychotherapy*. New York: Gardner.

Pinsoff, W.M. (1994) An overview of Integrative Problem Centered Therapy: A synthesis of family and individual psychotherapies. Special Issue: Developments in family therapy in the USA. *Journal of Family Therapy*, 16, 103–20.

Prochaska, J. O. (1999) How do people change, and how can we change to help many more people? In M. A. Hubble, B. L. Duncan and S. D. Miller (eds), *The Heart & Soul of Change: What Works in Therapy* (pp. 227–55). Washington DC: American Psychological Association.

Prochaska, J. O. and DiClemente, C. C. (1992) The Transtheoretical Approach. In J. C. Norcross and M. R. Goldfried (eds) *Handbook of psychotherapy integration* (pp. 300–34). New York: Basic Books.

Ridley, C. R. (1995) *Overcoming Unintentional Racism in Counseling and Therapy: A Practitioner's Guide to Intentional Intervention*. Thousand Oaks: Sage.

Rogers, C. R. (1955) *Client-Centered Therapy*. Boston: Houghton Mifflin.

Rogers, C. R. (1957) The necessary and sufficient conditions of psychotherapeutic personality change. *Journal of Consulting Psychology*, 21, 95–103.

Rogers, C. R. (1961) *On Becoming a Person*. London: Constable.

Scaturo, D. J. (1994) Integrative psychotherapy for panic disorder and agoraphobia in clinical practice. *Journal of Psychotherapy Integration*, 4, 253–72.

Schaufeli, W. B., Maslach, C. and Marek, T. (eds) (1993) *Professional Burnout: Recent Developments in Theory and Research*. Washington: Taylor & Francis.

Shillito-Clarke, C. (1996) Ethical Issues in Counselling Psychology. In R. Woolfe and W. Dryden (eds) *Handbook of Counselling Psychology*. London: Sage.

Steenbarger, B. N. (1992) Toward science–practice integration in brief counselling and therapy. *Counselling Psychologist*, 20, 403–50.

Street, E. (1994) *Counselling for Family Problems*. London: Sage.

Stricker, G. and Gold, J. R. (eds) (1993) *Comprehensive handbook of psychotherapy integration*. New York: Plenum.

Stuart, R. B. (2004) Twelve practical suggestions for achieving multicultural competence. *Professional psychology: research and practice*, 35(1), 3–9.

Sue, D. W. and Sue, D. (1990) *Counseling the culturally different – theory and practice*. New York: Wiley.

Tierney, G. T. (2003) Psychotherapy integration: examination of clinical utilization. Dissertation Abstracts International: Section B: The Sciences & Engineering, 63(8-B), 39–43.

Walter, J. and Peller, J. (1992) *Becoming Solution Focused in Brief Therapy*. New York: Bruner/Mazel.

Waterman, A. (1984) *The Psychology of Individualism*. New York: Praeger.

Watkins, C. E. and Watts R. E. (1995) Psychotherapy survey research studies: Some consistent findings and integrative conclusions. *Psychotherapy in Private Practice*, *13*, 49–68.

White, M. and Epston, D. (1990) *Narrative means to therapeutic ends*. New York: Norton.

Woolfe, R. and Dryden, D. (1996) *Handbook of Counselling Psychology*. London: Sage.

Worthington, E. (ed.) (1993) *Psychotherapy and Religious Values*. Grand Rapids: Baker,

Yang, K. S. (1997) Theories and research in Chinese personality: An indigenous approach. In H. S. R. Kao and D. Sinah (eds), *Asian perspective on psychology* (pp. 236–64). New Delhi: Sage.

Zinker, J. (1978) *Creative Process in Gestalt Therapy*. New York: Vintage.

Index

action plan, 212–15
action
  facilitating, 206–16
  planning for, 131
active listening, 22, 128
advice giving
  disadvantages of, 10
  need for, 11
Agnew-Davies, R., 15
Alford, B. A., 108
anger, repressed, 168
anxiety, as blocked excitement, 153
appointment times, 96
appointments
  contracting for, 99
  making, 95
  ongoing, 99
arousal, 208
Atkinson, D. R., 246
awareness, raising, 208–9

BACP, 4, 225, 259, 261
Bandler, R., 114
behaviour
  emphasis on, 131
  facilitating change in, 115
  need to address, 110
  normalising changes in, 145–7
Beitman, D. D., 108, 109
Beliappa, J., 238
beliefs
  involving unrealistic expectations,
    161–2

origins of, 160
unhelpful, 159–61
blocks
  dealing with, 211–12
  to progress, 209
burnout
  causes of, 285–6
  combating, 288–9
  dealing with, 290–2
  due to over-involvement, 287–8
  influence of isolation on, 288
  influence of suicidal or violent clients
    on, 288
  normality of, 289–90
  protecting yourself from, 286–7
  symptoms, 284–5
  the need to look after yourself, 283–303

catharsis, 57
cathartic release, 129
challenging self-destructive beliefs, 114,
    131, 157–64
change
  combining skills to facilitate, 122–133
  effective long-term, 158
  facilitating cognitive, 112
  promoting, 109
  related to exploration and
    self-discovery, 116–17
cheerleading, 182
choice, making a, 201–2
clarifying, 113, 130–1
  use of, 130